Developing Successful Diversity

Mentoring Programmes

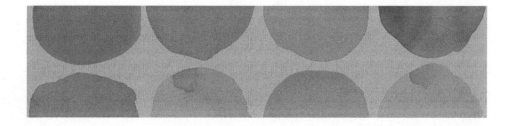

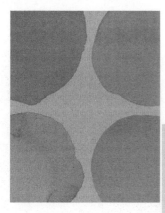

Developing Successful Diversity Mentoring Programmes

An international casebook

David Clutterbuck,
Kirsten M. Poulsen and
Frances Kochan

Open University Press

Open University Press
McGraw-Hill Education
McGraw-Hill House
Shoppenhangers Road
Maidenhead
Berkshire
England
SL6 2QL

email: enquiries@openup.co.uk
world wide web: www.openup.co.uk

and Two Penn Plaza, New York, NY 10121-2289, USA

First published 2012

A catalogue record of this book is available from the British Library

ISBN-13: 978-0-33-524388-4 (pb)
ISBN-10: 0-33-524388-6 (pb)
eISBN: 978-0-33-524389-1

Library of Congress Cataloging-in-Publication Data
CIP data applied for

Typesetting and e-book compilations by
RefineCatch Limited, Bungay, Suffolk
Printed and bound by CPI Group (UK) Ltd, Croydon, CR0 4YY

The **McGraw·Hill** Companies

"This book provides insightful analyses of diversity mentoring principles and their application to real world practice. It is highly timely, internationally relevant and should appeal to scholars, policy makers and practitioners. In these pages you will find a rich mixture of the best examples of mentoring case studies, which show intersections between diversity groups. The book is particularly significant in amplifying differing voices by not attempting to standardise language used by case study contributors. Through the reflective questions in all sections, I think the authors have done an outstanding job in promoting engagement with readers."

Professor Uduak Archibong, Professor of Diversity, University of Bradford, UK

"Developing Successful Diversity Mentoring Programmes *fills a gap in the mentoring literature. The editors introduce the topic of diversity with sensitivity and awareness. They then bring together a comprehensive range of real case studies that provide a wonderful resource of examples of diversity mentoring programmes across a wide range of disability, gender, race and culture contexts. The case studies themselves examine necessary programme processes, such as matching and also consider the challenges and lessons learned. The book is informed, insightful and inspiring and will be of immense use to the mentoring community."*

Dr Elaine Cox, Director of Postgraduate Coaching and Mentoring Programmes, Oxford Brookes University, UK

"As a diversity practitioner working for a multi-national organisation, I found this a great manual to dip into for ideas and advice on how best to use mentoring as a means of driving behavioural and organisational change. The case studies are many and varied and offer bite-sized and very practical lessons. When mentoring works, it affords both parties the opportunity for personal growth, increased self awareness and increased understanding of different perspectives – all of which are essential to truly value difference. These qualities are the foundations for that sense of inclusion that we all strive for in our daily lives."

Human Capital Director, Head of Diversity, Inclusion & Employee Wellbeing, PricewaterhouseCoopers LLP, London, UK

This book is dedicated to Barbara Burford, pioneer of diversity mentoring in Europe's largest employer, the UK National Health Service. Barbara, who will be sorely missed, inspired many researchers and practitioners and demonstrated the power of positive challenge to change lives and organisations.

Contents

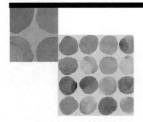

About the editors

David Clutterbuck brought the concept of supported mentoring to Europe some 30 years ago and pioneered the developmental mentoring movement. A co-founder of the European Mentoring Centre, which became the European Mentoring & Coaching Council (the main body representing coaching and mentoring in Europe), he is the author of hundreds of articles and 15 previous books on coaching and mentoring. These include *Everyone Needs a Mentor* (1985), now a classic text and soon to go into its fifth edition. David is visiting professor in the coaching and mentoring faculties of Sheffield Hallam and Oxford Brookes Universities and external examiner on a number of other coaching/mentoring programmes. He led the research team behind the International Standards for Mentoring Programmes in Employment. His doctorate (Kings College, London University) was a longitudinal and cross-sectional study of the dynamics of mentoring relationships, from the perspective of both mentor and mentee. He has helped hundreds of organisations around the world design and implement sustainable mentoring programmes. David lives in the Thames Valley in the UK and enjoys being a multiple grandfather. He continues to set himself a major learning challenge each year – from mountaineering to becoming a stand-up comic!

Kirsten M. Poulsen is passionate about professionalising and bringing best practices into the design and implementation of mentoring programmes. As co-founder and first president (2007–2009) of EMCC Denmark, Kirsten was and is still active in the public debate on the quality of coaching and mentoring. She is an international speaker and has written numerous articles on mentoring, career navigation, leadership and talent development. She is author of the book *Mentor+Guiden*, published in Danish, in 2008, which has set the standard for mentoring programmes in Denmark and emphasised the importance of training mentors and mentees. Kirsten is a partner in the International Cross-Mentoring Program, an associate professor at Copenhagen Business School, and the founder (in 2000) and owner of the consulting company KMP+. She has more than 20 years of experience as an international management consultant and holds an MBA from IESE Business School, Barcelona, Spain.

Frances Kochan views mentoring as a vital aspect in improving individual lives, organisations and societies. She is the editor of a book series on mentoring published by Information Age Press, and has published numerous journal articles on the topic. She served as a school and school system administrator in a variety of locations. She also served as Dean of the College of Education at Auburn University, Alabama, for eight years and is presently a Distinguished Professor in leadership at that institution. Dr. Kochan is presently involved in researching the influence of culture on mentoring processes and programmes.

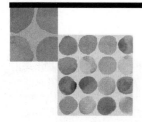

Contributors

Penny Abbott is Founding Director and Partner of Clutterbuck Associates South Africa, providing organisational consultancy for coaching and structured mentoring programmes in organisations. She has conducted Master's research in the role of the coordinator of structured mentoring programmes in South Africa and has recently co-authored a Guide for Coachees. She is an active member of Coaches and Mentors of South Africa, serving on the Research and Definitions Committee as well as heading up the Mentoring Special Interest Group.

Olu Alake is President of 100 Black Men of London, a charity dedicated to the education, development and uplifting of youth and the wider community. He has held senior management positions in the UK's Equalities and Human Rights Commission, the Commission for Racial Equality and the Arts Council England. He has chaired the UNESCO East Asia Forum on Cultural Diversity resolution drafting working group and was a member of the International Advisory Board of the World Cultural Forum, and currently sits on the board of African-British Theatre Company Tiata Fahodzi. He holds an MSc in Race & Ethnic Studies (Birkbeck); a Postgraduate Diploma in Management Studies and BSc (Hons) in Economics.

Raymond Asumadu is a second-year BA HRM student at Middlesex University and student representative.

Dellroy O. Birch is a Mentium mentor and Vice President, Information Services, at Fortegra Financial. He holds a PhD in Organization and Management, an MS and a BS in Technology Management as well as a Lean Master, Lean Six Sigma Master Black Belt certification.

Merridee Bujaki holds a PhD in Management, is a Chartered Accountant, an Associate Professor of Accounting at the Telfer School of Management, University of Ottawa, and a member of the Centre for Research and Education on Women and Work at the Sprott School of Business, Carleton University, where she teaches in the Management Development for Women program.

Maggie Clarke is senior lecturer at the University of Western Sydney, Australia. She is an executive for the Australian Teacher Education Association. In July 2010, she was awarded an Australian Learning and Teaching Citation for Outstanding Contribution to Student Learning and a University College of Arts Award for her outstanding contribution to student learning in 2009.

Jane Cordell holds an MEd and an MA. She is Head of Access, Training and Consultancy at the British NGO, Action on Hearing Loss. She is a member of the European Mentoring and Coaching Council. She has published *Cambridge Business English Activities* (Cambridge University Press, 2000) and a paper on coaching people with disabilities.

Giulia Corinaldi is Programme Manager at the Cherie Blair Foundation for Women 'Mentoring Women in Business' project. Giulia previously worked for TIEUK, as the Chapter Manager, responsible for restructuring the UK mentoring programme and launching a programme for young aspiring entrepreneurs. She holds a Master's degree in International Politics from SOAS.

Patricia Pedraza Cruz leads the Integrated Women Mentorship Program at Immigrant Services, Calgary. She holds a Bachelor's Degree in Psychology and is a specialist in Higher Education Teaching. Originally from Colombia, she now works in Canada with women in the Latin American community, helping them to reach their professional and personal goals and integrate into Canadian society.

Tulsi Derodra is a second-year BA HRM student at Middlesex University.

Pamela M. Dixon is Director of Talent Development, Research and Assessment at Menttium Corporation. She has been Assistant Professor at Colorado State University and visiting professor at the University of Wisconsin, River Falls and UW-Stout. She has a Master's degree in Instructional Design and Adult Learning Theory, and a PhD in Organization Performance and Change.

Nora Dominguez is Director of the International Mentoring Association and of the Mentoring Institute at the University of New Mexico. She is a PhD Candidate in Organizational Learning and Instructional Technologies at UNM. Last year she co-edited the book *Mentoring: Perspectivas Teóricas y Prácticas*, one of the few mentoring resources in Spanish.

Jennybeth Ekeland is Senior Consultant and Programme Director in AFF at the Norwegian School of Economics, responsible for professional mentoring. She qualified as an educational psychologist at the University of Oslo and as an Advanced Organizational Consultant at The Tavistock Institute, London. She has 30 years of experience in leadership and organizational development. She currently works with mentoring, coaching, leadership development programmes and management groups.

Gifty Gabor is a second-year BA HRM student at Middlesex University and student representative.

Coral Gardiner holds a PhD in Mentoring and is Extended School Manager at Joseph Leckie Community Technology College. She introduced mentoring in 1992 to young offenders on probation in the West Midlands, the UK. Her extensive research resulted in an approach to mentoring, known as 'Professional Friendship Mentoring'.

Tim Gutierrez is Associate Vice President of Student Services at the University of New Mexico, implementing federal and state-funded programs to support under-represented students. He received his Doctorate in Educational Leadership from UNM.

Julie Haddock-Millar is a lecturer in HR Management and Development at Middlesex University Business School and a member of the Chartered Institute of Personnel and Development. She founded the Middlesex University Mentoring Network and is currently working with the UK Cabinet Office to develop a mentoring programme for Fast Stream Civil Servants and undergraduate students.

Christina Hartshorn was one of the founding cohort of the Master's in Entrepreneurial Studies programme from the University of Stirling. A qualified Careers Adviser, she is a Fellow of the Royal Society of Arts and currently Head of Enterprise and Competition Policy, South East England Development Agency. She was also founding director of the Women's Enterprise Unit at the University of Stirling.

Susanne Søes Hejlsvig is a career consultant at the Career Centre at Aarhus University, Business and Social Sciences, responsible for the mentoring programme, which matches former students (alumni) from the business community with Master's students. She holds a Master's degree in business languages and international market communication, is a trained process consultant and an ICF-certified life and business coach.

Rachelle Heller is Associate Provost, Mount Vernon Campus of the George Washington University and Professor of Computer Science. She holds a PhD from the University of Maryland in the educational uses of computers. She has been co-principal investigator of many US National Science Foundation grants and is co-editor of the peer-reviewed *Computers & Education: An International Journal* (Elsevier Science).

Malcolm Johnson possesses Bachelor degrees in History and Psychology and an MBA from Warwick University Business School. He developed the UK University Transitions Programme in conjunction with the Careers Service at Nottingham University. The programme seeks to assist students with Asperger Syndrome identify a suitable career and transition effectively into the workplace.

Rita Knott holds a university diploma in Coaching and Supervision from the University of Applied Sciences in Frankfurt/Main in Germany. She is a board member of the European Mentoring and Coaching Council (EMCC) in Luxembourg and accredited coach with EMCC Luxembourg and the German Association of Supervision. She leads her own coaching/mentoring consulting company. In cooperation with the Centre for Corporate Governance, University of St. Gallen, Switzerland, she launched the Luxembourg FEMALE BOARD POOL initiative in 2011.

James W. Koschoreck is Associate Professor in the Educational Leadership Program at the University of Cincinnati and Graduate Program Director for the doctoral program in Urban Educational Leadership. He holds degrees from University of Texas at Austin, Purdue University, and University of Wisconsin-Madison. He was President of the University Council for Educational Administration, 2008–09.

Alan Li is a primary care physician at Regent Park Community Health Centre, Ontario. He is the founding co-chair of the 'Committee for Accessible AIDS Treatment' (CAAT), a coalition group of many health and community service providers working to eliminate treatment access barriers for people with HIV/AIDS with precarious migration status in Canada. He received an Ontario HIV Treatment Network Community Scholar Award and is lead investigator in the Canadian Institute of Health Research-funded study: Community HIV Champion Advocate Mobilization Project.

Catherine Mavriplis holds a PhD in Aeronautics from MIT. She joined the University of Ottawa as an Associate Professor of Mechanical Engineering. She has had four US NSF ADVANCE grants to advance women in the professoriate and to leadership levels in academia. She has recently completed a study of women in career gaps, published in the *Journal of Technology Management & Innovation*.

Norma T. Mertz is a professor of Higher Education Administration at the University of Tennessee. She is the editor of the 2009 book, *Breaking into the All-Male Club: Female Professors of Educational Administration*, and co-editor of *Theoretical Frameworks in Qualitative Research* (Sage).

Elisabeth Møller-Jensen is a Danish scholar on Nordic Literature and editor in chief of the *History of Nordic Women's Literature 1000–1990* as well as Managing Director of KVINFO, a leading institution dedicated to inform the general public about breakthrough research in gender studies and women issues. For the past nine years Elisabeth has been actively promoting the value and practice of mentoring to support immigrant women living in Denmark.

Silvia Inés Monserrat is a full professor at Unicen, Argentina, and has been a visiting professor at Cal State University, San Bernardino. She serves as a Judge at a Family Law Court in Tandil, Argentina.

Françoise Moreau-Johnson is the Activities Coordinator at the Centre for Academic Leadership, University of Ottawa, organizing activities and workshops for full-time faculty on leadership and career development. Françoise received the 2010 Prize for Excellence in Service for the University of Ottawa's support staff. She holds a MSc in Experimental Psychology.

Catherine Mossop is a Fellow Certified Management Consultant, and leads the consultancy Sage Mentors Inc., Canada. She is co-author of several resources guides for mentors and mentees and is working with the University of Ottawa, Faculty of Admin. Studies on creating a common body of knowledge for the certification of leadership mentors.

Loshini Naidoo is a senior lecturer in Sociology in the School of Education at the University of Western Sydney, Australia. Her current research is in mentoring of pre-service teachers as literacy tutors for refugee and indigenous high school students in Greater Western Sydney secondary schools and at Tennant Creek High, Northern Territory. She received a citation from the Australian Teaching Learning Council for her outstanding contribution to student learning.

Jonelle Naude is an international coach and change facilitator. Her company, Leadership Lab, operates in Cape Town and London. As an international faculty member of the Coaches Training Institute, she trains coaches across the UK and greater Europe in the co-active coaching model. Jonelle is also a director of Recovery Coach Training and Consulting. She has served on both the Research Committee and Standards of Competence committees of Coaches and Mentors of South Africa since 2006.

Leyla Okhai is a Senior Equality Advisor specializing in race, religion and belief in the Equality and Diversity Unit of Oxford University. She is Vice Chair of the Higher Education Race Equality Action Group, an inter-institutional group that shares best practice.

Nwamaka Onyiuke is a Learning and Development Consultant, Qualified Life Coach and Mentor, working with Jesus House, London, currently completing her MA in Human Resource Development with Middlesex University.

Louise Overy is a consultant with Summers Consulting. Until April 2011 she was the South West Regional Coordinator for the National Breaking Through initiative for the NHS Institute for Innovation and Improvement.

Martin Parsonage is the founder and CEO of the INDIGO Dyslexia Centre in Norwich, named a top 100 business in the 2010 Barclay's Trading Places Awards 2010. His BA degree is in Philosophy, Politics and Culture, and he holds qualifications in psychology, teaching, counselling and management.

Shari Lawrence Pfleeger is the Director of Research for the Institute for Information Infrastructure Protection at Dartmouth College, a consortium of 27 universities, national laboratories and non-profits, engaged in research to make the information infrastructure more reliable, dependable, safe and secure. She is associate editor of *IEEE Security and Privacy* magazine and author of several leading textbooks and was first director of the Association for Computing Machinery's Committee on Women and Minorities.

Cherry Potts has worked with Leonard Cheshire Disability as a Business Mentor and advisor since 2008, first, on the Ready to Start programme and now on Be the Boss, mentoring disabled veterans of the armed services who are starting businesses; and on Enabled4Growth, as a Business Advisor to established disabled-led businesses in London. She heads her own life coaching and training consultancy.

Peter Quinn is head of Oxford University's Disability Advisory Service, responsible for disability-related academic study support throughout the Collegiate University of Oxford. He is a Director for the National Association of Disability Practitioners. He chairs the University's Buildings and Estates sub-committee on access, and was recently on the University's Working Party on Specific Learning Difficulties.

Ann Rolfe founded the consultancy Mentoring Works in 1987, assisting organizations to set up mentoring programs. She has worked with Aboriginal people in mentoring programs in government agencies, professional and community associations and is author of ten books on mentoring.

Michail Sanidas is Equality and Human Rights Manager for South West Strategic Health Authority, UK. Previously Patient and Public Involvement lead for Avon, Somerset and Wiltshire Cancer Services, his interest in equality issues developed as secretary of the NHS Bristol BME Staff network (2005–07).

Clive Saunders (JP) has over 20 years of experience in equality, diversity and inclusion. He is Managing Director of Equality Associates Limited and heads the African Caribbean Supplementary School in Watford, providing voluntary developmental support for children and young people aged 5–16. In 2005, he was appointed a senior manager at Transport for London (TfL) where he initiated, developed and managed the TfL Mentoring Programme.

Kolarele Sonaike is the Vice President Programmes for 100 Black Men of London. A barrister for 13 years, specializing in Employment and Commercial litigation, he is an accredited mediator and associate member of the Institute of Arbitrators. He is a speechwriter and public speaking consultant and the founder of GreatSpeech.Co – The 'Great Speech' Consultancy. Kolarele holds a degree in Philosophy and Politics from the University of Birmingham.

Lynn P. Sontag is President and Chief Mentoring Officer of Menttium Corporation, where she has overseen development of all mentoring models for nearly a decade. She leads the renowned Menttium 100® program for high-potential women, recognized by the US Department of Labor as 'the model for mentoring systems nationwide'. Lynn has a Master's in Business Administration in Organizational Development from the University of St. Thomas in Minneapolis, Minnesota.

Charlene Sorensen is Professor and Chair of Chemistry and Physics at Gallaudet University, a liberal arts university for the Deaf and hard of hearing. She holds a PhD in Physical Chemistry from the University of Tennessee in Knoxville. She has encouraged women, Deaf individuals and other underrepresented groups to seek advanced degrees in the science, engineering, and mathematic fields through the FORWARD program.

Jenepher Lennox Terrion holds a PhD in Communication and is an Associate Professor in the Department of Communication, University of Ottawa. Her research examines the impacts of peer mentoring, leadership development, family support, and communication skills training programmes.

Kimberly Vappie is Chief Executive Officer and co-owner of Menttium Corporation, which promotes mentoring to help women breach the glass ceiling. She is on the board of directors for Graywolf Publishing, and on the Executive Committee and Planning Committee for the University of St. Thomas Multicultural Forum. She is a past co-chair for the Programs Committee for Minnesota Women Lawyers, a non-profit organization whose mission is to secure the full and equal participation of women in the legal profession and in a just society. Kim received a Bachelor of Arts in Economics and Management from Augsburg College in Minneapolis, and her Juris Doctorate from Hamline University School of Law in St. Paul.

Cynthia Miller Veraldo is a doctoral student in the Urban Educational Leadership Program at the University of Cincinnati and holds a graduate assistantship in the Educational Leadership Program.

Helen Villalobos is a freelance learning and development facilitator and lecturer in the Human Resource Management Department, Middlesex University Business School. She is currently completing her MA in Human Resource Development with Middlesex University.

Dieter Wagner is professor and Vice President for Knowledge and Technology Transfer at the University of Potsdam and is responsible for the Career Service Mentoring program. He holds the chair of Business Administration, with special focus on Organizational Behavior and Human Resource Management.

Nelli Wagner is head of Career Services at the University of Potsdam and leads its mentoring programme. She is a fellow of the Stifterverband (Association for the Promotion of Science and Humanities in Germany) studying extra-occupational 'Management of Higher Educational Institutions and Sciences' in Austria.

Carol Whitaker has an MBA and Postgraduate Diploma in Coaching and Mentoring Practice from Oxford Brookes University, where she is also Associate Lecturer and a Coach/Supervisor for the MA Coaching and Mentoring Practice.

Keith Whittlestone is Headteacher at Joseph Leckie Community Technology College in Walsall, West Midlands. He is trained by the National College for School and College Leaders as a Local Leader in Education.

Shaun Wilson-Gotobed is a Project Development Worker in Community Services at Norfolk County Council. As a dyslexic, he has a passion for supporting other dyslexic people in the workplace. As a result of his work, Norfolk County Council won a Commended Equalities Award 2010.

Helen Worrall is Learning & Development Manager UKMEA for Arup, a global firm of Engineers, Architects, Designers and Consultants. Helen is particularly interested in the impact of implicit bias within a professional environment and continues to implement progressive diversity strategies within development initiatives and mentoring programmes.

Derek Yee is a long-term survivor infected with HIV since 1988, presently employed as a coordinator for Committee for Accessible AIDS Treatment in Toronto, Canada, with the Legacy Project, to which he brings personal experience of homelessness, addiction and depression.

Foreword

How difference makes a difference in mentoring

In a sense, all developmental mentoring involves diversity. As a relationship of mutual learning, it is the difference in experience, knowledge, perspectives and values of the two people that fuels the learning exchange. When one of us interviewed mentoring programme managers more than a decade ago, to understand how they matched prospective mentors and mentees, we found a distinct pattern in the way they thought when they achieved successful matches. From knowledge of participants, they instinctively assessed how much similarity and difference there was between them. The more mature as a learner, and the more open to challenge (two connected criteria) the participants were, the greater the amount of difference they could absorb and the higher the potential for learning. Recent experiments by the Swiss company Mentorable, using motivational profiling to assist matching, tell a similar story. While perceived similarity is important to achieving rapport in the mentoring relationship, difference is important in stimulating learning and fostering growth and development.

When you add to the catalogue of differences between the members of a mentoring pair diversity in terms of race, religion, gender, sexual preference and disability (to name just the most obvious issues), both the potential problems and the potential learning opportunities become magnified. Building rapport with someone, who sees the world radically differently, can be hard work. Yet the process of self-growth, through increased self-awareness and through the ability to recognise and embrace other perspectives, is at its strongest when people can explore how others make meaning of the world around them, in an intellectually challenging but emotionally supportive conversation. There are many facets of wisdom, but perhaps one of the most important is the ability to live with and value the ambiguity of difference, while sustaining and nurturing one's ethical core. A decade or less ago, the term diversity mentoring was not readily recognised, particularly among academics. But frequent use has acculturalised it. While individual mentoring programmes typically identify themselves with reference to the groups they target (for example, the Women's Mentoring Network), when programme managers talk about the wider use of mentoring to support corporate diversity or talent management objectives, the phrase diversity mentoring is a convenient shorthand.

In this book we have tried to cover a wide spectrum of diversity issues, but we have not been exhaustive. We have been limited in our search by the areas, where mentoring has been applied. We could not, for example, find any examples of mentoring programmes directed at countering discrimination based on sizeism, or ageism, although we are aware that both have been proposed. We have also not explicitly dealt with issues of inter-generational diversity, not least because so many mentoring programmes have this implicitly built in to their structure. Indeed, all the early writing about mentoring, by Daniel Levinson, tacitly assumed a difference of perspective based on generational factors. (Not to be confused with 'the generative effect', which is the intrinsic motivation of people in older generations to pass on their wisdom to members of succeeding generations.)

The literature on Generations X and Y, and on millennials, would lead us to believe t hat the scale of difference between successive generations is increasing and that baby boomers and post-millennials are almost different species of humanity. Whatever the level of truth in that, it is clear from the research that millennials place a relatively high value on mentors as resources, upon which they can draw in managing their careers. And, research is also suggesting that the millennial generation is more alike across national boundaries that ever before because they all have access to the same media and are influenced by the same media – the internet. This, we hope, is a positive indication that mentoring will continue to thrive and grow in the decades to come.

Central to all the cases of diversity mentoring we have gathered is a recognition that, where relationships work, learning is a two-way process. The most effective diversity mentoring relationships can be cathartic for those involved.

The areas of diversity mentoring we have covered in this book are:

- *Disability* – itself a highly diverse area, with some disabilities being very obvious to an observer and others not. Our cases range from general disability to deafness, HIV and dyslexia.

- *Gender and sexual preference* – we explore a range of programmes in a variety of countries, aimed at enabling the career advancement of women. A particularly strong theme we have found is the growing use of mentoring to support women as entrepreneurs. In 1987, one of us carried out a study of 100 successful women, half of whom had become entrepreneurs and half of whom stayed with large companies and rose to senior positions. A majority of women in both groups pointed to the role of a mentor in facilitating their career choice.

- *Race and culture* – ranging in target audience from immigrants into Europe and Canada, to Australian aborigines. Our cases cover both highly successful and much less successful programmes. One of the observations from the latter is that the mixture of racial difference with intergenerational difference can raise barriers, which are very hard to overcome.

Lessons from our case studies

The final chapter of this book is an analysis of the lessons from the cases. Here we have adopted an unusual approach. We have invited all of the authors, who have contributed to a section, to extract their own lessons and observations from all of the cases in that section. The result is an intriguing and valuable set of insights for anyone wishing to launch a diversity mentoring programme or to improve an existing one.

A note on terminology

Since this is a book about diversity, it might be seen as strange, if we attempted to standardise the language used. The lexicon of mentoring around the world provides a richness of culture and perspectives, models and approaches and we have aimed to reflect this by retaining the terms and spellings used by the case study authors. The most noticeable spelling differences will be seen between US and UK English (for example, program versus programme). In terminology, authors refer variously to mentoring and mentorship, and to the recipients of mentoring as protégé and mentee (and sometimes mentoree – Australia). Protégé tends to be primarily a US preference and to reflect a more directive, hands-on model of mentoring than mentee. However, the shades of meaning surrounding all of these terms are subtle and highly contextual – the culture(s), the programme purpose, and the assumptions of the organisers and participants all influence how the language of mentoring translates into meaning and behaviour. So we leave these terms as the authors use them as another means to celebrate diversity and honour differences.

Finally, we wish to express our appreciation to Joseph Pascarelli for his valuable assistance in this project.

David Clutterbuck, London, Great Britain
Kirsten M. Poulsen, Copenhagen, Denmark
Frances Kochan, Auburn, Alabama, USA

The authors would like to thank Catalyst for a kind permission to reproduce Figure 4.1, p. 69. Founded in 1962, Catalyst is the leading nonprofit membership organization expanding opportunities for women and business. With offices in the United States , Canada , Europe, and India , and more than 500 preeminent corporations as members, Catalyst is the trusted resource for research, information, and advice about women at work.

CHAPTER 1

Understanding diversity mentoring

David Clutterbuck

This book focuses on issues related to diversity mentoring. *Diversity mentoring is a developmental process of open dialogue that aims to achieve both individual and organisational change through shared understanding and suspending judgement within a relationship of mutual learning in which differences that exist are perceived as integral to learning, growth and development.* Let's deconstruct that.

Diversity mentoring is a process within the context of a mentoring *relationship* which takes place within the larger context of the organisation and sometimes also within society. As a process, it may be carried out in various ways, some of which will be more effective and/or efficient than others. Given the diversity of the participants, their work and life contexts and the issues they confront, it is inevitable that this process will be difficult to pin down. One of the common factors we can point to, however, is that, like all developmental mentoring, this form of mentoring works *by enhancing the capacity and quality of participants' thinking about issues that they perceive to be important to them.*

It requires *open dialogue*, which depends significantly on the level of psychological safety within the relationship. Thus, it is essential that both parties are comfortable about revealing their thoughts and concerns. Likewise, it is vital that they can challenge each other's assumptions, behaviours and actions.

Diversity mentoring is an instrument of personal change aimed at helping mentees identify how they and their circumstances could be different; and how they will bring changes to fruition. It is also an instrument of social change. In the workplace, it helps organisations achieve equal opportunities objectives, tap into a wider talent pool and become more representative to and better able to listen to their customers. In society, it helps integrate disenfranchised groups. It involves awakening awareness of personal potential – both in the individual and in those around them – and facilitating the blossoming of that potential within a context that is also changed.

Diversity mentoring builds understanding in at least three levels in the workplace:

- Mentees become more aware of their potential; gain greater clarity about themselves and their environment; and achieve greater self-motivation and support to achieve their dreams.

- Mentors gain awareness of how people from differing backgrounds or situations perceive and experience the working world. This frequently results in the mentors recognising how they and others create artificial barriers to the advancement of talented people, who happen to be different. As the mentors gain a better understanding and appreciation of people, who are different from themselves, they modify and widen their view of talent.

- Diversity mentoring builds understanding of the value of diversity on a strategic level – how the company as a whole can benefit from inclusion and from ensuring that the talents of disadvantaged groups are developed and utilised. It has become strongly connected to corporate social responsibility, adding value to corporate branding and helping to attract a diverse workforce.

Diversity mentoring on an organisational level is closely associated with stronger communications and more interaction between groups and strata, giving disadvantaged groups a stronger voice than they have been used to. It requires mentor and mentee to *suspend judgement* about each other, though this can sometimes be difficult. When the parties involved come from communities which have a deep hostility towards each other, the relationship may never develop the depth of trust to be effective. Carl Rogers (1961) talks of *unconditional positive regard*. To this we add *respectful curiosity about the other person's world and their perspectives*. Respectful curiosity provides the psychological safety, where both parties can learn about each other and experiment with ways of thinking and behaving across the gulf of difference. Engaging in diversity mentoring involves *mutual learning and growth*. All developmental mentoring seeks to stimulate learning in both parties. In some cases, programmes are designed specifically with the learning of mentors as a primary focus. In diversity mentoring, however, the differences between partners provides fertile ground for much richer and substantive mutual learning and growth.

Diversity mentoring involves a *relationship*. This implies that the conversations between mentor and mentee are more than transactional. They may operate at all seven levels of dialogue, as described elsewhere by one of the editors (Megginson and Clutterbuck 2005) – social, technical, tactical, strategic, for self-insight, for behaviour change, and integrative (the 'what is the meaning of life?' conversation). As we shall discuss later in the chapter, difference can sometimes be a partial impediment to building rapport, yet, as in all mentoring, rapport-building is an essential first stage of the mentoring process.

Finally, difference is positioned within the relationship as a resource of learning, rather than as a problem or something to be avoided. The mutuality of the learning exchange is fundamental to the process. Indeed, in one of our cases, the failure of the programme is related closely to mentors' unwillingness to learn from mentees.

The style of diversity mentoring has evolved differently on the two sides of the Atlantic. In North America, the dominant model has been, and still largely is, one in which the mentor plays the role of sponsor, using their influence on behalf of the protégé. This model did not work well in Northern Europe, where a different style of mentoring, called developmental mentoring (as opposed to sponsorship mentoring) emerged. This style is very similar to modern developmental coaching – and was one of the sources, which gave rise to this form of coaching – in that it is primarily about helping the mentee (the word protégé is seen as too indicative of a directive relationship) build self-awareness and improve the quality of their thinking about issues that are important to them. This enables them to make better decisions, to perform better and achieve personal goals through increased self-awareness and self-motivation. However, as one of the authors has experienced working with mentoring programmes for women in leadership, the sponsor role of coaching and advising about visibility, providing guidance on office politics and actively promoting the mentee among other top managers can also in some circumstances play a very important role in achieving results of the mentoring programme. And since in diversity mentoring the mentees are facing very real barriers in their environment, they may also need sponsorship mentoring to achieve their goals.

Multinational organisations such as the World Bank were instrumental in bringing developmental mentoring to North America. As a result, we see a spectrum from strongly developmental to strongly sponsorship-oriented mentoring programmes around the world. In general, countries and cultures with high power distance, or where individual power is valued highly, tend to have more sponsorship mentoring.

In our broad overview of diversity mentoring programmes, we have been unable to find any reliable data about who owns these initiatives on behalf of organisations. In some cases, it is human resources; in others, a head of diversity; in yet others, it is a shared responsibility. Relatively few programmes have a steering committee, containing administrators, champions and representatives of the target mentees and mentors.

History of diversity mentoring

The first, widely used definitions of mentoring were anything but reflective of diversity. Drawn from observations of mentoring relationships that supported the advancement of young, white, male professionals, these definitions in the early 1980s talked of 'overseeing the career of a young man' (Gray 1986). Significantly, most of the research into mentoring at that time, including the seminal study by Kathy Kram (Kram 1983, 1985), were in the context of informal relationships, brought about through the mutual attraction between older, experienced professionals, with a desire to share experience, and younger, ambitious colleagues, who valued them as a source of access to information, networks, influence and, in some cases, protection. Key to these relationships was a sense of shared identity, with both parties having similar backgrounds. The mentor often saw the younger person, known as a protégé, as a version of them decades before. With the formalisation of mentoring into programmes supported by organisations, came the opportunity to address a more diverse audience. While the first structured mentoring programmes were aimed at much the same audience as informal mentoring (and hence tended to reinforce inequalities in companies and professional bodies), the potential for overcoming disadvantage was soon recognised and the next generation of mentoring programmes aimed or partially aimed at supporting equality objectives. They began to appear first in the world of employment, then became rapidly integrated into the wider community.

In employment, diversity mentoring tended to evolve from an initial focus on race, to embrace a wider range of sources of disadvantage. Many companies' programmes started with a racial focus and then opened the doors to a limited number of other 'mainstream' disadvantaged groups, such as the disabled and women; then to all disadvantaged groups. Sometimes, the programmes then lost their diversity branding entirely, as mentoring became part of the corporate culture, with the result that anyone who wanted a mentor could have one. In recent years, we have seen some reversion of this trend, as shortages of resources to support mentoring have caused companies to refocus on specific audiences.

As Table 1.1 shows, the perception of diversity in an organisational context has changed dramatically over the past 30 years. This is in line with the evolution of diversity as an issue in the organisational psyche. In many recent programmes, the focus has shifted yet again, from a focus on redressing disadvantage to one of leveraging difference. By and large, these evolving perspectives on diversity have shaped the role, purpose and style of associated mentoring programmes. Equal opportunities was essentially a legalistic, compliance-based approach. Diversity management recognised that there was more to be gained for both the organisation and its disadvantaged employees (and potential employees) by focusing on the business benefits of supporting talented people, whatever their background. Leveraging difference, which extends in application to both organisations and society more generally, increases the emphasis on valuing difference as the engine of creativity and innovation. The scope of difference also evolves with

TABLE 1.1 From equal opportunities to leveraging difference

Equal opportunities	Diversity management	Leveraging difference
Issue (problem) focused	Opportunity focused	Individual focused
Tactical emphasis	Strategic emphasis	Tactical and strategic
Focused on a small number of defined groups	Aimed at everyone in a wider range of groups	A wider definition of talent
An HR issue	Issue owned by everyone	Valuing difference in all its forms
'Hard' targets (get the numbers)	Changing thinking and behaviours to change the culture	About the quality of conversations between employees and the organisation
About enforcing the distribution of power, privilege and advantage	About increasing collaborative endeavour and sharing	Driven by alignment between individual and organisational needs
Driven by legislation	Driven by organisational need	

these movements. Equal opportunity was mainly about easily defined groups (predominantly on the basis of colour or gender). Diversity management extended the construct to include a much wider range of difference, from social class to size. Leveraging difference extends it again, recognising that everyone is different and, while obvious differences such as colour or gender have a major impact on social interchange, they are merely superficial compared, say, to differences in personality or life experience.

Benefits of diversity mentoring

As programmes involving diversity mentoring seek to change individuals and the organisation, they often come under scrutiny to demonstrate their value. Diversity mentoring programmes form the majority of those accredited by the International Standards for Mentoring Programmes in Employment. It appears that they are more likely to come under scrutiny and need to prove the value they bring, than, say programmes aimed at graduate recruits. This emphasis on measuring the effectiveness of diversity mentoring is valuable in that it has provided an extensive database on the impact of both programmes and relationships engaging in this type of endeavour. From a societal and business perspective, diversity mentoring addresses in a powerful way issues of marginalisation, inequality and waste of talent. Each of these issues has a significant cost attached, in both monetary and broader societal terms. For example, the cost to taxpayers of keeping young people in idleness makes little economic sense. In the late 1990s, the Irish Government pioneered a programme, which brought thousands of these people into employment in sectors such as retail and airport logistics, through a mixture of mentoring, coaching and vocational training. As we write, the UK Government is looking to mentoring as a means of bringing hundreds of thousands of people back into the working economy, while in Denmark a law was implemented several years ago financing the use of mentoring to support 'weak unemployed' of all nationalities in the workplace and to retain disadvantaged young people in school.

From a mentee perspective, diversity mentoring offers a range of outcomes, which can be defined in terms of career, or as developmental, enabling and emotional. Career outcomes are the readily measurable transitions that occur when someone gains a promotion, or achieves substantial new responsibilities within the same job role, or makes a career move outside of the organisation. While developmental mentoring typically does not promise advancement of this kind, it does promise to help the mentee with the personal and professional development, which is normally a precursor to career progress.

Developmental outcomes relate to learning and the impact of learning. Learning can take a variety of forms: (1) learning directly from the mentor (tapping into their experience and wisdom); (2) learning from dialogue with the mentor (having their assumptions challenged, challenging back in turn, becoming more self-aware and contextually aware, gaining insight into their own and other people's behaviour, learning how to learn, and so on); and (3) learning from their reflection on the mentoring sessions.

Enabling outcomes consist of changes and achievements on the way towards the mentee's goals. Some examples are: creating and beginning to implement a career development plan; or establishing more extensive and more robust networks of influence (for getting things done through others) and information (for gathering intelligence about opportunities). These outcomes might also include taking a professional qualification; setting more ambitious goals in their personal development plan, and clarifying their own values and ambitions.

Finally, emotional outcomes are an important benefit of diversity mentoring. Such outcomes involve personal, internal transitions, such as increasing in self-confidence, becoming more positively assertive, understanding and valuing one's own contributions and culture, developing relationships of trust, feeling more comfortable about working with power differentials, and achieving greater authenticity. Of such outcomes, one mentee in a recent programme shared, 'I have learned to trust my own judgement and to be more forgiving to myself.'

Many of these outcomes for mentees are reflected in the outcomes for mentors. For example, a mentor in a mentoring programme for women leaders says: 'I have learned a lot from the fact that my mentee is a woman. Women do look differently at the world than men especially in relation to career and children. I realised before that there were these difference, but I had no idea how much time and effort women spend in making ends meet. I think about this a lot in my role as a manager today.' Another example is a mentoring programme aimed at helping the transition of women middle managers into directors, which found that approximately half of the mentors reported that they had gained greater confidence in their ability to perform their current job role (as did more than four out of five of the mentees). But perhaps the most common benefit for mentors is the opportunity to be challenged. The more senior people become in an organisation, the less people in more junior positions are willing to disagree with them. In the developmental mentoring relationship (though much less so in sponsorship mentoring), authority of position is largely put aside. Authority of experience is important, but because both parties bring different experience, there can be a much more equal exchange. More and more diversity mentoring programmes are designed with the mentor's learning as much, or more in mind than that of the mentee.

Issues from the diversity mentoring literature and our personal experience

From the cases gathered for this project and others, and from our own work with literally hundreds of organisations in dozens of countries, we (the editors) have been able to observe a great deal of good and poor practice and to identify a range of issues that influence the efficacy of diversity mentoring. In this section, we review some of the main recurring issues, in the light of that experience.

What makes the diversity mentoring relationship work?

A study by the US Minority Corporate Counsel Association (Anon 2003) found that diverse mentoring relationships that worked had a number of common characteristics. This research did not distinguish between developmental and sponsorship mentoring styles, though it suggests that the data are based primarily on a sponsorship mentoring approach. In the most effective mentoring relationships, the partners did the following:

- established confidence by beginning with work-related issues;
- identified common interests and values;
- made efforts to learn about each other;
- showed empathy;
- were clear about needs and expectations;
- avoided stereotypes and untested assumptions;
- risked discomfort to make the relationship work.

In order to answer the question more fully, however, it is necessary to examine as many as possible of the influencing variables. Some of these will be internal to the participants, some internal to the relationship and some to the context or environment.

Issues relating to the individual client include why they have come to mentoring (how clear are they about how they want to be different in themselves and in their circumstances?), the level of personal competence they have in the role and personal qualities that may aid or hinder rapport building and working together. In the book *The Situational Mentor* (Clutterbuck and Lane 2004) the chapters include an analysis of both mentor and mentee competencies, which suggests that mentor competencies remain relatively stable across the lifetime of the relationship, while mentee competencies evolve with the phases of relationship development. The analysis also suggests that some mentees, who come from a deprived background, may lack the initial competencies – such as communication skills – to get the most out of mentoring. Pre-mentoring can sometimes be a practical option to help them establish a mindset and basic competencies, which will allow them to work effectively with a mentor, i.e. to help the mentor help them. Some gender- and/or race-based mentoring programmes have found that offering assertiveness training to mentees before they begin their relationships has a positive impact on relationship quality and outcomes, although we have not been able to find empirical data to support this. The Mentor+Survey[1] used by one of the editors to evaluate the quality and results of mentoring programmes shows that mentors almost always experience personal development – and that the mentoring process has a positive influence on their active listening skills.

Personal qualities that facilitate success include behaviours, which are likely to foster rapport, or to contribute to effective collaborative management of the relationship. For example, there is some evidence to support ingratiation – in the sense of working to earn the good opinion of another person – as an important factor in making mentees attractive to mentors (Aryee et al. 1996). On the other hand, for the mentor, altruism has been negatively associated with relationship efficacy, on the basis that 'wanting to put something back' is more about the needs of the mentor than those of the mentee.

Factors internal to the relationship relate, for example, to the contract between mentor and mentee. These include such issues as expectations of how frequently to meet, how deeply to probe issues and concepts about their respective roles. Factors external to the relationship include the level of supportiveness from the organisation, which appears to be positively correlated with relationship success; and logistic issues, such as the opportunities to meet. The latter may be affected by the culture – for example, in busy, high energy cultures there are many distractions from setting and keeping to meetings, stronger skills of relationship management may therefore be needed.

Positioning difference and disadvantage

The MCCA study referred to above also found that 'discussion of race and gender diversity was often avoided when one of the parties was white, even in mentoring relationships, which were strong'. The problem with this is that it can be demeaning to the person from the minority or disadvantaged group, either to ignore the source of difference or to over-emphasise it. Here's a poignant comment from the report: 'As a mentee, it doesn't hurt my feelings if someone acknowledges the [racial] difference between us. In some ways I like those relationships better. It makes me feel more comfortable – we're not dancing around the issues in some artificial way. What's uncomfortable for me is when we have to pretend there isn't a difference.'

The keys, in our experience, are to do the following:

- Agree, between mentor and mentee, what role the mentee wishes difference to play in the relationship.
- Agree that mentor and mentee will challenge each other around the role of difference, where appropriate. So, for example, the mentor might question the mentee's perception that their failure to achieve a promotion is a result of racial bias (or vice versa).
- Educate and support participants in the skills of managing difference.
- Provide avenues for assistance when difference seems to cause difficulties.

One of the reasons positioning difference is so difficult is that it often depends on subtle, elusive perceptual variations. For example, linguistic difference affects the way that people perceive time. Asked to put pictures of themselves at ages from childhood to older age, English speakers will sort them from left to right. Someone, for whom Hebrew is their main language, would arrange the pictures from right to left. Mandarin Chinese speakers see time horizontally – they associate up with the past and down with the future (Ross 2011).

Mentors and mentees need to be open to such subtleties, developing a high level of attentiveness and awareness of both their own and the other person's reactions and assumptions. The skills of diversity dialogue do not always come easily, so the programme may need to be supported with opportunities for learning how to have productive and respectful conversations across the barriers of difference. A particularly useful tool, developed by one of the editors and now increasingly widely used in diversity training is the Diversity Awareness Ladder (Table 1.2). This is a model of two conversations – the inner conversation, which represents instinctive, emotional responses to difference, and is not normally spoken out loud; and the outer conversation, which offers a way of engaging with the other person, once the level of awareness has been acknowledged. While the inner conversation may sometimes emerge as spoken comment, this is typically not in the context of conversation with the person, who is seen as different.

The diversity mentoring relationship helps both parties take steps up the Diversity Awareness Ladder, in respect of their own relationship and ability to converse openly, and often in respect of relationships with the entire category of person, that the mentor or mentee perceives the other person to represent.

TABLE 1.2 Diversity awareness ladder

Stage	The inner conversation	The outer conversation
1. Fear	What do I fear from this person? What do I fear learning about myself? What might I be avoiding admitting to myself?	What do we have in common? What concerns do you have about me and my intentions?
2. Wariness	What if I say the wrong thing? Is their expectation of me negative and/or stereotyped? How open and honest can I be with them?	How can we be more open with each other? How can we recognise and manage behaviours that make each other feel uncomfortable/unvalued?
3. Tolerance	What judgements am I making about this person and on what basis? What boundaries am I seeking/applying in dealing with this person?	How can we exist/work together without friction? How can we take blame out of our conversations?
4. Acceptance	Can I accept this person for who they are? Can I accept and work with the validity of their perspective, even if it's different from mine?	What values do you hold? How do you apply them? How can we make our collaboration active and purposeful?
5. Appreciation	What can I learn from this person? How could knowing them make me a better/ more accomplished person?	What can we learn from each other? How will we learn from each other?

A useful exercise in exploring difference in the mentoring relationship is as follows: mentor and mentee define together the group, to which the mentee belongs. For example, 'educated male Ghanaians' or 'female ex-offenders'. They make a list, down the centre of a page, of descriptors that apply to the mentee, both positive and negative. In the left-hand column, the mentee writes a list of more negative characteristics of specific people, whom she sees as peers in the context of the group description; and in the right-hand column, the positive characteristics of other (or the same) peers. The first observation from this is that what seemed like a homogenous group is anything but. The second is that the mentor has an opportunity to recognise some of their own prejudices and to reframe them. The third is that the process emphasises the innate individuality of mentoring participants. Reversing the process (focusing on the mentor's 'group') enriches the conversation even further.

Stereotypes and implicit bias

Diversity mentoring provides a safe environment, in which people can learn to face up to, accept and manage their stereotypes and stereotypical assumptions. Project Implicit is a Harvard-based, continuing exploration of the hidden biases that people carry with them. Even if at a rational, conscious level, we are diversity-aware and extend goodwill to people, whom we see as different, at a subconscious level our instinctive responses may be very different. In the same way, our minds are full of associations, many of which we may not consciously agree with or give credit to, about 'types' of people. When caught off-guard without time to think of a 'proper' response, these implicit associations shape what we say and our instinctive response.

An exercise here is to ask mentors and mentees on their first meeting to offer each other three rapid and unreflective assumptions about the other person – for example, what kind of car they drive, or how tidy their home is. They then explore how accurate the assumption was and – more importantly – the reasoning process that led to that assumption. Most of the time, the assumptions are based on images and associations gleaned from newspapers, films or casual; or on encounters with somebody, who shares some characteristic with the other person. That characteristic may be their name (for example, 'I always think of Malcolms as being effete'), some physical attribute, their job ('professors are dull and have no sense of humour'), and so on.

The good news is that the more people get to know peers from other races or backgrounds, the more positive their attitudes tend to be towards them. Indeed, even having a friend who has positive social contact with people of a different race, for example, can improve a person's attitudes. Research exploring this phenomenon has recently shown that simply imaging positive contact with someone different can have a positive impact on how you regard them.

It's also possible, of course, to be over-empathetic. We have encountered relationships, which have struggled or failed because the mentor tried too hard and empathy became sympathy, which was not conducive to an adult-to-adult conversation! Another related issue here is privilege. For example, it is often difficult for people in senior positions to recognise the frustrations of people lower down, who have less control over their work and time and who are not trusted to work at home one day a week. It is likewise sometimes difficult for people on reasonable incomes to relate to the difficulties of having to rely on buses to get to work, rather than drive in their own car. Diversity mentoring provides the opportunity to bring such issues into the open. When an entire top team of an organisation understands the nature of privilege – something that can happen, for example, as a result of reverse mentoring[2] – it lays the grounds for quite radical change in the corporate culture.

Managing the diversity dialogue

Diversity dialogue can be defined as 'finding the appropriate language to engage with another person'. This is often easier said than done. Indeed, much institutional racism can be put down to conversational avoidance – choosing not to have conversations, particularly about difficult issues, with people of difference, for fear of giving offence. (Giving clear feedback and handling conflicts are behaviours managers often avoid, so when diversity becomes part of the picture, the issue becomes even more complex.)

One of the more unfortunate effects of our instinctive attempts to avoid saying the wrong thing is that we become more distant and less able to engage with the other person. One recent study (Norton et al. 2006) found that the harder people try to be colour-blind, the worse the communication with people of different colour.

Some ground rules that can be useful in terms of contracting for diversity dialogue include:

1 *Build agreements that allow mutual feedback about the impact of language.* Agree with people you work with that you expect them to tell you if you appear to be prejudiced or using language that has the potential to offend.

2 *Develop greater awareness of your own and other people's reactions to language.* Body language is an important clue. In most cultures, avoidance of eye contact is an indicator of emotional discomfort, for example.

3 *Recognise and respond appropriately to slip ups you make.* No matter how well we think we have buried or displaced racial or other stereotypes, there are almost always residual traces that surface from time to time without warning. If you do say something that offends, or which you know on reflection to be inappropriate:

● Admit it to yourself.

● If relevant, admit it to the other person(s) as well. (It's OK to say: 'I'm really surprised at myself. I do apologise. I think I need to reflect on this.')

● Talk it through with someone whose wisdom you trust.

- Don't feel guilty – feel intrigued about the potential to learn more about yourself.

4 *Don't confuse avoiding offence with abdicating responsibility.* Tough feedback can be very painful and quite upsetting. If a person dislikes a message, that doesn't mean it's offensive. It's very easy to back off from saying what needs to be said, using fear of giving offence as an excuse. If you do need to have hard words:

- Think about them beforehand, wherever possible.
- Ensure that the feedback you give is focused on specific behaviour or actions.
- Ensure that you don't import broader prejudices.
- Choose language that will not hinder the other person in addressing the issue.

Power dynamics

Power differentials are viewed differently in different cultures (Hofstede 1994; Trompenaars 1998; Rosinski 2003). Likewise there may be some preconceived power issues inherent in the environment or relationship (i.e. gender, race, socio-economic differences), which may affect the ability of mentor and mentee to engage in meaningful dialogue.

People acquire power in a variety of ways. Some of the most significant in this context (Garvey et al. 2009) include:

- *Reward power* – the ability to provide rewards such as promotions, pay rises or developmental projects.
- *Coercive power* – the ability to withdraw or withhold the rewards mentioned above or to make life difficult or unpleasant for those who do not comply.
- *Legitimate power* – derived from someone's formal authority or position within the organisation.
- *Expert power* – derived from being perceived to hold knowledge, experience or judgement that others value but do not yet have.
- *Referent power* – based on personal qualities, i.e. likeability, being respected, charisma.

One person in a mentoring relationship may have a great deal of all of these sources of power, while the other has very little. In such circumstances, the person with least power will tend to be deferential towards the other. This will lead to behaviours such as:

- reluctance to put forward their own opinion, for fear of appearing presumptuous;
- inability to challenge what is said;
- feeling obligated to follow the recommendations of the other person;

- expecting the more powerful person to 'have the floor' and to do most of the talking.

However, although someone may have power, they do not necessarily have to use it. In a mentoring relationship, it helps if both mentor and mentee agree to leave any power differential outside the relationship – as much as that is possible, if the formal power is still there.

In sponsorship mentoring, however, the authority and influence of the mentor are central to the relationship. The mentor uses his or her power to do the following:

- make introductions;
- intervene on behalf of the protégé;
- 'promote' the protégé by putting their name forward;
- protect them.

In developmental mentoring and developmental coaching, power is 'parked'. Both mentor and mentee attempt to minimise any effects of the power differential between them.

Some practical ways of reducing the negative impact of power in the learning relationship include:

- Agree learning goals for both parties.
- Recognise that power is often best exercised through influence rather than authority and make the development of influencing skills in the learner (as well as for the mentor) a sub-goal of the relationship.
- The mentor should encourage the mentee to put forward their view, before expressing their own; ask and show respect for their opinions.
- Don't meet in places that emphasise the mentor's status (e.g. mentor's office, mentor's club, restaurants beyond the mentee's budget).
- Use language that emphasises equality, rather than authority.
- Avoid a directive style, wherever possible – depending on what the mentee needs at the time.
- Ensure that the mentee retains responsibility for managing the relationship and for actions arising from the mentoring conversations.
- Review the relationship regularly to identify any situations where the mentee has felt a power imbalance.

Closely associated with the issue of power is that of rank. Rank may be conferred by:

- *Social status* – the relative value society places on their attributes (skin colour, gender, physical height and ability/disability, age, and so on).
- *Psychological status* – how confident you feel in your ability to function effectively in an environment or society (i.e. integration with the external world).

● *Spiritual status* – having a sense of personal purpose and meaning (integration with the inner world).

As with privilege, when people have high rank, they are usually unaware of it. They feel comfortable (integrated) and cannot understand why people of lower rank do not feel the same. They have little awareness of the stereotypes and prejudices they apply to others of lower rank. Other people respond by listening to them – their opinion has high credibility.

When people have low rank, they are very aware of it. They lack confidence, feel uncomfortable and have lower self-esteem. Other people respond by attaching less significance to what they say – their opinion has less credibility.

It's easy to see this scenario playing out in a mentoring relationship. Hence it's important in the contracting and review processes, and in the training of participants, to integrate these themes into the relationship dialogue.

Individual and shared stories

One of the simplest and most powerful ways to build understanding between diverse mentors and mentees is for them to share their stories. By this we do not mean their biographical history. These stories operate at a much deeper, emotional and values-laden level. Some practical ways to approach this include:

● Identifying the metaphor that they feel best describes them and their relationship to the world they currently inhabit. For example, one highly qualified professional, who was a refugee and was unable, in his adopted country, to work in his area of expertise, because his qualifications were not recognised, described his life as being a tiny person holding on to the leg of a big table.

● Finding and exploring the story, from the mentee's own culture, which expresses something of the mentoring theme.

● Sharing their personal journey of self-discovery. A useful framework for this is The Hero's Journey (Campbell 1949), an analysis of the common elements of epic stories, which has reportedly been used, for example, to design the *Star Wars* films. The steps of the journey pass through the comfort of normal, uneventful life, through the call to adventure, the support of a mentor, trials and tribulations, to self-discovery and personal change.

Choosing the media

Most of the cases in this book are based on traditional face-to-face mentoring. However, mentoring using other media is increasingly common, especially in the context of diversity and in cross-cultural programmes, where the participants may be both from different cultures and in different continents. E-mentoring – defined as mentoring through e-mail – has proven to be a highly effective medium, although it differs in many ways from face-to-face mentoring (Clutterbuck and Hussain

2010). One of its positive advantages is that it has built-in reflection time, which can be hard to create in the flow and excitement of a face-to-face mentoring session. Another is that e-mail correspondence is associated with lower power distance – people are less conscious of and hence less influenced by power differentials in the relationship (Hamilton and Scandura 2003), and since the mentor and mentee are unable to see each other face-to-face, this adds to the feel of being anonymous and thus make it easier to talk about 'intimate' subjects. However, e-mentoring has come to include many other. In practice, the trend in mentoring media appears to be towards multi-media solutions, including face-to-face (Skype and similar programs), e-mail, telephone, text/chat and many other media.

Maintaining the relationship

A phenomenon we observe frequently in mentoring and especially in the context of diversity mentoring is 'relationship droop'. It occurs when the relationship deals mainly with transactional and relatively superficial issues to begin with, perhaps because one or both parties feels uncomfortable or constrained about exploring deeper issues, and then runs out of things to talk about. In the diverse relationship, reluctance to make personal disclosure can be greater at the beginning, because trust takes longer to build with people, who are seen as different. At this point, there is often a dip in interest and motivation, due in part at least to a lack of any sense of progress towards the relationship goals, or a failure to agree goals, which are sufficiently challenging.

The cause and the cure go back to the selection stage of the programme and the contracting stage of the relationship. The relationships that have most resilience to relationship droop are those in the top right-hand box of the mentee purposefulness matrix in Figure 1.1 – where there is a clearly defined and

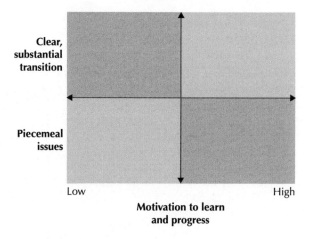

FIGURE 1.1 Mentee purposefulness

significant transition for the mentee and where the mentee is strongly motivated to progress and learn.

Closely related to this issue is: How long should the diversity mentoring relationship last? The simple answer is 'as long as it needs to'. However, the danger of relationships that go on past their sell-by date is that they develop into a state of dependency (Scandura 1988; Eby and McManus 2004). Research into endings of both coaching and mentoring relationships (Clutterbuck and Megginson 2004) has found that relationships that drift away, as opposed to having a clear ending, with recognition of each party's contribution, tend to be regarded by both mentor and mentee as unsatisfactory. We surmise that diverse mentoring relationships may encounter greater than normal difficulties in respect of mentees being able to tell mentors that they have gained all they need from the relationship and need to move on. In the authors' experience, having a defined period for the formal part of the relationship helps remove most of these problems – mentor and mentee still have the freedom to continue, if they wish, but do not have to negotiate an end point.

Conclusion

This short introductory chapter cannot hope to cover the full spectrum of issues relating to diversity mentoring. However, we have raised some of the primary concerns and most of these themes you will find echoed and re-echoed through our case studies. Some of the themes we will revisit in the light of the analysis of the case studies. All are potential areas for further research and experimentation.

Notes

1 See Poulsen and Wittrock (forthcoming 2012), for additional information, see www.kmpplus.com.
2 Reverse mentoring upturns the traditional hierarchical approach by making the mentor more junior to the mentee. For example, in the UK's Cabinet Office, junior black and minority ethnic managers mentor members of the top 50, helping them to become more aware of diversity issues.

References

Anon (2003) *Mentoring Across Differences: A Guide to Cross-Gender and Cross-Race Mentoring.* Washington, DC: Minority Corporate Counsel Association.

Aryee, S., Wyatt, T. and Stone, R. (1996) Early career outcomes of graduate employees: the effect of mentoring and ingratiation, *Journal of Management Studies*, 33(1): 95–118.

Campbell, J. (1949) *The Hero with a Thousand Faces*. San Francisco: New World Library.

Clutterbuck, D. and Hussain, Z. (2010) *Virtual Coach, Virtual Mentor*. Charlotte, NC: Information Age Publishing.

Clutterbuck, D. and Lane, G. (eds) (2004) *The Situational Mentor*. Aldershot: Gower.

Clutterbuck, D. and Megginson, D. (2004) All good things must come to an end: winding up and winding down a mentoring relationship, in D. Clutterbuck, and G. Lane (eds) *The Situational Mentor*. Aldershot: Gower.

Eby, L.T. and McManus, S.E. (2004) The protégé's role in negative mentoring experiences, *Journal of Vocational Behavior*, 65(2): 255–75.

Garvey, R., Stokes, P. and Megginson, D. (2009) *Coaching and Mentoring: Theory and Practice*. London: Sage.

Gray, W. (1986) Components for developing a successful formalized mentoring program, in W. Gray and M.M. Gray (eds) *Mentoring: Aid to Excellence in Career Development, Business and the Professions, Proceedings of the First International Conference on Mentoring*. Vancouver: Corporate Mentoring Solutions, Inc., 2, pp. 15–22.

Hamilton, B.A. and Scandura, T.A. (2003) Implications for organizational learning and development in a wired world, *Organizational Dynamics*, 31(4): 388–402.

Hofstede, G.H. (1994) *Culture's Consequences: International Differences in Work-Related Values*. New York: Sage.

Kram, K. (1983) Phases of the mentoring relationship, *Academy of Management Journal*, 26(4): 608–25.

Kram, K. (1985) *Mentoring at Work: Developmental Relationships in Organizational Life*. Glenview, IL: Scott, Foresman.

Megginson, D. and Clutterbuck, D. (2005) *Techniques for Coaching and Mentoring*. Oxford: Butterworth Heinemann, pp. 32–6.

Norton, M.I., Sommers, S.R., Apfelbaum, E.P., Pura, N. and Ariely, D. (2006) Colour blindness and inter-racial interaction, *Psychological Science*, 17: 949–53.

Rogers, C. (1961) *A Therapist's View of Psychotherapy: On Becoming a Person*. London: Constable.

Rosinski, P. (2003) *Coaching Across Cultures*. London: Nicholas Brealey.

Ross, V. (2011) Which way is the future? How we imagine the movement of time depends on what language we speak, *Scientific American MIND*, 10: 8.

Scandura, T.A. (1998) Dysfunctional mentoring relationships and outcomes, *Journal of Management*, 24(3): 449–67.

Trompenaars, A. (1998) *Riding the Waves of Culture: Understanding Cultural Diversity in Global Business*. New York: McGraw-Hill.

CHAPTER 2

The learning and development processes of diversity mentoring

Kirsten M. Poulsen

The complexity of diversity

In traditional corporate mentoring, where programmes are implemented to support new employees and new managers, to develop and retain talent, and to add value to formal training programmes, the mentee is usually less experienced than the mentor – and this is often, though not always, reflected in the mentor being older than the mentee. However, in diversity mentoring, the picture is more complex: the mentee might be older than the mentor while the mentor might be more experienced in what it is like to deal with diversity issues in the workplace (e.g. black or gay); the mentee might be younger than the mentor and come from a completely different socio-economic background, while the mentor might have more experience in the job market; the mentee might be very highly educated and have a disability, while the mentor could have less education but with experience in handling the same disability.

Adding more complexity is the fact that the mentees are part of a disadvantaged minority group – and their diversity issues may be very personal and very sensitive (e.g. health, disability and sexual preference). According to social identity theory, individuals classify themselves into social categories that shape their personal identities and allow them to define themselves in relation to their social environment (Clutterbuck and Ragins 2002: 29). And people prefer to relate to people whom they perceive as similar to themselves. Similarity is safe, there are no surprises, it is easy to communicate and understand each other, and members of such a group continuously validate each other's identity and self-image. Valuing and learning from differences is a challenge for both the mentor and the mentee as well as for the programme manager – and the perception of difference vs. similarity, the strength of stereotypes and the perceived level of discrimination in the organisation/society will affect the relationship and the learning process.

In Figure 2.1, we seek to illustrate the complexity of diversity mentoring by listing diversity dimensions and the characteristics of the organisational and societal context that can influence the relationship and the learning process.

We have experienced many diversity mentoring programmes over the years where well-meaning organisations and individuals wanted to do something special

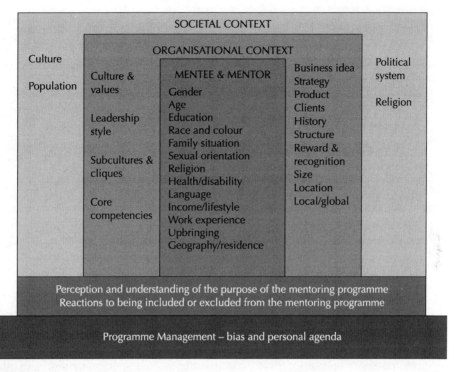

FIGURE 2.1 The complexity of diversity mentoring

for a group they perceived as disadvantaged and in need of help, and the potential mentees did not wish to participate because they did not wish to feel like a 'problem' – and because being invited into the programme made them feel even more disadvantaged. In the words of Edgar H. Schein (2009): 'Helping . . . is to enable others to do something that they cannot do for themselves. The dilemma of helping is that in most cultures we do not like to need help or ask for help.'[1] Schein talks about the need to create 'cultural islands', where the normal rules of the social order are temporarily suspended to create the psychological safety to explore and to be able to talk about subjects that are usually not thought to be polite. In diversity mentoring, the ability and willingness to place oneself in this 'cultural island' are fundamental to achieving a mutual process of learning and development. Building on the MBI (Mapping–Bridging–Integrating) model (diStefano and Maznevski 2000, 2004), diversity mentoring, even more than mentoring at large, is about recognising and articulating differences as the basis for self-discovery and new learning. It is about mapping how we are different in all the diversity dimensions. It is about bridging the gap by suspending our assumptions and prejudice and by using our empathy to see the world from each other's perspective. It is about realising how we are alike as human beings with dreams and feelings and needs. Finally, it is about integrating this insight into our knowledge and understanding of ourselves, thus developing a new self-image and empowering patterns of behaviour.

The learning process

The learning process in mentoring builds on the experiential learning process as described by Kolb (1976, 1981, 1984) and his associate Roger Fry (Kolb and Fry 1975) and has been expanded on by many others since. The experiential learning process creates new knowledge 'from the combination of grasping experience and transforming it' (Kolb 1984: 41). Through the experiential learning process the individual makes sense of concrete experience and develops an understanding of what shapes specific events and how the outcome of these events might change through different understandings and different behaviour.

The experiential learning process is seen as a circular four-step process that in principle can start at any of the four steps described below:

1 *Concrete experience* – specific experiences have shaped the mentee's understanding of the world and colour the mentee's expectation and perception of future events. In the mentoring dialogue, the mentor helps the mentee identify all the factual aspects of the concrete experiences they have had, thus helping the mentee overcome their selective focus on specific aspects of the experienced events.

2 *Reflective observation* – after experiencing a specific situation or a number of similar situations, the individual needs to explore the lessons learned. When doing this alone, the mentee may focus entirely too much on the aspects that confirm their former – and negative – perception of the situation, thus enhancing their existing understanding and preconceived notions of the world. Through the mentoring dialogue the mentee is challenged and supported in looking at themselves, at others and their experiences from many perspectives, adding depth and quality to the process of reflection.

3 *Abstract conceptualisation* – based on the learning from the reflective observation, abstract conceptualisation transforms new understanding of self and the relationship to others into meaningful concepts. The mentee is building new mental models of 'how the world works' and their own role and concludes how this learning can be applied to similar or new situations in the future.

4 *Active experimentation* – the next step is putting the new learning into action, about creating an action plan for what to do or not to do and finding the courage to actually do it. Through the mentoring dialogue, the mentor and mentee discuss how to put the learning into action in different ways and the mentor supports the mentee in exploring the potential value and risk of each alternative decision and action.

Chapter 1 explained how developmental mentoring works through enhancing the capacity and quality of a participant's thinking about issues that they perceive to be important to them. The experiential learning process provides a platform to identify and challenge the mentee's thinking patterns and to find out how they can escape from their own self-fulfilling prophecies. The way you think about yourself and others shapes your actions and your communication – as well as the stories you tell about yourself. So to change your actions and communication, first, you need to change the way you think and the stories you tell yourself and others, which may also result in a change in which issues are important to you. We could actually talk about the learning process of mentoring as finding and telling the identifying stories of the mentee and finding ways of reconstructing and transforming these stories in ways that create a new and empowering self-image, instead of the mentee continuously seeking out situations or searching for information that confirms his/her existing preconceptions.[2] As you cannot change your past and your past experiences, learning through mentoring – and especially through diversity mentoring – is about rewriting the meaning of your past experiences and creating new meaning of your future experiences.

The double learning process of diversity mentoring

In the words of one of the editors (Poulsen 2008): 'Mentoring is a synergetic learning partnership between two people with different levels or kinds of experience, where both can achieve new learning, new insights and personal growth.' In diversity mentoring, the initiative for establishing the programmes may come from a wish/a need to help a specific minority group. However, the programmes also present learning opportunities for the mentors – especially about their own (and others') unconscious use of stereotypes and how that affects relationships and collaboration.

It is through this 'double' learning process (Figure 2.2) that diversity mentoring can have a greater effect on society: by developing understanding, relations, mutual interest and respect among diverse groups of populations, thus making it easier to interact as neighbours, as colleagues and as people in the same community.

In the following pages we will describe some of the vital elements in enabling the double learning process of diversity mentoring.

Stereotypes, bias and social identity

This editor has been especially keen to focus on gender, i.e. women and leadership and there is a number of interesting research reports describing the effect of bias in regards to gender. In an older research report from 1983 (Paludi and Bauer 1983), a scientific article was reviewed and judged much more positively by both men and women when they thought it was a man who had written the article – and the

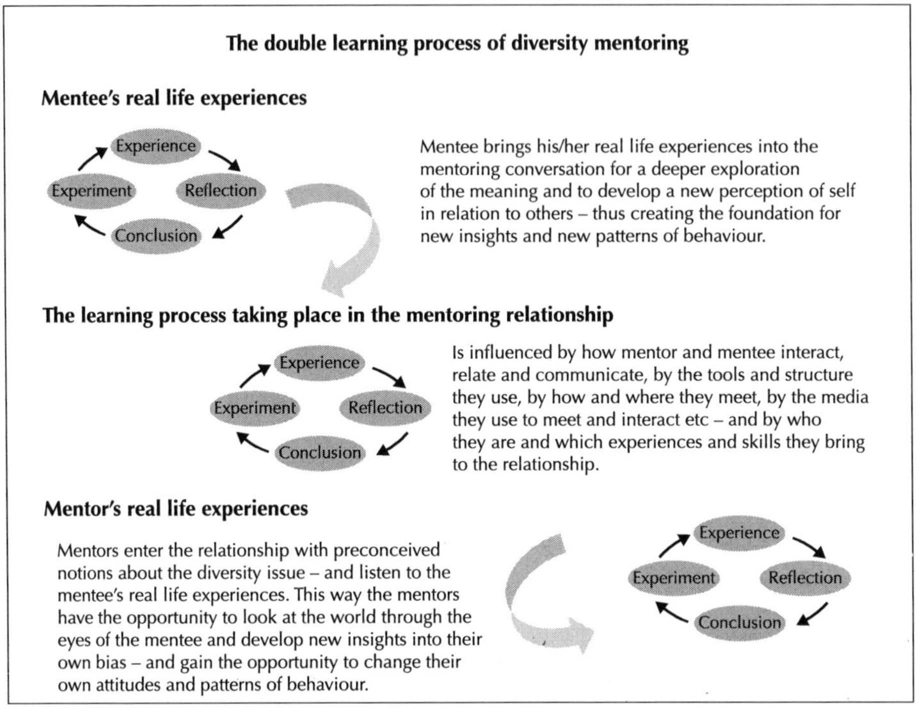

FIGURE 2.2 The double learning process of diversity mentoring

men were even more positive in their judgement than the women. In 1997, two Swedish researchers conducted a similar analysis of peer reviews of research fund applications (Wennerås and Wold 1997). It showed that the members of the review committee in general were more positive towards men, even when men and women had the same publication rate.

In the completely different area of symphony orchestras, Goldin and Rouse (2000) analysed the impact of changing from the music director hand-picking new musicians to a process of advertising the positions, using a hiring committee and letting the candidates play behind a screen, so the committee members could not see the applicants. Using the audition data, the authors find:

> That the screen increases – by 50% – the probability that a woman will be advanced from certain preliminary rounds and increases by severalfold the likelihood that a women will be selected in the final round. By a use of the roster data, the switch to blind auditions can explain 30% of the increase in the proportion of females among new hires and possibly 25% of the increase in the percentage of females in the orchestras from 1970 to 1996.

This research is a very obvious demonstration of bias and stereotyping as an automatic response to certain circumstances mainly based on our personal history, our upbringing, our earlier experiences and the norms of the society that we live in.

> Stereotypic beliefs about women's roles, for example, may enable one to see correctly that a woman in a dark room is threading a needle rather than tying a fishing lure, but they may also cause one to mistakenly assume that her goal is embroidery rather than cardiac surgery.
>
> (Gilbert and Hixon 1991)

The psychology of bias is valid for all the diversity dimensions. We may want to believe ourselves to be open, unbiased, inclusive and conscious about not stereo-typing others. However, just look at how at every conference or training course people will gravitate towards those that they already know or who are similar to themselves, unless the instructor tells them to do something else, of course. This is an effect of wanting to be in the comfort zone and of wanting to belong – to confirm our social identity. This happens in large groups and in small groups – you gravitate towards those people with whom you feel that you have something in common whether it be gender, race, profession, nationality, disability, personality, clothes style or dialect and which is a defining issue for yourself in the specific situ-ation (depending on the situation, the defining issue may change). Young people are doing this all the time today over the internet, networking with each other to feel part of a larger group – the 'right' group also called the in-group – building their self-esteem and identity also through excluding others and distancing them-selves from these others – the out-group. From social identity theory, we learn that the in-group will discriminate against the out-group to enhance their self-image – the more different and negatively we view the others, the more similar and right we see ourselves. Since the advent of the internet we have seen some very serious examples of how active discrimination and exclusion can have tragic effects, e.g. hate mails that lead to teenage suicides.

Matching vs. learning potential

Psychological safety describes the individual's perceptions about the consequences of interpersonal risk in the mentoring relationship – or any interaction with other people. It consists of the assumptions and beliefs about how others will respond when you expose your ideas and feelings, e.g. by asking a question, seeking feed-back, reporting a mistake, or proposing a new idea. 'How will my mentor react if I tell her about how I really feel . . .? Will she laugh at me, think I am stupid, and how will it affect our relationship?' In corporate mentoring, this is usually a ques-tion of considering career and social consequences in the job. In diversity mentoring, it is a question of the mentee's identity in society – and thus the risk is perceived as much higher.

When mentors and mentees are matched in diversity mentoring programmes, the issue of social identity and creating the foundation for trust and psychological safety is in focus. When you match a disabled mentee with a similarly disabled mentor, they may easily connect because of their similarities. However, they may also have the tendency to confirm their minority in-group situation and a distrust of others of the majority groups. When you match a disabled mentee with a not-disabled mentor, the mentee may feel unsafe, inferior, distrustful, while the mentor may come across as condescending, superior, insensitive, and it will take longer and require more effort to develop a safe and trustful relationship. However, the potential for learning for both is tremendously higher.

The whole purpose of diversity mentoring is for the mentee to gain new perspectives on his/her own identity, competencies and opportunities while at the same time influencing the mentor's perception of the in-group of the mentee and developing a new understanding of his/her own patterns of behaviour and how these can change to create a community where diversity is valued and put to good use for all. Building psychological safety and trust when there are few similarities to build on is a key element for success in diversity mentoring – so the question is, how do we prepare mentors and mentees for the challenges of the diversity mentoring learning process?

Preparing mentors and mentees for diversity mentoring

Building on the cases in this book and our own experiences, the following key mentor/mentee characteristics shape the development of the relationship and enable the double learning process:

- personality as well as personal history and social identity;
- motivation and readiness to enter the relationship and the learning process;
- social and emotional intelligence, such as self-awareness, empathy, impulse control, etc.;
- communication skills.

The influence of the mentor on the mentee's perception of psychological safety is paramount – the mentor's behaviour, communication style, accessibility and/or a failure to acknowledge the mentee's vulnerability can contribute negatively to the mentee's motivation for the relationship and the learning process and inhibit the mentee from opening up. Likewise, the mentee's approach to the relationship influences the mentor's perception of what is appropriate to do and say – and may lead to the mentor feeling awkward, over-analysing his/her intentions, words and actions, and loosing motivation for the relationship.

By training mentors to observe their own behaviour and to recognise discrepancies between their espoused values of equality and openness and their biased behaviours and communication, you can motivate and prepare mentors to enter diversity mentoring with open eyes and humility towards their own imperfections. By providing communication training and cultural awareness, mentors can learn new strategies to deal with differences and to understand the consequences of these strategies, e.g.

- *destructive* – using negative stereotyping, displaying mistrust, creating poor relationships and conflict;
- *equalising* – suppressing and ignoring differences, creating mediocre and superficial relationships;
- *appreciating* – recognising, accepting, exploring and building upon differences, creating positive and well-functioning relationships.

> As a mentee, it doesn't hurt my feelings if someone acknowledges the [racial] difference between us. In some ways I like those relationships better. It makes me feel more comfortable – we're not dancing around the issues in some artificial way. What's uncomfortable for me is when we have to pretend there isn't a difference.
>
> (Mentoring Across Differences, 2003)

However, it is not always enough to train the mentors, also the mentees may need preparation and training for meeting and working with their mentor. Especially in cases with very sensitive diversity issues and mentees with low self-esteem, it becomes crucial to support the mentees in daring to trust and open up. Even for the mentees to believe that mentoring can bring about valuable outcomes requires a huge effort in such a situation.

Some valuable tools for training mentors and mentees were mentioned in Chapter 1. Other relevant tools are personality profiles or preference tests such as MBTI, Big-5 and DISC. Working with profiles gives the mentors and mentees a common tool to focus on in identifying their similarities and differences as people and how these similarities and differences can help or hinder the mentoring process.

An innovative and easy to use new tool is the Diversity Icebreaker,[3] which identifies three behaviour preferences called red, green and blue. The Diversity Icebreaker dimensions are partly unconscious, they are created by language, and create a basis for developing in-groups, leading to intergroup dynamics and prejudice. People have emotions related to these dimensions and they often are tightly intertwined with identity. So are cultural descriptions and dimensions. Using the Diversity Icebreaker to train mentors and mentees creates a shared experience around less sensitive diversity dimensions in a positive and fun atmosphere that establishes a common language of egalitarian and complementary qualities. It promotes individual and collective reflection, highlights individual contribution and leads to better ideas of how diversity can be viewed and managed. In contrast to personality tests, the Diversity Icebreaker dimensions are traits that one can easily see in different ways in real life, due to a variety of contexts, tasks and people involved in interaction, and they provide the participants with words and concepts to consciously observe and describe their thoughts and actions.

Conclusion

Diversity mentoring is a very valuable tool for corporations and for society to encourage all employees and citizens to learn from each other, about each other and with each other. In this chapter we have outlined the main dimensions defining and influencing this learning process, which is brought to life through the case studies in the book.

It is our hope that this book will serve as inspiration for all who wish to develop a workplace and a society where diversity is valued as a resource that can make corporations stronger and better able to face the global market and create cohesive and inclusive societies.

Notes

1 Conference at CBS, Copenhagen Business School, 16 March 2010, on his new book, *Helping: How to Offer, Give, and Receive Help.*
2 Also called confirmation bias, a phenomenon where you actively seek out and assign more weight to evidence that confirms your hypothesis and ignore or undervalue evidence that might prove the hypothesis wrong.
3 See www.diversityicebreaker.com. The Diversity Icebreaker (DI) is not a personality profile, however, significant correlations with Big5 dimensions have been found, especially 'Openness to experience' with .5 plus correlation with green and .5 negative correlations with blue. Neuroticism was not found to be significantly correlated with any of the colours. The three other dimensions have significant correlations but not higher than .3. This indicates that DI dimensions are related to, but not the same as, general personality dimensions.

References

Clutterbuck, D. and Ragins, B.R. (2002) *Mentoring and Diversity: An International Perspective*. Oxford: Butterworth Heinemann.

diStefano, J.J. and Maznevski, M.L. (2000) Creating values with diverse teams in global management, *Organizational Dynamics*, 29(1): 45–64.

diStefano, J.J. and Maznevski, M.L. (2004) Synergy from individual differences: Map, Bridge and Integrate, *IMD Perspectives for Managers*, 108, March.

Gilbert, D.T. and Hixon, J.G. (1991) The trouble of thinking: Activation and application of stereotypic beliefs. *Journal of Personality and Social Psychology*, 60(4): 509–17.

Goldin, C. and Rouse, C. (2000) The impact of 'blind' auditions on female musicians, *The American Economic Review*, 90(4): 714–41.

Kolb, D.A. (1976) *The Learning Style Inventory: Technical Manual*, Boston, MA: McBer.

Kolb, D.A. (1981) Learning styles and disciplinary differences, in A.W. Chickering (ed.) *The Modern American College*, San Francisco: Jossey-Bass.

Kolb, D. (1984) *Experiential Learning: Experience as the Source of Learning and Development*. Englewood Cliffs, NJ: Prentice-Hall.

Kolb, D.A. and Fry, R. (1975) Toward an applied theory of experiential learning, in C. Cooper (ed.) *Theories of Group Process*. London: John Wiley.

Mentoring Across Differences (2003) *Creating Pathways to Diversity® – Mentoring Across Differences: A Guide to Cross-Gender and Cross-Race Mentoring*, Washington, DC: MCCA – Minority Corporate Council Association, Available at: http://www.mcca.com/index.cfm?fuseaction=page. viewpage&pageid=666.

Paludi, M.A. and Bauer, W.D. (1983) Goldberg revisited: What's in an author's name?, *Sex Roles: A Journal of Research*, 9(3).

Poulsen, K.M. (2008) *Mentor+Guiden*. Copenhagen: KMP+ Forlag.

Schein, E.H. (2009) *Helping: How to Offer, Give, and Receive Help*. San Francisco, Berrett-Koehler Publishers.

Wennerås, C. and Wold, A. (1997) Nepotism and sexism in peer-review, *Nature*, 387: 341–3.

Mentoring in the context of disability

Frances Kochan

Introduction

The case studies presented in this chapter deal with mentoring programmes designed to assist individuals who may require some type of accommodation to function in a manner that will foster their independence, productivity and success. We turn to the Disabled World website (http://www.disabled-world.com/disability/types/) to define a disability as 'a condition or function judged to be significantly impaired relative to the usual standard of an individual or group'.

While, in the past, the concept of disability carried a negative perspective of the person or their limitation, a newer view is that a disability is socially constructed. The website describes this social model of disability by suggesting that 'an individual may be impaired by a condition that requires daily living adaptations, but the bulk of his problem – his disability – can be found in the attitudinal and physical barriers erected by society'.

The writers of our case studies appear to accept this social model as the world in which people served by their programmes exist. They have created programmes that seek to provide their mentees with an understanding of their abilities and how to overcome barriers that limit their opportunities. At the same time, these programmes seek to change the organizational, cultural and societal milieu in which mentees exist.

As a group, these case studies help to broaden our understanding of the world from the perspective of those classified as having a disability. They provide a broadened perspective of the role the environment plays in limiting people and propose strategies that will enable them to apply their strengths and gifts, no matter what environment they encounter.

Case study 1: Great Britain

'Aimhigher': encouraging young people with disabilities

Leyla Okhai and Peter Quinn

Introduction

In 2006, the Disability Rights Commission, now merged into the UK Equality and Human Rights Commission, noted that only 1 in 20 disabled people were in post-18 education[1] compared with 1 in 10 of the general population. In the academic year 2006–2007 the University of Oxford's Disability Advisory Service (DAS) sought to address this issue by developing a mentoring programme to encourage local pre-university students with disabilities to consider entering higher education (HE).

The Project, labelled the Aimhigher[2] Mentoring Project, was initiated as a pilot programme. The pilot was a success but was very resource-intensive. The University already had experience of engaging with Aimhigher schools throughout the county of Oxfordshire and it was decided to use internal expertise from the University's Widening Participation Team, with whom the DAS had some existing collaborative links, to further the programme. Guided by participant feedback and a review of the previous year's scheme, it was decided to repeat the programme in academic year 2007–2008 with some adjustments.

Design of the programme

The programme consisted of three half-day workshop sessions for the mentees supported by their mentors. The mentors were students with disabilities at the University of Oxford. The mentors were trained in their role as a mentor. In addition, training was given on the e-mentoring system used for maintaining contact between mentors and mentees throughout the project.

The programme's objectives were to ensure that all students would do the following:

- be confident that they could succeed in higher education study;
- know how to access information about further and higher education;
- be aware of the higher education institutions which could offer appropriate study environments and the range of delivery modes;
- be able to evaluate information and develop a personal action plan;
- be able to identify a subject of study and suitable study route and be supported in the application process.

Recruitment of mentees

Programme information was circulated via the Special Educational Need Coordinators networks (SENCo). Information was shared through a wide variety of media venues. However, although information was distributed widely, the schools that eventually became involved did so as a result of historical working relationships and extensive work with individual teachers, parents and SENCos.

We also found that parents could be barriers to student progression into higher education. Parents are often the pivotal support for their children and cannot envisage anyone else being capable of providing suitable support. Sometimes, they assume that support in higher education mirrors school support, which is less resourced. They may also want to shield their child from discrimination that they fear might occur.

Another barrier encountered was terminology. In universities, 'disabled student' is a common term. In pre-university study, also known as Further Education (post-16 study taking place in a college) 'students with special educational needs' is the preferred descriptor and we initially encountered confusion when attempting to attract participants, thus resulting in us having to translate and clarify our terminology.

Once interested schools had been identified, members of the DAS and Widening Participation Team interviewed each applicant. This entailed several visits to schools. From a total of nine interviewees, seven students were identified as suitable (one student put forward was not disabled, but had English as a second language, not legally a disability in the UK), and this is an example of the misunderstandings encountered in this work. One student who was eligible decided not to participate.

Recruitment of mentors

The DAS nominated a number of champions from within the disabled student body who had expressed an interest in outreach work. As soon as the core group of mentees was established, the potential mentors were approached, agreed to participate, received the necessary training and were allocated mentees. Much of the training had already been delivered within training for other roles students had undertaken for their College. Specific training on mentoring skills was delivered by an experienced mentoring trainer. Tables 3.1 and 3.2 show the disabilities and the courses for the mentees and their mentors.

TABLE 3.1 The mentees' disability and their aspirations

Mentees	Disability	Aspiration
1	Chronic fatigue syndrome	Performing Arts
2	Hearing impairment/unseen disability/mental health	Business Studies
3	Hearing impairment	Childcare
4	Severe SpLD	Youth Work
5	Visual impairment	HE (subject undecided)
6	Mobility difficulty	Dentistry
7	Unseen/mobility difficulty	Unknown

Note: SpLD – Specific Learning Disability.

TABLE 3.2 The mentors' disabilities and their course of study

Mentors	Disability	Studying
1	Visual impairment	Politics, Philosophy, Economics (3rd year)
2	SpLD/visual impairment	History (1st year)
3	Severe SpLD	DPhil Psychology (3rd year)

Implementation

The three half-day workshops were an opportunity for mentees to meet mentors, who were successfully studying in HE as well as interacting with other young people with disabilities. One of the University's Colleges, Trinity College, hosted the first two workshops while the third included a guided tour of Oxford Brookes University, which is a modern campus-based university in Oxford. The tour provided an opportunity for the mentees to see another type of university. The project was mindful of the atypical environment of the University of Oxford which may have been perceived as a barrier without the context of the tour of Oxford Brookes University.

During the programme, we became aware that a significant knowledge gap for parents could and would become a barrier to their supporting their son or daughter into HE. Parents were unaware that they would not have to cover costs relating to reasonable adjustments as they had done for their child throughout school. In HE there are generous, non-means-tested government-funded finance packages to cover all disability related to study support costs. In recognition of this, we hosted an evening information session for the parents in a prestigious venue covering financial support and the student experience. Time was allocated for one-to-one meetings with the DAS team.

Assessment

The project was monitored and evaluated using questionnaires to gather feedback from students and their parents, career guidance teachers, and staff speakers/student ambassadors. The Coordinator compiled a written evaluation and final report and there was a follow-up with the school after the programme was completed.

The results from these evaluations showed that all programme objectives had been met. All participants found the workshops useful. Although some participants came to understand that HE was not for them, they also came to realise that there are other options available. This programme also provided these students with a good opportunity to discuss HE issues in a safe space with other students who face similar difficulties.

Another interesting outcome was the realisation from the mentors that their disability, something they described as having to compensate for, was now something they could contribute. Students also appreciated that the programme included materials in accessible format; funded travel; provision of accessible venues and refreshments.

Lessons learned

The feedback from teachers, participants and mentors was very positive. The Oxford Brookes University campus tour was particularly popular, as was the opportunity to visit one of the colleges at the University of Oxford. However, there was clearly an information gap. Teachers did not seem aware of the aims of the project despite targeted information. This resulted in confusion on the part of participants, who could not understand why they had been selected for the programme.

The university was disappointed that there were not more participants available to take part. This was in the main due to lack of communication within the Aimhigher schools' partnership. There may also have been a perception within schools about which type of participants would be appropriate for the programme.

Reflection questions

1. What would you propose to ensure recruiting more participants for the programme?
2. Were you surprised that parents and teachers were barriers to the participation of disabled students?
3. Can you think of disabilities where participation would be problematic and actually create a further barrier to participation in higher education?

Notes

1 See: www.skill.org.uk/page.aspx?c=32&p=139.
2 For more information, see: http://www.direct.gov.uk/en/EducationAndLearning/UniversityAndHigher Education/DG_073697.

Case study 2: Great Britain

The Asperger Transitions Project: fostering workplace success
Malcolm Johnson

Introduction

The Asperger Transitions Project began as a pilot initiative at Nottingham University in 2008. Asperger syndrome (AS) is a predominantly male, mild and high-functioning form of autism. Named after the Austrian pediatrician Hans Asperger, the condition remained largely ignored from its discovery shortly after the Second World War until the early 1990s when it began to receive greater prominence. This programme seeks to address the distinct character traits of AS such as an introverted personality, less developed social skills and desire/ability to interact with others, and a preference for routine and lower ability to cope with change.

However, sufferers of Asperger syndrome also have a number of exceptional abilities and advantages. Among these are a highly original mode of thinking and cognition and exceptional levels of honesty and integrity. This makes them loyal and dedicated employees. For this reason, it is thought that some of the most influential individuals in history 'might' have been afflicted by the condition, including Isaac Newton, Albert Einstein and Bill Gates.

The aim of the Asperger Transitions Project is to fill the gap that existed in the provision of support for students with AS in the UK Higher Educational sector. At the time of its inception there was an absence of any national programme that guided the career search process and transition into the workplace for students with AS to effectively prepare them for workplace entry.

The programme consists of four stages:

1 *Knowing Yourself* – explores specific Asperger traits such as how they manifest themselves both internally and in the workplace. This provides the individual with greater self-understanding about how the traits may impact on them during the course of their work. These provide the basis for constructive adjustments going forward.

2 *Careers Search* – covers the careers search process and investigates why some careers are suitable/unsuitable for the AS personality profile.

3 *Workplace Issues* – explores how factors such as disclosure and reporting structures/objectives can be managed to enable smooth transitions into an organisation role. As change is something that a person with AS typically feels uncomfortable with, and finds hard to adjust to, providing insight into the change and practical advice on how to deal with the process can contribute significantly to career success.

4 *Action Plan* – the student is supported to develop a Personal Development Plan. As a person with AS benefits from clear, explicit instructions and defined objectives, providing these in the form of a personalised development outline can act as a reference point and provide necessary reassurance as to what is professionally required.

Assessing outcomes

At the end of the project, students are interviewed individually and also complete a questionnaire about the programme. Feedback has shown that students have gained a much higher level of self-awareness and knowledge about how AS affects them and what they can do to manage their professional and career development/ choice. This awareness enables students to make better and more informed decisions about what they need in relation to a career. However, rather like the move from university into the world of work, little specialist support exists currently once they have assumed an actual role.

Lessons learned

The outcomes identified from the project make us believe that a mentoring programme could be of major assistance to provide support once individuals have entered the workforce. A mentoring programme in the world of work could do the same. Such a programme could draw upon mentors from a wide variety of professional backgrounds.

Providing effective mentoring support would result in numerous benefits for both the employee and the employing organisation. For the former, it would provide the direction, guidance and reassurance that would enable them to perform effectively and to their full potential. For the latter, it would enable them to secure an effective and loyal worker, one who provides skills and insights that many mainstream employees are unable to deliver. Just as important is the opportunity to prevent difficulties arising that can be more difficult and costly to address at a later stage.

Implications for training

The starting point for training would be for both students and mentor to achieve a shared understanding of the purpose of mentoring and the roles followed by the development of specific mentoring skills. For the mentees, this would include focus on their role and responsibility, on how to manage the relationship and to show appreciation to their mentor. For the mentors, it would include skills-specific accounting for AS and what the employee with AS requires. Training should be mainly face-to-face/small groups and in the form of a modular approach: short but frequent sessions.

Telephone mentoring sessions can be an option, though they may not be as challenging/developmental for mentees with AS as they will not have to maintain eye contact or interact as fully interpersonally, i.e. by picking up on non-verbal language, and, therefore, this would make learning less impactful.

Reflection questions

When considering whether an individual or organisation should take advantage of implementing a mentoring scheme, you may consider:

1. How could the individual benefit from having a formal structure and support mechanism to enable them to transition into, and perform effectively in, a given role?
2. How is providing specialist, specific support any different to training mainstream employees in the art of negotiation or conflict management – and is it?
3. Does having a satisfied, contented, loyal and productive employee, one who can offer exceptional talents and insight that could uniquely benefit the organisation, appeal to the organisation?

Case study 3: Great Britain

Access to Work: workplace support for individuals with dyslexia

Martin Parsonage and Shaun Wilson-Gotobed

Introduction

Three organisations – the INDIGO Dyslexia Centre (a charity), the Norfolk County Council (NCC) (a Local Authority) and the Department of Work and Pensions (DWP) – developed the Access to Work (AtW) programme in the UK as a 12-month pilot project supporting individuals with dyslexia to help them overcome work-related obstacles resulting from their disability. The programme is run by the DWP which supplied funding and referred the clients.

NCC is a Local Authority with 28,000 employees. The organisation recognises that dyslexia is often a condition misunderstood both by those with dyslexia and those who do not suffer from it. Although most people view dyslexia as focusing upon one's ability to read, write and spell correctly, the effects of dyslexia are broader and in today's workplace where one must do more with less, employees with dyslexia are potentially at a significant disadvantage. A total of 50 NCC employees participated in the support offered through this pilot project. NCC agreed to grant the employees (customers/clients) 10 hours of release time to participate.

The INDIGO Dyslexia Centre is a Norwich-based charity dedicated to helping any individual or organisation with dyslexia-related issues. Although there are many definitions of dyslexia, the one used by this group is 'a specific learning difficulty which mainly affects the development of literacy and language related skills'. The Centre supplied the specialist mentors, counsellors, dyslexia advisors, IT expertise and access to a fully equipped resource centre to support the AtW programme.

Background and aims

NCC was looking for mentoring support for its employees to help overcome work-related obstacles caused by their dyslexia. The INDIGO organisation was seeking to expand and develop its provision of active services. DWP/AtW wanted to explore the cost effectiveness of empowerment of dyslexics through mentoring.

Together, the aims of all three partners were:

- to help dyslexic people (NCC employees who are in paid employment) by providing practical support to overcome work-related obstacles resulting from their dyslexia;
- to provide customer-/client-focused support and mentoring;
- to improve the effectiveness of current Access to Work provisions;
- to increase awareness within the NCC of dyslexia and to value its positive aspects for employees;
- to increase the confidence level of employees with dyslexia;
- to improve the effectiveness of any identified adjustments, and ensure that they are better targeted;
- to the needs of the individual, thereby achieving cost savings;
- to encourage employers to recruit and retain dyslexic people.

In each organisation there were individuals willing and prepared to take on the role of primary contact and leadership. There was good communication between these individuals and regular meetings were held. A customer journey diagram was produced and distributed to all involved, in order to assist with clarity for the organisations and beneficiaries of the project.

The INDIGO Dyslexia Centre's working definition of mentoring is: 'to support and encourage people to manage their own learning in order that they may maxi-mize their potential, develop their skills, improve their performance and become the person they want to be' (Parsloe, cited in Rao 2010: 60) – and in the AtW programme the mentor and mentee normally work in similar fields or share similar experiences.

The project began in 2009 and the target output for the pilot was 50 clients in a six-month period. Dyslexia was the shared experience of the mentors and mentees. This assisted in building a relationship based upon mutual trust and respect. Mentors were considered to be guides helping the mentee find the right direction and assisting them to develop solutions to career issues. INDIGO mentors relied upon having had similar experiences which enabled them to offer empathy to the mentee, helped them to understand issues facing the mentee and fostered their ability to facilitate the mentees' understanding of how dyslexia might affect them in the workplace setting.

The authors developed the concept for the project. Shaun Wilson-Gotobed had previously encountered mentoring support himself. They approached AtW and offered to take part in a pilot scheme. They suggested providing NCC employees with dyslexia the opportunity of taking part in five one-hour sessions of dyslexia skills-training prior to AtW workplace assessment, followed by a further five sessions. This was the start of the pilot project.

Project processes

The AtW programme begins by having a workplace assessor conduct a needs assessment with the client. This assessment usually results in recommendations for the use of assistive technology equipment. It was noticeable, however, that employees often failed to utilise equipment to its full potential. It was clear that the crucial aspect of support was missing from the existing AtW provision. The assumptions behind the pilot programme was that the individuals needed help to gain a better understanding of their difficulties, which would then assist them to benefit fully from the assistive technology equipment.

The mentoring support was provided in one-to-one sessions by an INDIGO associate mentor with a wide range of skills, including counselling, mentoring, IT, and needs assessment. The INDIGO mentors aimed to assist AtW customers to develop coping strategies and organisational skills which were transferable between job roles, reducing the reliance on the technical solutions, while also helping individuals to use what was essential.

The pilot project included ten mentoring sessions per client. Maximum flexibility was available for the client/customer and the mentor to travel in the optimum direction for the individuals' situation. In recognition of the fact that individuals with dyslexia may experience very different issues, at the start of the programme, the INDIGO mentor explained what dyslexia is and shared how it affects people in the workplace.

All clients/customers who participated were referred by their employer. The lead person within NCC undertook work to market the pilot project to raise awareness of the service and encourage employees to join the programme.

Assessment strategies

The project was assessed for impact and cost effectiveness by AtW. The project clients/customers and a control group of 50 people were compared. A customer/client questionnaire was used. Feedback was supplied from NCC from an employer's point of view and by INDIGO's own review.

The questionnaires aimed to record customer experiences of support offered on the pilot versus customer experience of those not involved in the pilot. Clients/customers of both groups were asked specific questions about the impact of the support they had received in their working life. An individual, who was involved in delivering the workstation/workplace assessments for the pilot customers, also gave his observations.

Once the customers in the AtW pilot group had completed their mentoring sessions and participated in a workplace assessment, they were telephoned to complete the questionnaires. The same process was used with the control group following their participation in the workplace assessment and receipt of their equipment.

NCC conducted a similar exercise with the line managers of the customers/clients who had participated in the pilot. Once all the data collection was completed, it was analysed by AtW personnel. The financial data from both groups was also compared. At INDIGO, clients who participated were requested to review each session they attended. The sample of the AtW workers who responded consisted of 78 out of 100 participants.

Outcomes

It was not possible to measure the impact of the pilot upon customers of various employers. However, when the comparison was made between the average costs of both groups, a saving of £332.16 per customer was achieved with the pilot customers.
Additionally,

- Some 19 per cent of pilot customers felt that a positive impact had been made on their ability to complete the tasks in their job role due to AtW mentoring support.
- Line managers of the pilot customers reported positively on the impact the mentoring sessions had on the employee.
- Most participants believed that the skills they had learned were transferable to other situations.
- There was a significant difference in the customer experiences reported between the control group and the pilot group, with the pilot group reporting more positively.
- Employers and the ICT (technology) group were educated about how to deal with dyslexia in the workplace.

- Pilot clients reported more confidence in using the technical equipment supplied than the control group.

The ICT teams at Norfolk County Council have welcomed the introduction of the INDIGO mentoring sessions. They find that users are now much better informed as to how they can benefit from ICT in their day-to-day jobs. When they were assessed by AtW, prior to the introduction of the mentoring sessions, many users had little or no knowledge of what is available in terms of IT to assist them and they were often recommended a lengthy list of ICT equipment which, in many cases, ended up in a drawer not being used.

We believe that the improved level of consultation and involvement between all parties will persist into the future. The project added substantial value and innovation, and the actual impact of the project on the client is clear. The project challenged the status quo for all three stakeholders and improved it. Others recognised the value of the work, and NCC was commended in the regional equality award competition by the regional council.

Lessons learned

Additional key learning points for INDIGO about the project were:

- Mentors/counsellors require knowledge of a variety of learning difficulties not just SpLD. Dyslexia in some clients presents itself with other difficulties, an example being Tourette's syndrome.
- It is essential that the employer supports the participants who need 10 hours of employee time for the mentoring sessions.
- Mentors need to have a high level of expertise and access to a dyslexia resource centre for diagnostic screening if this has not been completed previously. Such a centre also needs to be able to demonstrate assistive technology.
- Mentors need professional supervision.
- Clear referral processes and communication need to be maintained in order for the service to work properly.
- Contractual arrangements need to be in place and the contract monitored.
- Flexibility must be maintained.

Looking ahead

In conclusion, this mentoring pilot highlighted several important issues with the types of support AtW delivers to its customers with dyslexia. The learning from this project can help improve provisions for dyslexic people in employment. Although there were many positive aspects to the programme, it is recommended that prior to rolling out the INDIGO approach nationally a test project be established in two regions to identify further lessons to be learned from working with various employers in a wider geographical setting.

The mentoring sessions instilled self-confidence, productivity and a general sense of well-being in the individuals. We believe disability groups need a better model of service provision and greater awareness and understanding across all organisations. We hope that this programme provides guidance in doing so.

Reflection questions

1. How can we bring about change in policy, planning, personal practices, service delivery and customer satisfaction by using the mentoring approach? How can it be used for other disability groups? Are we prepared to implement specialist mentoring for disability groups?
2. Are employers doing enough to help dyslexic employees in the workplace? What could be done differently?
3. How could this example of a third sector (charity) organisation providing specialist disability services be duplicated in other settings? What are the barriers, and how could they be overcome?

Reference

Rao, M.S. (2010) *Soft Skills Enhancing Employability: Connecting Campus with Corporate.* Greenwich, CT: International Publishing House Ltd.

Case study 4: Great Britain

Deaf mentoring: a personal view

Jane Cordell

Introduction

The case describes my experience as a deaf person mentoring a deaf colleague Anne[1] at our workplace in 2004 and 2005. The mentoring helped the mentee develop confidence in a mainstream, predominantly non-disabled organisation. She subsequently took on leadership roles among deaf colleagues, including informally mentoring them.

This case affirms the importance of diverse role models and the multiplier effect these can have, but given the lack of senior disabled (particularly deaf) role models, it also raises questions about how to promote this type of practice. For me, as a mentor it also highlighted certain risks including over-empathising and assuming too great a responsibility as one of a very small number of role models who are deaf.

The government department Anne and I work for is rated as a top-choice employer for graduates. Entry is highly competitive. Quantitative data on levels of disability in the department is not readily available. The Annual Table of Civil Service Statistics 2010[2] shows 78 per cent of the department's staff did not provide their status (disabled or not). My own observation is that it is rare to encounter a visibly disabled colleague; however, many disabilities are not visible.

The mentoring programme and the context

At the time Anne and I started our mentoring relationship, the department provided a mentoring programme to any interested staff. An external provider offered a half-day introductory course explaining how mentoring worked, the benefits and potential pitfalls, followed by a 'matching' exercise for potential mentors and mentees. A few months later there was a progress review. When Anne and I decided to start a mentoring relationship, we contacted the department's programme, which was happy for us to access the training, even though we had already 'matched' ourselves as mentor and mentee.

The political backdrop to this mentoring relationship was pro-diversity. In 2004, there was interest across Whitehall – under the then Labour government – in promoting diversity in the Civil Service. The Cabinet Office ran talent-promotion programmes for specific minority groups, including the Bursary scheme for high-potential civil servants with disabilities. I entered the scheme in 2004. It gave me my first experience of being mentored. That experience was positive. None of my mentors (I have had three over seven years) was disabled.

The mentee

Anne became deaf gradually as a young person. She is comfortable communicating in English, British Sign Language (BSL), or both. While working at a college as a young adult, she received mentoring-type advice from a deaf colleague, who then went on to run her own successful business.

Anne was appointed to her position in the government department at higher level support grade. She then went on to pass the internal promotion competition to the next (operational) grade. She is one of a small group of deaf staff (10 at the time of writing), half of whom work at support grade.

Some time before Anne and I met, she had been given a new role in a different office. A difficult visit to the place where she was to work left her feeling worried about the job. When I interviewed her for this case study she said, 'I wasn't able to stand up for myself at the time in the way I feel I can now.' She described the situation with the future colleagues as 'not reassuring'. After some thought, Anne made the difficult decision to withdraw from that particular job, but remained employed by the department.

When I met Anne, her morale – and confidence in her employer – seemed low. She had started a new role and was finding it a challenge to get her colleagues to understand her needs as a deaf officer and her way of working. She told me a couple of times she was thinking of leaving the organisation.

The mentor

I became profoundly deaf as an adult. I joined the department in 2001 as a mid-career entrant at middle management grade, one level below the senior management grade.

How the mentoring worked

Anne and I agreed to meet initially every three to four weeks for 60–90 minutes. We communicated directly in these meetings. This would be unremarkable for a non-deaf person, but if Anne's mentor had been hearing, Anne would have probably required a support worker (lipspeaker or sign-language interpreter) to support communication. As we were able to communicate with each other directly (using a combination of lip reading, finger-spelling some English words, and some sign language), communication between us could be fluent and open. This probably helped us to develop a rapport with one another.

Between meetings we used e-mail to communicate. Anne set the agenda for each session, reviewing progress and noting any new challenges or questions. Sometimes Anne would request help in wording particularly sensitive or tricky e-mails to colleagues, often concerning her needs as a deaf member of staff. Anne was keen to convey these in a clear way which would encourage her colleagues to take a positive attitude towards her requests. Getting the tone of written communication right was a particular challenge for her.

Anne seemed to find it useful to be able to discuss face-to-face why a particular phrase or structure was more effective than another. When Anne was experiencing practical challenges, for example, speaking up at meetings and conveying her views, we would use the safe environment of the mentoring meeting to rehearse how she would handle the situation, including engaging in role play.

This seemed to be helpful. Anne said, during our interview in January 2011:

> I became more confident than I was in the first couple of years at the department. I wouldn't say I am *very* confident as a person, e.g. in large groups. But after the mentoring I could approach my line manager and explain my needs. And at team meetings I will now interrupt if I need to, for example to ask for clarification. I would not have done that before.

Timetable and methodology

The mentoring relationship lasted approximately 20 months and became less formal as it progressed. As Anne gained confidence in handling the various challenges she faced, she would often send me quick requests to check her own decisions, rather than ask for advice on what to do. I felt this was a sign of her greater self-reliance, and of the success of the mentoring, as we had defined it. In January 2011, as part of the research for this case study, I sent questions by e-mail then used those questions as the basis for an interview with Anne.

Objectives

We developed objectives together. I set out what I thought the role of mentor was. Then Anne outlined that she wanted to use mentoring to increase her confidence in a variety of areas, learn to become more assertive, deal with specific problems that arose, and help raise deaf awareness among her co-workers.

We agreed to define mentoring as:

- regular access to a volunteer with useful professional and personal experience to share;
- contact with someone who had your interests at heart and who could draw on their experience to suggest new approaches to problems;
- a relationship based on mutual respect and confidentiality.

Outcomes

After the mentoring relationship ended, Anne did the following:

- showed a marked increase in confidence and assertiveness;
- demonstrated stronger self-belief, including readiness to question action taken on her behalf as a deaf member of staff, or assumptions made;
- voluntarily led a deaf team of staff to run a successful public event in the department celebrating deaf awareness;
- wrote and led a petition from deaf staff to the department's Minister about a decision which they viewed as discriminatory;
- took on the role of Chair of the staff disability body's deaf sub-group;
- promoted dialogue between department deaf staff and external contacts, including encouraging contributions to Civil Service-wide research on the experience of civil servants with disabilities;
- advised BSL users when in difficulty, including going to meet them to explain important messages in complex written English.

Lessons learned

While the benefits of such a mentoring relationship seem clear, there are also risks worth highlighting.

First, when both mentor and mentee are members of a small, well-differentiated minority group, especially when they work for the same organisation, it is possible for the mentor to over-empathise with the difficulties the mentee experiences. By this, I mean the mentor may subconsciously adopt an approach to mentoring which takes a 'them against us' angle on the work situation. The mentor in such a relationship needs to be aware of this risk and of the need to obtain a balance between using common experience positively (e.g. to demonstrate understanding and create rapport) and potentially biasing the mentee.

There is a concomitant risk linked to being a role model. Diverse role models are of course valuable, but their very scarcity can mean that their behaviour and choices may be scrutinised too closely by mentees and taken wholesale as 'the model' for them. Individuality is important and it would be risky, for example, for an introverted mentee to assume that they should adopt the apparently extravert demeanour of their role model/mentor and view extraversion as the path to achievement or confidence. Equally the mentor may feel pressure to fit the model of an ideal rather than being able to be themselves, warts and all. The two risks could also be mutually reinforcing. I found myself aware of both risks while mentoring Anne.

The factors Anne and I have identified in making this mentoring partnership a success were:

- I offered to mentor Anne because I perceived that she might need support.
- Anne did not have to join the formal mentoring structure at the government department where we work where she would have been 'matched' to an available volunteer. Anne admitted that if she had not been offered mentoring, she probably would not have considered it.
- I am deaf, so Anne and I could communicate directly, and I understood the issues relating to her disability and could discuss them with confidence and without the hypersensitivity that could have constrained a non-deaf mentor.
- Mentoring offered Anne regular access to a positive role model, who shared her disability and could offer experience with which Anne could identify and with advice that she could therefore more readily use.
- My positive experience of being mentored within a government-organised leadership scheme to promote diversity helped me understand the process and its benefits.

The ongoing challenges

After the formal mentoring relationship had ended, Anne and I stayed in touch. On one occasion, after Anne had started a new and particularly challenging job, I was concerned that she seemed to be feeling daunted, inadequate, and said she wanted to leave. When we discussed why, it seemed that Anne may not yet have received sufficient access to the large amounts of new information she needed to do her new job confidently.

I felt myself then to be near the 'danger zone' (over-empathy) described above, but having taken a mental pause, I decided to offer to facilitate a meeting between Anne and her managers *if* Anne agreed to lead the meeting itself. She did. As I suspected, Anne's colleagues were surprised at how low Anne's confidence was and reassured her of her competence and potential to do the job well. When, subsequently, more intensive support was arranged, Anne flourished in the job (even though she admitted it was not one she particularly enjoyed). Evidence of this was that during a manager's prolonged absence, Anne was given sole responsibility for much of their work, including approving very high-value projects. This demonstrated high levels of trust in Anne's ability.

This incident brought home to me two points:

- The need for an ongoing mentoring support 'net' for Anne (and possibly, by extension, others who were deaf, or in a small minority with specific needs).
- The risk, without such support, of misunderstandings between hearing and deaf staff, including a reversion by the deaf person to 'self-blame' – assuming problems were somehow their own fault, or due to their lack of competence.

Reflection questions

1. How might the outcomes have differed in this case if:
    1. Anne had not been offered mentoring?
    2. Anne had been offered mentoring by someone who did not share Anne's disability?

2. If you were running a mentoring programme, how could you adapt it to ensure someone with Anne's disability benefited from it?

3. If you planned to draw on the example this case study offers, how could you make best use of potential disabled mentors without:
    1. placing a disproportionate responsibility on them?
    2. making assumptions about their readiness to perform such a role?

Notes

1 Anne is not her real name.
2 See: http://www.statistics.gov.uk/downloads/theme_labour/civilservice2010tables.xls.

Case study 5: Great Britain

Ready to Start: fostering self-employment for people with disabilities

Cherry Potts[1]

Introduction

From 2006 to 2009, Leonard Cheshire Disability, a leading disability charity which was established over 60 years ago, set up and ran Ready to Start, its first enterprise and financial inclusion project. This was made possible by £2.6 million funding from Barclays which enabled a three-year programme to be implemented across the country. The objective of the project was to improve the financial inclusion of disabled people, through engagement in enterprise. Some 50 per cent of disabled people of working age are unemployed. Self-employment can be an important option for many of them. In fact, 20 per cent of disabled people in our country have chosen this option (Employers Forum on Disability figures, 2006). The programme was designed to provide advice, support and mentoring to people with disabilities, who wanted to start up businesses to provide an alternative route to financial independence. It was designed to address the lack of support for disabled entrepreneurs, provide much-needed signposting to training and advice, and challenge and change attitudes towards disabled people in the business world.

The structure of the project

A National Steering Group was formed consisting of the key stakeholders from Leonard Cheshire Disability and Barclays, and included representatives from several partner organisations including the Prince's Trust, Action for Blind People and Business Link London, and from our clients, the entrepreneurs themselves. This forum enabled the management team to discuss and agree upon delivery models, processes and joint working methodologies that were endorsed by the Steering Group. The wide representation of the group proved exceptionally helpful throughout the project life as, beyond monitoring and supporting the project growth, members' external views were able to guide ongoing development.

An internal infrastructure was created and adapted as the delivery modes and practices evolved and the project developed. We found we were being contacted by clients from outside the geographic areas that we were able to cover with the original 27-location model. Creating a distance mentor model meant we were able to open the programme up to disabled people from across most of England and South Wales. Initially services were provided by three external partner agencies:

Meganuxus, Northern Pinetree Trust, and Destiny. However, more mentoring hours were required and there was a need for a central overview of how mentoring was being delivered, so the RTS Distance Mentoring team, comprising a Mentoring Coordinator and a dedicated in-house team together with the existing partner agencies, was developed.

Establishing referral partnerships across the country was a key part of the implementation strategy of the Ready to Start (RTS) programme. Nearly 43 per cent of RTS clients have been referred by partner agencies. These partnerships have flourished, with excellent cross-referral of clients and partnering together for future projects.

Programme operations

People with a disability are often likely to see starting a business as a route to work which complements their values or enables them to balance their lives, rather than as an end in itself. To address this, rather than focusing primarily on profit, we sought to identify and address what help an individual needed, and to treat business start-up in a holistic manner placing the client at the centre of the business proposition. It was important to recognise that, for some disabled people, start-up would take a long time.

From the outset, it was clear that a vital feature of RTS would be its client-centred, flexible approach. This allowed us to start from where the client was, and what the client needed. It enabled us to be much more organic in our approach and to change and mould the project as the client's needs dictated. It was part of our ongoing approach to listening to what our clients were telling us and responding to changing needs and issues.

A significant number of the RTS clients were in receipt of incapacity or other benefits. The issues implicit in coming off benefits needed to be considered. Although permitted work regulations allow someone to continue to claim benefits for up to a year once they start earning an income, the regulations assume that the person is starting employment rather than a business. Thus, participants had to consider how they would cope with the fluctuations of income once their business had grown to a point where they were no longer entitled to some of these benefits. For many clients, this was seen as a high risk, and for some, who had been benefit-dependent for a long time, the potential loss of this income was very alarming. They had to be confident that they could earn sufficient money from their business to keep a roof over their heads while managing their health. This required careful thought and planning.

A small Development Fund was instigated part-way through the project, when we recognised that clients were often prevented from launching their business because they needed very small amounts of money for business critical purchases such as equipment, insurance, or marketing materials. We also provided refurbished computers with appropriate disability adaptations and software, and a year's membership of either the Federation of Small Businesses or a similar trade body to provide ongoing support and networking opportunities once the business was launched.

Initially the project was centred on 27 locations across England and South Wales. Regional Coordinators recruited clients and developed relationships with key partner organisations to both refer and provide services to our clients. Alongside this, they motivated, supported and coached clients to move through an individual development path and linked them with appropriate local support and services, and referred those who wanted it to the mentoring team. The mentoring element was an 'opt in' service, and about 60 per cent of the clients took up the offer.

The mentoring element was set up to be run with volunteer mentors known as 'Buddies'. They were employees of Barclays, the funding partner, who provided their expertise to support the start-up process on a local face-to-face basis. Training was provided to volunteer buddies covering disability issues, equal opportunities, personal safety, confidentiality and mentoring skills and boundaries. Buddies signed a volunteering agreement for 4 hours per month (for at least six months). Approximately 150 buddies supported RTS clients in the programme.

The mentoring processes

Half-way through the project, the mentoring was expanded to include support by our internal team of Distance Mentors (working by phone or e-mail rather than face-to-face) and mentors from partner organisations: Destiny, Northern Pinetree Trust, and Meganexus. These mentors had experience in coaching and backgrounds in local authority, corporates, other large charities, international development, and in running their own businesses. This mix enabled intensive, individual support focused upon meeting the varied needs of the clients.

The new businesses were set up in a huge range of sectors and many were set us as social enterprises. However, most were sole traders, working alone and taking sole responsibility for their business, making the support of the mentor all the more important.

As coaches, we know and respect that the clients are the experts in knowing what they can handle and how inventive they can be in finding solutions, whether it be how their disability affects them, or what resources they can bring to the business. This means that we do not make assumptions about what it means for the client to have a disability, nor what it means to them to be working towards financial independence. The clients do not have to put on their best face for the mentors as they are neither a funder for whom they have to be professional, nor a family member whom they don't want to burden. The mentors are a sounding board for ideas, a fellow explorer of possibilities, an enthusiastic supporter, but also that critical someone who will tell them the truth if they believe they are getting in too deep.

Clients came from widely differing backgrounds, and all forms of physical and mental disability were represented. Some 43 per cent had a physical disability, and 24 per cent had a mental health disability. The rest had a variety of disabilities in a wide array of categories. Most clients were between 30 and 65 years of age. They were offered an average of 2 hours a month mentoring during start-up, and 2 hours every three months, once they were trading. The clients were also referred to local providers for training and advice specific to their situation.

Mentors worked with clients creating action plans, reviewing business and marketing plans and helping them to establish the vision for their business. They also provided opportunities for them to explore all the options available and to reassess essential skills needed for themselves and the future development of their business. We used coaching techniques to ensure the clients owned their decisions, and although the direction of the project was towards businesses, we were able to support clients on a wide range of issues that were affecting their ability to run a business, whether that was other financial issues or how they handled their disability. This was done to provide a stronger foundation to work from when they started trading.

The three Distance Mentors worked mainly on the phone (using SkypeChat for deaf clients) and by e-mail, which meant that they could work with a great many clients far more intensively than they would have if they had been travelling to meet clients all around the country. This permitted them to be far more proactive and flexible in responding to clients.

Developing a business idea through mentoring

In the early stages, we were looking at the viability of the business idea. The client explained the idea and how far they had progressed, and there was a lot of 'fact finding' going on. Some of their questions were straightforward, others less so. What we provided was not just 'business advice'. While we worked with clients on their business plans, their marketing and their vision for their business as a matter of course, these were, in some ways, the least important part of the work.

Some clients had a very clear idea of their business and exactly how they wanted to achieve it, and a very business-focused approach worked well with them. However, for others, the prospect of self-employment, particularly for individuals who took this path because they were unable to secure paid employment elsewhere, was very daunting. Disabled people who have received countless rejections for paid employment often have low self-esteem and need assistance to acknowledge their capabilities. To start a business from this low ebb is a monumental task, and the support of a mentor to recover self-belief and confidence was critical.

Because we used a coaching approach, the client was asked to find their own answers and explore the best use of their strengths, rather than having 'ready to wear' solutions and suggestions offered to them. This meant that they were convinced by their own solutions. This helped them to realise that they had the ability to achieve the goals they set themselves.

Once the client's business model was established, we addressed the personal blocks to success. Issues centred on their fears and concerns about, e.g. going into debt, letting others down, and coping with the complexity of it all.

As the project progressed, we introduced group distance mentoring around themes. This included sector-specific sessions – creative, construction, catering, retail, etc. – and Business Skill sessions like marketing, maximising your web presence, and dealing with the Inland Revenue. We also began to record these sessions so that we could pod-cast them to reach a wider audience. Additionally, this allowed clients who were geographically isolated to network and sometimes collaborate with each other.

Providing ongoing support

Once their business had been launched, many clients were reluctant to leave the support offered by the programme. To address this issue, we instigated a second phase, which provided a continuing but reduced level of support and mentoring to clients, along with a one-year's subscription to a business support organisation.

A number of methods were used to maintain contact with clients and to get client feedback during this time. Regional Coordinators set up a series of network events in their region. Often these comprised small groups of RTS clients meeting together to share their experiences and challenges. Sometimes they included input from a guest expert on a subject of interest. Some network events involved joining forces with partner organisations to put RTS clients in contact with other budding entrepreneurs in larger-scale meetings.

Staying in touch with clients and partners via regular quarterly newsletters was a key element of the project. The newsletters showcased some of the many client successes and achievements, as well as giving project updates and reporting progress.

We were keen to encourage entrepreneurs to work peer-to-peer and support each other and we set up an online network to facilitate this. The network subsequently developed into an Online Business Directory for RTS clients to showcase their businesses and gain work from one another.

Outcomes

Project targets were to recruit 1200 clients and for our support to result in 600 new businesses being set up, 120 other employment, 50 further education, and 30 voluntary work outcomes. All these targets were exceeded, with 735 clients self-employed by the end of the project, and 126 employed, resulting in 100 per cent decrease in numbers claiming job seekers allowance, 62 per cent decrease in those claiming income support, and 46 per cent reduction in those claiming incapacity benefit.

In April 2009, we commissioned an independent evaluation of the project. This included client questionnaires, in-depth one-to-one interviews with several clients from each region, and a client Focus Group. A similar exercise was carried out with Barclays and LCD staff involved in the project as well as a number of partner organisations. Clients felt that the RTS programme was a positive and helpful experience, with 82.4 per cent of clients stating the service overall was useful and almost a third (31.1 per cent) stating it was very useful to them. Some 24.6 per cent said mentoring was the most useful part of the service. Clients particularly valued that they were working with people who understood people with disabilities and they did not feel they were treated like a number.

For our clients, success was not determined by turnover/profit alone. It also included creating a sustainable and hopefully rising income for the business owner and their family and enabling them to maintain good health and well-being in an environment of their own choosing that is fully supportive of their individual needs. The most valuable thing that we could offer clients through mentoring was to support them to make a shift in how they saw themselves, and what they felt they were capable of achieving in a realistic and sustainable way, as evidenced by this client quote:

> I am ill often and so my business is very small but it has given me an empowerment I couldn't have predicted would be so personally valuable. I could at last give an answer to 'What do you do?' and for this I will be eternally grateful.

Paul's story also captures the essence of the programme's impact on the mentees. Paul has had many careers, both in the army and as a private investigator, but his true love is comedy and when we started mentoring him on RTS, he wanted to be a comedy writer, preferably for the BBC.

Paul's epilepsy affects his memory and limits his options for employment and the idea of working at his own pace on something he loved appealed enormously. We managed to match him with a mentor who was also a writer. Paul's mentor provided insight into the creative process and the publishing world, and supported him to improve his management of his memory and time. Paul has subsequently had several articles published. Paul says:

> It is vital that you have faith in the mentor; that she/he/it knows of what they speak. I come from the North East, speak with a Pitmatick accent and am very interested in the linguistics and humour of that area. My mentor's grandparents also come from that area and she understands both the accent and humour of the North East. This has been invaluable to some of my writing. Whilst most of my writing has been article-based, I am also interested in script writing and mentoring has been of help to me here too.
>
> My mentor has been of great help to me in providing an independent 'ear' for my writing. Her background guarantees that any suggestion she makes is pertinent and her manner assures that it is NEVER impertinent. The whole process is both enjoyable and very, very worthwhile indeed.

Lessons learned

In terms of what we might have done differently, getting professional mentors working on the project much sooner would have improved the delivery of the service. Making use of the group sessions sooner would also have supported clients better, as it allowed often quite isolated clients to build up networks of people working in the same sector around the country as well as making use of peer mentoring.

Starting a business can be overwhelming, and it is important to keep some perspective on what the point of it is. For those clients, whose business was a passion for them, they could become engrossed in it. For those who were less focused, there was a possibility that great amounts of effort are put into unproductive side issues, so exploring what was going to have the greatest effect for the least effort is part of the process. We also asked clients to remember to leave time for fun, relaxation, family and friends.

A client's ability to cope with their condition, whether physical or mental, could vary from day to day. Focusing on business issues could be difficult at times and there was the possibility of clients either 'switching off' or becoming incoherent during appointments. In recognising that and not insisting that we stick to the purpose of the call, and instead discussing what was causing the current difficulty, we built up trust. This gave the client the space to feel he/she could come back to us when they were ready to continue, at the same time as potentially resolving the underlying issue.

It can take a significant amount of time and effort to get a business off the ground, and if the business becomes successful, resources of time and energy can become limited. It can be harder for someone to be able to manage their health condition when the business is also making demands.

There is a key point in the development of a new business when expansion through taking on staff or larger premises or other assistance is needed but this is not yet financially possible, and managing the effort required by the business owner to keep going at this point can make or break a fledgling company. Our awareness of this key tipping point informed our efforts to come up with our replacement for RTS – 'Enabled 4 Growth' – which is aimed at businesses that need a financial injection to get over this hurdle.

Although we did not routinely disclose our own situations to clients, some clients have benefited from the knowledge and personal experience of disability of the internal Distance Mentors. Questions regarding disability might be perceived as intrusive by a client, but without making a big deal of it, mentors could give personal examples of how to overcome barriers.

Reflection questions

1. How do you build a project that meets the diverse needs of individuals with diverse disabilities?
2. How often can rigid expectations and policies of government or EU funders be addressed to allow the flexibility of a truly customer-focused mentoring service?

Note

1 This case study uses material from Kim Dalton, Catherine Casolani, Terri Wilson, Linda Holland and Jane Jutsum.

Reference

Employers Forum on Disability (2006)

Case study 6: The USA

FORWARD to Professorship: academic mentoring for women and deaf scientists

Catherine Mavriplis, Rachelle Heller and Charlene Sorensen

Introduction

'FORWARD to Professorship' is a career development workshop, first held in 2003, supported by a series of grants from the US National Science Foundation ADVANCE program (National Science Foundation 2010). The program aims to help women and other underrepresented groups in Science, Technology, Engineering and Mathematics (STEM) succeed in tenure-track faculty positions. The workshop was designed as a derivative from the 'FORWARD to Graduate School' workshop, also supported by NSF, where female and deaf students learned successful strategies for gaining access to a graduate STEM program with funding. As a result the FORWARD workshop is held annually at Gallaudet University, a university for the Deaf and Hard of Hearing, in an environment that forces participants and speakers alike to experience the considerable hurdles that deaf scientists and engineers face.

The main objective of the program is to increase the number of women and minorities, particularly the deaf, in tenure-track STEM professorships, and then to ensure their success through the tenure process. We determined that this objective would be best met through a workshop format for pre-tenured scientists and engineers coming from wide geographical, scientific and career-level backgrounds, including a range of disciplines and types of institutions. The workshop includes graduate students in their final years of dissertation work, postdoctoral associates, untenured faculty, non-tenure-track faculty and researchers, professionals in industry and some on a career break. These individuals come together to share their experiences and acquire new strategies to enable them to succeed. Most participants are female but some men, either on their own or accompanying their partners, do attend.

Having a range of experiences among the participants with opportunity for near-peer mentoring and learning from those slightly ahead enhance the community building and networking that go on at the workshop and in future years. The cross-fertilization of ideas and practices also prepares participants for an ever-changing and adapting environment, in particular, one that is becoming more interdisciplinary.

The workshop addresses skills, resources, and strategies to enter, survive and excel in academia. Topics of discussion include how to do the following:

- apply for a position and negotiate salary and startup packages;
- navigate the tenure-track process, including an investigation of teaching strategies, securing research funding and engaging in appropriate levels of service;
- achieve a career/home balance in life.

Activities include presentations from experts as well as activities designed to help participants develop their own approaches to their success. A personalized career plan is the desired outcome for those attending this workshop. Participants also have the opportunity to discuss their particular ideas and issues with administrators in a non-threatening environment.

Mentoring context

The program uses traditional senior–junior, near-peer, and peer mentoring processes. While senior academic mentors can offer important career-advancing advice as well as provide important contacts for job searches and research funding, since the landscape for women entering STEM fields has changed considerably, peer or near-peer mentoring is equally, if not more, important. Among these changes are increased numbers of women in the field; the acceleration and progress in the way science is done; and advances in technology to support the work. Near-peers who have lived through difficult situations recently can offer special insights and rapport that senior mentors cannot.

The personal contact between the participants and the (approximately) 20 speakers and the workshop organizers is a major component of the mentoring activity. Because women and other minorities such as the deaf are so isolated in

STEM fields, we created the opportunity to meet many potential mentors in one place over an intense two-and-a-half-day period. The lack of critical mass in STEM fields of these minorities often means that people new to the field either feel compelled to follow the paths of the very rare existing trailblazers, or turn away if they cannot see themselves making those same sacrifices. By presenting a wide range of examples of minority players who have adapted and succeeded in different ways, we open up the realm of possibilities for the newer players so that they often can then more easily see and create a path for themselves.

From anecdotal evidence, it seems close mentoring relationships endured between some of the speakers and some of the participants. As organizers, we kept in contact with several of the participants providing mentoring especially in the realm of securing a position and navigating the dual career situation. Each year we invite past participants back to act as new near-peer mentors. Very valuable information is transferred by these past participants as they can identify with being in the same position as the current participants several years before and they point to instances at the workshop that led them through their career progression.

Another level of mentoring is directed toward the trainees, who are mentored through a training program outlining the major activities necessary in planning a workshop. These trainees are then given the opportunity to be a participant-observer in a workshop. This is followed with a day of debriefing about what they saw as the workshop unfolded. Finally, the trainees are mentored throughout the year as they design, implement and assess their own workshop. This mentoring is conducted primarily by regular e-mail contact, video-conferencing and then by observation and feedback during and after their inaugural workshop.

Workshop processes

The workshop addresses the three 'legs' of academia: Research, Teaching, and Service. Success in each of these areas is vital to obtaining tenure. However, as we look at the entire path of our target group – from entry into a tenure-track position, to evaluation of performance in that position, and finally to becoming tenured – other elements also need to be addressed. These include: writing and interviewing skills for obtaining a position; negotiation when receiving an offer (e.g. for startup packages); dealing with life situations (dual career issues and family or other personal life–work balance); understanding the differences between larger and smaller institutions; and looking at the process from an administrator's perspective. Brief descriptions of how the workshop addresses all of these key elements are given in Mavriplis et al. (2005) and on the website (see FORWARD 2010). Here we concentrate on the delivery of this information as it relates to mentoring.

The first way one interacts with an institution is via *writing*: the cover letter, the résumé and the research and teaching statements. Participants are asked to submit samples of their writing that are then critiqued by the organizers (written comments are remitted to them at the workshop) and by peers in a one-to-one activity. Participants are very grateful for this personal advice.

One of the next steps on the path to tenure is the job offer. The session on *negotiation* is enlightening for both the participants and the presenters. Many participants said they did not realize they could negotiate.

The session on *research* includes presenters from common granting agencies as well as those familiar with private foundation funding. Again, giving the participants access to the information and the people controlling the flow of information is key. These individuals give participants information relevant to obtaining funding before and after procuring a position, instructions on writing strong proposals, how to interact with program officers, indicating differences between federal and non-federal agencies (e.g. private foundations), and outlining issues of intellectual property.

The session on *service* addresses various concerns regarding the amount and types of service as well as the varying requirements of service for different institutions. The session touches on the types of service that are considered significant, the emphasis or lack of emphasis on service depending on size and type of institution, time commitments, and knowing who to ask about service requirements. Also, this session focuses on the ever present and all-important trap women seem to fall into: that of over-commitment and hence participants practice how to say 'No!'

The '*Having It All*' session is a safe place to look at the crosspoints of professional and personal lives. This session includes information about dual career situations, having a family before, during and/or after tenure, and having outside activities whether or not you have a family. Many presenters as well as participants discuss options for balancing family and work responsibilities. Career breaks are also discussed with the aim of crafting a path that would lead back to an academic career after interruption of full-time STEM employment.

The final session of the workshop is a *meeting with chairs and administrators* from various colleges and universities. Participants are eager for a time and place to ask administrators about situations (e.g. how things might be perceived if . . .) and perspectives. Participants feel it is 'safe' to ask questions in this type of setting, questions that they 'don't dare ask' in their own departments. Furthermore, this is a way to effect systemic change in institutions by affecting chairs, deans and other administrators. Many of the speakers for this session, both male and female, report feeling changed by the experience.

Evaluation

Participants are asked to complete an evaluation form at the end of each of the three days of workshop activities. The participants are also sent an e-mail evaluation and inquiry six months after the workshop. A pre-workshop questionnaire also assesses their expectations and level of experience in certain fields such as negotiation in order to measure the effect of the workshop. A five-cohort survey was administered in 2007. Results are reported in Mavriplis et al. (2010).

The response from participants has been overwhelmingly positive (available in Mavriplis et al. 2005, 2010). Overall, participants feel this is an opportunity not easily found elsewhere. A typical response was of a participant who noted that the workshop 'provides information nowhere else available'. Others find the overall mentoring experience empowering: 'Probably the most inspiring and confidence building thing I've ever done as far as science goes,' reported one respondent.

Participants reported several positive outcomes at different polling times. At the workshop, participants reported that the experience of being in a room with so many other women scientists and engineers was very uplifting. Most had never experienced this feeling before. In terms of specific mentoring interventions that helped participants stay in STEM academia, several reports indicated the program was instrumental in their staying.

The workshop speakers themselves reported unexpected outcomes. One presenter from a prestigious university said: 'Wow, I never thought I could give a talk like that' (i.e. a non-science talk). Another speaker realized after the 'Having It All' session that she had been living in a two-body (dual-career couple) problem for 30 years! Some male presenters found themselves considering for the first time the very real challenges of women in tenure-track positions.

Outcomes

Over the years, we have learnt the power of offering personal mentoring and networking opportunities to women in disciplines starved of female contact. The importance of multi-level mentoring and community building cannot be over-stated. For deaf scientists and engineers, the issues of access to suitable positions and communication are far more difficult than for mainstream women. More continuous support is most helpful, especially in identifying places of employment and people and budgets that might be accepting.

The mentoring that we have been involved with in the case of deaf scientists is a very intense process. The Gallaudet University environment is itself a very small community at just over 1500 undergraduates, most of whom are deaf or hard of hearing and approximately 400 graduate students, many of whom are hearing. The number of science majors hovers around 50 with a professor to student ratio of 1:5. Graduate degrees in science are mostly in audiology or related fields.

Since most of the students rely on sign language as their 'first' language, commu-nication with the hearing world, in standardized tests, for example, represent an additional challenge. Intense mentoring and coaching, for example, in how to take the Graduate Record Examinations required for admission to graduate programs across the US, produced several graduate school-bound students. Through these workshops, many of our deaf participants told us they realized for the first time that they could be 'smart' and compete with the 'outside' world.

On the graduate and professorial side, we have known few students to persist all the way through to the tenure track, but one past participant did return to our workshop to offer advice. He mentioned his love and determination for study in science. With a Bachelor's degree from Gallaudet and a fellowship at a national institute under his belt, he was able to pursue his PhD at a hearing university. While he investigated working in industry, he found little support there for Deaf scientists. He credits the workshop with opening his eyes to the possibility of being a professor and delineating the pros and cons while differentiating adjunct from tenure-track positions. Through sign language interpretation he has been a full participant in our workshops and the participants learn tremendously from his experiences. He has found the workshops extremely helpful in many aspects, including salary negotiation, networking and particularly in learning to say no to service requests, which he considers a weakness of deaf scientists who, like women, he sees as 'eager to prove their worth'. He sees his greatest challenge, as do many other participants, in securing the first research funding award. Again, communication with the agency program manager presents new challenges for deaf scientists. Mentoring to explore ways to make those first contacts is important at this stage.

Lessons learned

As organizers of the workshop, we learned the power of a sincere keynote speaker to open up the way for an open and meaningful mentoring atmosphere. For example, in 2003 and again in 2005 at MIT, Maria Klawe, then Dean of Princeton University's Engineering School, gave an honest and sincere keynote speech on the first night of the first workshop. Participants rated her talk 100 percent excellent at the meeting. Six months later, 70 percent of the e-mail survey respondents mentioned her talk as one of the most memorable events of the workshop.

We also learned that working with other minority groups, e.g. the deaf, and more recently with minority women across the US, either regionally or culturally, e.g. Pacific Islander women and racially diverse women in the Midwest, that there is much to be learned about our own challenges by considering others' more daunting ones.

Over the 13 years we have been working in this area, we have noticed a definite improvement in networking and access to information for women entering the doctoral STEM job market, no doubt due to proliferation of communication through the Internet and more recently social media, as well as concerted funding to address gender issues in scientific and other male-dominated fields. The discussion of gender imbalance has gone beyond numbers and simple progression through the ranks and has turned to a woven fabric of several issues affecting women's progress, at once systemic, social and personal. Mentoring, although less recognized for scientists and engineers, especially in academia, can start to have a profound effect on improving career development and hence institutional progress.

In terms of support, the funding has been a tremendous help for the designed activities. Support has been mostly directed at participation expenses, e.g. travel and subsistence expenses, meeting room expenses and materials. These are essential: without them, there is no workshop – people will not come. Most speaker-mentors are very enthusiastic and generous with their time. In the first years, the budgets were slim and we relied heavily on the goodwill of our speakers. We felt this was an unfair scenario, however, one in which women and minorities were being burdened more than their majority counterparts by volunteering their time and effort. This is time taken away from career-advancing activities. So we argued that these mentors should be compensated, as this is truly worthwhile work for the benefit of the disciplines. We suggest that compensation (financial or other) be incorporated in structured mentoring activities.

Reflection questions

1. Does mentoring have to be continuous to be beneficial (or how can one provide small bursts of mentoring that are beneficial)?
2. How does one promote near-peer mentoring in the context of everyone's busy schedules?
3. Bridging the gap to a far different culture (e.g. deaf or racially different) in mentoring is difficult.
4. There are few mentors available in these underrepresented groups. How can a majority group mentor gain experience and understanding and then acceptance in such a mentoring relationship?

References

FORWARD to Professorship (2010) Available at: http://www.seas.gwu.edu/~forward/.

Mavriplis, C., Heller, R., Sorensen, C. and Snyder, H.D. (2005) The FORWARD to professorship workshop, in *Proceedings of the 2005 American Society for Engineering Education Annual Conference and Exposition*, Portland, OR, pp. 6537–49.

Mavriplis, C., Beil, C., Dam, K., Heller, R. and Sorensen, C. (2010) An analysis of the FORWARD to Professorship workshop: what works to entice and prepare women for professorship? in A.S. Godfroy-Genin (ed.) *Women in Engineering and Technology Research: The PROMETEA Conference Proceedings*. Berlin: LIT Verlag, pp. 443–60.

National Science Foundation (NSF) (2010) ADVANCE: increasing the participation and advancement of women in academic science and engineering careers. Available at: http://www.nsf.gov/funding/pgm_summ.jsp?pims_id=5383.

Case study 7: Canada

The Legacy Project: mentorship to support long-term empowerment of people living with HIV/AIDS

Catherine Mossop, Alan Li and Derek Yee

Introduction

The Committee for Accessible AIDS Treatment (CAAT) is a coalition of more than 30 Ontario-based organizations from the legal, health, settlement and HIV/AIDS sectors. This coalition accounts for approximately 20,000 people living with HIV/AIDS (PHAs) in Ontario, with the highest concentration being in the Greater Toronto Area. The coalition was created to improve access to treatment and support services for the most marginalized people living with HIV. Over the years, CAAT has played a key role in advocating and facilitating service access and promoting capacity building and civic participation for these individuals.

The diversity of PHAs in Toronto include people in many marginalized communities such as: refugees; new immigrants; individuals fleeing domestic violence and persecution; former and currently incarcerated persons; lesbian, gay, bi-sexual, transgendered persons; sex trade workers; and people without full legal status in Canada. These populations face complex challenges in accessing social and health services[1] to help them live with HIV and enable them to contribute to and participate in society.

There were minimal ongoing structured supports in place for PHAs to apply their learning in areas of overcoming complex barriers of social and economic exclusion; managing personal and professional transitions; and achieving their goals in building a meaningful life. To address this ongoing need, in 2008, CAAT approached other community agency partners involved in running PHA capacity-building programs to champion the idea of creating a structured mentorship program to support the ongoing capacity building of PHAs to further pursue their life goals. Thus, the Legacy Project was born.

Program initiation

CAAT established a project advisory group with membership from various community partners involved in delivering PHA capacity-building programs. Key partners include: the AIDS Bereavement and Resiliency Project of Ontario, the African and Caribbean Council on HIV/AIDS in Ontario, the Ethno-racial Treatment Support Network, the Ontario AIDS Network, the Ontario HIV Treatment Network, and the Toronto People with AIDS Foundation. Additional program participants were recruited through outreach to CAAT's many member organizations such as: the

Alliance of South Asian AIDS Prevention, the Asian Community AIDS Services, the Canadian Aboriginal AIDS Network, the Africans in Partnerships Against AIDS, the Black Coalition for AIDS Prevention, the Prisoners AIDS Support Action Network, Latinos Positivos Ontario and 2 Spirited (Canadian Aboriginal people prefer to be identified as 2 Spirited). Participation now reaches into every ethno-racial group and encompasses every orientation and status of people living in Canada.

The Legacy Project serves to provide an avenue for development, participation and hope to those who have experienced multiple losses, such as loss of country, community, family, career, and assumptive self-identity. PHAs often experience persecution, stigmatization, and marginalization. This program supports the formation of a new sense of self and renewed hope, seeks to enable them to restructure their identity as they learn and grow in new communities, and enhances their confidence to engage meaningfully in society.

Working with community members, the Legacy Project is designed to provide three crucial support systems:

1 Mentorship.
2 Career and employment practicum opportunities.
3 Capacity building through establishing relationships across and within diverse communities.

The Legacy Project's objectives are centered on the participants' ability to develop their networks of support and thus build resiliency into their lives.

Engagement of community stakeholders

A premium value of the program is to honor the lived experience of PHAs. As such, we began the program design process with a workshop that brought together PHAs who had graduated from capacity-building programs from the collaborating partner organizations. Thirty PHAs from diverse backgrounds, many meeting each other for the first time, came together to design a unique mentorship program to meet their collective needs. This was a highly engaging, emotionally cathartic and empowering experience for all involved.

The facilitation process began with a series of exercises wherein participants drew pictures representing their own personal journey and their new vision for their lives, and then for the program. This process generated innovative ideas and built trust among the participants and enabled them to join together with one common goal – supporting each other to live a meaningful life. The process began to break down barriers and alleviate the feelings of isolation many PHAs experience in their daily lives. Over the ensuing months of program development, the material generated and captured in these early exercises was incorporated into vision and values statements, the conceptual frameworks of all supporting workshops, mentor and protégé support materials (entitled: Walk with Me), as well as program marketing, and an evaluation framework.

At key points in the design process, various members of this community stake-holder group were brought together to provide input, feedback, and insights. These insights were valuable in building an understanding of how the different communities would view and interpret activities, processes, communications, and how to gain and maintain their engagement. Several elements of the program required fine-tuning to assure openness, transparency and accountability to diverse population needs. All traditional mentoring program elements, such as applications and matching processes, needed to be examined and adapted within the complex web of issues within PHA communities.

Following the launch of the program, we discovered that latent issues with self-esteem created an invisible barrier related to self-stigmatization and impacted the ability of some protégés to build early-stage trust within the mentoring relationship. This led to the need to address the question: 'How do we establish a safe, supportive environment that will allow for the development of early-stage trust to take hold and that will allow people to summon the courage to take the leap of faith needed to build a healthy relationship?'

Program design

As a community-driven program, it was considered paramount to engage PHA participation in a variety of ways regardless of their stage of life, background, or socio-cultural affiliation. A PHA could be a mentor, protégé, have multiple mentors, be a mentor and a protégé at the same time, be a resource, workshop facilitator, or an outreach facilitator. To suit the learning styles and participant needs, different mentoring models were used: individual one-on-one, group mentoring, group events, and reflective practice sessions for ongoing development. The following model represents the flow and key components of the program.

Program coordinator

The program coordinator is the lynch-pin in this program. The coordinator is highly credible, well regarded, and well networked across communities and agencies. A dynamic personality, well organized and an inspiring leader in his/her own right, his/her infectious enthusiasm set the platform for gaining the agency support needed to recruit the protégés and mentors. His/her role in building bridges across these highly diverse service provider agencies, bringing key community leaders into the program as mentors, special resource people, or advisors, has been one of the major factors contributing to program success.

Mentor recruitment

Mentors consist of PHA and non-PHA leaders who are recruited through community networks of long-term survivors, service partner agencies, and long-term community allies. Networking efforts focus on engaging mentors in the roles that suit their personality, style, and the time they have available to devote to mentorship. Some mentors offer a specialized knowledge that is valuable as a workshop resource, a facilitator, one who may do further outreach for the program, or as one-on-one mentors. Mentors are encouraged to identify the goals they have for their own learning and development as a result of participating in the program.

Through outreach activities such as presenting at conferences and attending community events, a credible database of long-term PHA and non-PHA mentors (community leaders, professors, professionals, active volunteers, and retired people) is being created. The community network is essential as the issues of privacy and confidentiality are always at the forefront of all activities. Many long-term PHA survivors (10–20 years) have reintegrated into the mainstream and are fairly 'invisible' (their colleagues, friends and associates may not be aware of their health status). This outreach and creation of a database are one of the foundations that will set the stage for the growth of the program outside of Toronto into other centers and communities across Canada.

Protégé recruitment

The protégés of the program are PHAs who are recruited through different service agencies and peer networks. For the pilot phase of the project, the focus was outreach to PHA peers who had completed one of the other capacity-building programs provided by collaborating partners. These programs include an extensive range of workshops on everything from how to use the legal system, to wellness management, anti-oppression/anti-stigma, and life skills. Once the PHA has completed these programs, they are eligible for and encouraged to participate in the mentorship program.

As intake into the program can be at any stage in the developmental process of a PHA, three phases of mentorship were defined to assist with personal goal setting and matching:

- *Phase 1 Walk with Me – Orientation to Mentorship*: This phase incorporates protégés' learning goals. The mentorship begins with a two-day joint mentor and protégé orientation session. Fifteen matched pairs are brought together to get to know each other, begin the process of building community, and establish the foundations for relationships to grow.

  In addition to mentor/protégé orientation, considerable time is dedicated to goal setting, building trust, and the exploration of the complexities of boundary identification and management. Issues such as the multiplicity of community roles (service supplier/ recipient), friend and family relationships, intimacy and falling in love with your partner are addressed.

- *Phase 2 Life-Work-Volunteering*: Once a PHA is managing their health, they are encouraged to continue their growth and development by re-engaging and participating in the community through education, re-training, volunteering, and becoming re-employed. Within this phase, practicum opportunities are identified and protégés are placed with an employer for an agreed time and role.

● *Phase 3 Leadership and Giving Back*: This phase of mentorship is for those ready to engage in community building, advocacy, and leadership development. PHAs who have managed living with HIV for many years indicated they would value mentors to help them grow as leaders in the community and organizations. Many of these PHAs are in the dual role of mentor to the newly diagnosed, and as a protégé in leadership development.

Progress made

A program evaluation was undertaken at the strategic design stage. It links and tracks progress of the individual learning goals to the program strategy and funder data requirements. The consistency makes ongoing outcome-tracking and reporting to funders possible.

The first year of the program included 50 mentors and 50 protégés. Since that time 130 individuals have participated. Several methods of tracking progress have been employed. Among them are: a formal online survey; informal feedback at the Mentor's Exchange and the Protégé's Exchange (reflective practice sessions) convened on a quarterly basis; and individual follow-up by the program coordinator.

The formal survey tracks progress against the learning categories that are selected for development by mentors and protégés on the application form. The application form uses a double-ended scale where a person may identify a strength they have to offer, or a learning need they have within a 'goal category'. The application form is used for intake and matching then the participant is asked to complete the online survey to establish a benchmark. At the sixth month and twelfth month date, participants are asked to complete the survey again and progress outcomes are identified.

Participants indicate they are feeling hopeful for their future, feel an increased level of confidence and have a renewed desire to develop, examine, and re-examine their career plans. They are building the resiliency needed to manage personal transformation. Additionally, the Legacy Project is building community capacity. The participants are creating learning relationships and sharing their experiences through narrative, dialogue and workshops.

Ultimately, program success must be about the way in which lives are impacted as a result of their participation. We now present two stories: Carlos and Daisy. All names are pseudonyms. We believe these stories capture the essence of this program and its impact on the lives of those involved.

Carlos' story

Carlos is a Latin American refugee living in Canada. He is in his mid-thirties, gay, and HIV positive. Carlos lived the straight life until he was 21 and completed his training and education as a lawyer. His lover of three years did not disclose he was HIV+ until Carlos became ill. A health service provider did not treat the information confidentially and disclosed it to Carlos' family members and the community. Persecuted, he was cast out, threatened and forced to flee the country to save his life. In his own words:

> I was afraid – I could no longer get work as an HIV+ gay lawyer and my life was threatened in my country. I had to go away to another place. I had no medical care, even in the hospital, once they knew I was HIV, they wouldn't look after me . . . Once I came to Canada, I was so surprised by how accepting people were – I am not used to that. I felt the compassion and empathy. When I was accepted [with refugee status], I felt like I had a chance to live a new life. Now I could access food, shelter, financial assistance and legal aid – it was very hard for me though . . . housing is a problem, living with drug addicts, sex workers, attempts on my life . . . very hard life and people don't know how to deal effectively with PHAs [language barriers] and I was sick, homeless and didn't know when I would eat again. That is when I became involved with the Legacy Project.
>
> At the session for Orientation, I met so many wonderful people, from all over the world, everyone coming from such a difficult place in their life . . . oh, my goodness . . . it has given me so much. With my mentor, we talked about goals – I went from not having a life and wanting to end my life, to finding my strengths and opening my eyes to new ideas. He helped me make plans and when I thought he would quit too – he wasn't, that was just in my head, he reached out and helped me stay on track, he inspires me. And the others in the program inspire me. [After 9 months with the program] I have a job I like now and I want to get more involved with adult education. I am having my credentials reviewed, I am working on my English, I am staying healthy. I found the love of my life and got married a month ago! You gave me hope – I can dream again.

Daisy's story

Daisy, now 44 years old, HIV+, came to Canada as a refugee from Kenya two years ago. She is a protégé in the Legacy Project. In her own words:

> I was diagnosed with HIV in the late 1990s as part of the routine testing because I was pregnant. I didn't know my husband gave me the virus and I was told I would die – soon. The stigma was so severe then, and it still is, so I kept the news from my family and community, and I had no support. I became severely depressed. I just waited to die. I took on the voice of dying. But I didn't die, and my baby didn't

have HIV. So I decided to do some research on the virus and began to volunteer with an agency helping women with AIDS.

It became more dangerous for me to live. I was getting very sick. I was cast out of my community; told to go by my family; lived in hiding – going from house to house; and the police could not protect me. I had death threats and threats to my family and friends. I sent my child to another country, and I fled.

I arrived in Canada and wandered the airport for hours because I didn't know anyone or what to do, and I was sick. I talked to a taxi driver who brought me to a shelter and from there, good Samaritans came into my life – they told me about the AIDS services organizations and I went to all the support groups – I had to start my life all over.

Now I am involved with Legacy – and my mentor has been fantastic in my life – I set goals; I want to know how to work better and improve my service to the community; I want to know how things are done in Canada; my mentor has guided me and directed me to everything – she is a friend and mentor. I was very open to her about my personal issues; problems in life and she has opened my eyes – she asks me tough questions; she puts me on my toes. She opened my mind in a way that is really special. I am becoming a mentor and doing something for my community.

Lessons learned

PHAs live within a complex and unique set of both personal and community parameters. Dialogue on boundary identification and management needs to be given considerable time in orientation sessions. We found it is one of the foundations for establishing and building trust. The dialogue begins with identifying all the roles the PHA has within the various communities and partner agencies – personally and professionally. Confidentiality issues can present themselves in innocent ways. Embracing a friend on the street with a warm hello might cause an uncomfortable question to arise from an innocent observer; or the mentor may be on the Board of Directors of an agency where the protégé is accessing services and it may be seen by others as preferential treatment; or, one PHA may be introduced to another PHA in the program and they may develop an intimate relationship. We found that taking the time up-front to work on boundary management issues significantly enhances sustained relationships.

Facilitating the building of trust between mentors and protégés – many of whom feel marginalized and disenfranchised is time-intensive, requires cultural sensitivity, and requires an ability to facilitate the building of bridges between people and communities. PHAs have a tremendous desire to connect with each other, yet their internal self-protection stance in the world creates an invisible barrier that is a challenge to surmount. It takes consistency, ongoing support, and patience to overcome these barriers. The impact of self-stigmatization, building trust, and the underlying influence of self-esteem were issues identified early in the process and course adjustments in the matching and follow up processes were made to the program structure to address these issues.

At the third month of the program, the Mentor's Exchange and the Protégé's Exchange (a process of reflective practice) were convened to address issues and add mentoring techniques to enhance the relationship development processes. It was identified, in a few relationships, that self-stigmatization related to very low self-esteem influenced the protégés' readiness to follow up and build relationships with mentors. To address this problem, special workshops were created to build trust such as 'Spotlight on You'. This is a large group communications and trust building workshop. We also developed small group mentoring sessions facilitated by peer participants on various topics such as 'HIV positive mothers', effective ways to cope and manage the day-to-day challenges of being HIV+ and a parent, and 'How to navigate social media'. These workshops have grown into a recurring series of trust and capacity-building sessions facilitated by participants of the Legacy Project.

In the future, additional sessions will be convened on topics related to mentoring techniques in coaching, compassionate communications and conflict resolution. We will also create community-based programs in anti-oppression and equity.

Reflection questions

1. How can group mentoring be used to reduce the experience of self-marginalization and build the self-esteem of participants in your own environment?
2. How could the program engage non-HIV individuals as mentors? What selection and matching criteria would you use?
3. The program coordinator is heavily engaged in community outreach to attract participants – mentors and protégés. How could the program be more broadly 'marketed' to assure a consistent intake of participants?

Note

1 Service providers include: community health workers; social workers; food banks; housing assistance; harm-reduction and outreach support workers; legal support.

Mentoring in the context of gender and sexual preference

Kirsten M. Poulsen

Introduction

Our aim for this section of the book was to combine gender and sexual preference cases. In practice, it has been remarkably difficult to source the latter, although we know they do exist.

Enabling the advancement of women in education, work life and society is a hot topic internationally. McKinsey's (2007) report *Women Matter* states that, in Europe, 'If the employment rate for women remains constant, Europe can expect a shortfall of 24 million people in the active workforce by 2040; if the rate can be raised to the same level as for men, then the projected shortfall drops to 3 million.' World Bank data from 64 emerging and developed countries indicates that women's share of university undergraduate and post-graduate degrees ranged from 23 per cent to 74 per cent – with most countries recording women's educational attainment as above 50 per cent of all degrees received.[1] In many countries there are now more women in higher education than men.

There is increasing evidence that a good mix of men and women at board level increases a company's performance. Analysis by Catalyst, an association focused on gathering information and doing research on gender, showed that Fortune 500 companies with higher percentages of women board directors, on average, significantly outperformed companies with the lowest percentages of women board directors (Catalyst 2007) (Figure 4.1).

In developing countries, it emerges that supporting women entrepreneurs with microloans results in higher repayment rates. Women tend to accept smaller loans than men – and make up 75 per cent of all microcredit recipients worldwide (Armendariz 2005). Women are more likely to put earned income to good use than their husbands, because they have the best perspective on the needs of the family. When women are economically empowered, children are more likely to be educated and healthy, and more money is likely to be reinvested into the family. This also supports the development of the society.

The first cases in this section are about mentoring in education. Wagner and Wagner (Case study 8: Germany) describe female PhD students, matched with female and male executives of small and medium-sized enterprises to prepare them

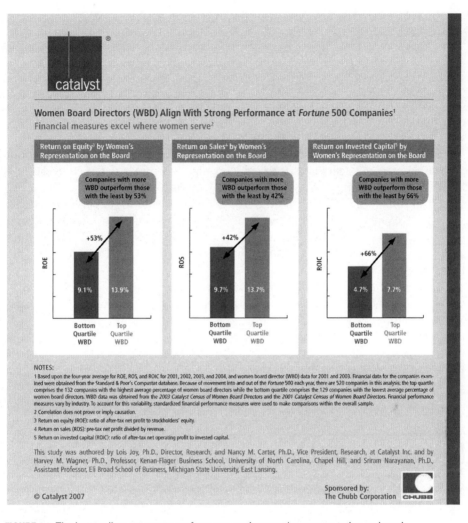

FIGURE 4.1 The bottom line: corporate performance and women's representation on boards
© Catalyst 2007, The Bottom Line: Corporate Performance and Women's Representation on Boards

for executive careers. Bujaki et al. (Case study 9: Canada) write about mid-career women associate professors mentored to accelerate their careers to full professorship. Koschoreck and Veraldo (Case study 10: the USA) focus on a professor mentoring his student to engage in conversations about sexuality and heterosexual privilege. This unusual perspective illustrates barriers that generally occur in diversity conversations. This case is followed by the reflections of Helen Worrall (Case study 11: Great Britain) on mentoring in the gay and lesbian population.

Next, we have two cases on mentoring immigrant women into employment and society in Denmark (Case study 12 by Møller-Jensen) and Canada (Case study 13 by Cruz) and one case study on mentoring women entrepreneurs in Africa, South

Asia and the Middle East (Case study 14 by Corinaldi). These programmes focus on building a role for women in society and adding value to society – and on creating opportunities for mentors to learn about other cultures. The Danish and the Canadian programmes are very alike in their purpose and are based on voluntary mentors. The case study by Corinaldi is an innovative e-mentoring programme in cooperation with Google, with volunteer mentors in the UK e-mentoring women entrepreneurs overseas. Case study 15 (Argentina) by Monserrat presents global virtual mentoring programmes.

Finally, are five cases on women and leadership. They tell stories about promoting women's leadership careers in computer science (Case study 16: the USA, by Mertz and Pfleeger), in small and medium-sized companies (Case study 17: Great Britain, by Hartshorn), in cross-company mentoring programmes (Case study 18: Luxembourg, by Knott and Poulsen), in the police force and in small and medium-sized companies in Norway (Case study 19: Norway, by Ekeland), and about promoting women of colour in their leadership career (Case study 20: the USA, by Dixon et al.).

This diversity illustrates the complexity of gender (and sexual preference) in society and in the corporate world and is an inspiration for those who wish to make an effort to promote the resources and competencies of women.

Note

1 See: http://ddp-ext.worldbank.org/ext/DDPQQ/member.do?method=getMembers&userid=1&que ryId=189.

References

Armendariz, B. (2005) *The Economics of Microfinance*. Cambridge, MA: The MIT Press.
McKinsey & Company (2007) *Women Matter: Gender Diversity, a Corporate Performance Driver*. New York: McKinsey & Co.

Case study 8: Germany

Mentoring for women: creating the future together!

Dieter Wagner and Nelli Wagner

Introduction

The federal state of Brandenburg surrounds the capital Berlin. Here are found primarily small and medium-sized enterprises (SMEs) mostly with fewer than 10 employees. Their innovation potential can be high, particularly due to their skilled people. These companies do not have HR or recruitment departments, recruiting junior employees mainly through personal networks.

Demographic changes are negatively influencing Brandenburg in East Germany, weakening the local economy. Among them is the low birth rate, which is intensified through the migration of the academic elite, who are seeking better future opportunities elsewhere. Particularly young women of the age to start a family are leaving the region, thus reinforcing societal and economic problems.

Additionally, women in Germany are still considerably underrepresented in top executive roles in the fields of economy, administration and science. Although approximately half of graduates at German universities are women, only about 11 per cent of them reach executive positions.

The programme

The programme 'Mentoring for women – creating the future together!' focuses on this problem. The idea was to offer female students a programme, tailored to their needs, preparing them for the working environment and to enter the workplace. It was developed to give them opportunities to gain insights into everyday working life and to have an experienced person with whom to discuss their individual career issues as well as providing networking opportunities.

The project also offers an advanced opportunity for regional enterprises and administration departments to benefit from the specific potential of qualified young women. As mentees, they can discover alternative kinds of work and how to enter them, through the relationship with an executive mentor or by getting to know other mentors. Additionally, participating mentors have the chance to meet the young generation of academics and get to know their expectations and demands in the future workplace. The mentees are not just looking for an adequate salary. They also have issues with the work–life balance, career advancement and how to deal with increased responsibility. Knowing these demands, companies in economically weaker regions can keep up with regions that offer more attractive salaries, by responding to the needs of young, highly qualified employees.

The general programme objective is to develop female undergraduate and PhD students for executive careers in the region Berlin-Brandenburg. This includes:

- raising the students' awareness of their potential and giving executives increased access to these talented individuals;
- supporting gender equality in recruitment;
- preventing the brain drain of potential female executives;
- supporting the cooperation between the universities and the regional economy.

Initially, the project had been funded through the European Social Fund since 2004. Since 2006, it has been co-funded by the universities in Brandenburg. Since the first round, the project has been overseen by an advisory board composed of representatives from the participating universities, regional company associations and relevant ministries.

The mentoring dyads are formed and supervised locally through the career service offices at the Universities of Potsdam and Frankfurt (Oder) and the office of the equal opportunity commissioner at the university in Cottbus. Since 2006, female students from the universities of applied sciences in Brandenburg can also take part in the programme.

Selection and matching

The programme is aimed at female students and PhD students, who see an individual career perspective in the regional economy Berlin-Brandenburg. While mentees are not selected on their field of study, their profiles are influenced by the universities. In Cottbus, there are mainly applications from engineers; in Frankfurt (Oder), applications from cultural studies and law; and at the University of Potsdam, applications come at random from arts, economy and social sciences to STEM-subjects.[1] The interdisciplinarity and heterogeneity of the mentee groups give participants a chance to look beyond their own field of study and to learn to work in interdisciplinary teams. Students, who are already mothers, further enrich the mentee group.

We use a three-step selection process, to choose those with the most potential, who will benefit the most (Figure 4.2). Mentors are male and female volunteers,

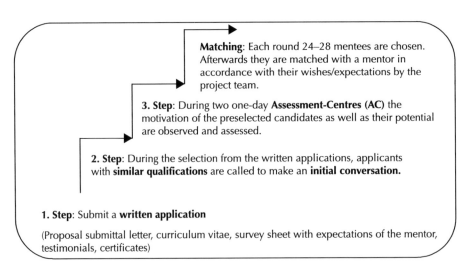

Matching: Each round 24–28 mentees are chosen. Afterwards they are matched with a mentor in accordance with their wishes/expectations by the project team.

3. Step: During two one-day **Assessment-Centres (AC)** the motivation of the preselected candidates as well as their potential are observed and assessed.

2. Step: During the selection from the written applications, applicants with **similar qualifications** are called to make an **initial conversation.**

1. Step: Submit a **written application**

(Proposal submittal letter, curriculum vitae, survey sheet with expectations of the mentor, testimonials, certificates)

FIGURE 4.2 The three-step selection process

who receive no payment. Having men in the programme helps sensitise them to the problems of young female academics, while female mentors provide role models.

Potential mentors are interviewed individually and presented with the programme goals and the enormous responsibility of taking on the mentor role. We explore their expectations of mentees and the programme and look for the following mentor characteristics:

- specialist or executive;
- in employment in the Brandenburg/Berlin region in:
  - business;
  - non-university academic institution;
  - public administration and politics;
- must agree to invest enough time for the mentoring programme;
- be able to give insights into the working environment and own working area;
- motivation to pass on their own experiences;
- openness and willingness to learn.

Preference is given to mentors from small and medium-sized enterprises in the region. Potential mentors also fill out a questionnaire describing their criteria for the kind of mentee with whom they would like to be matched, and they identify opportunities their company can offer to the mentees or the programme.

Matching is based on information gathered and assessment centre observation of the mentees. In total, this gives a good impression of personality, social skills, team spirit, ability to work under pressure, etc. The wishes of mentees and the mentors are respected.

Training and networking for mentees

Mentees benefit from vocational preparation training; work on projects in small groups; and meeting other mentees, mentors and former mentees from all project locations in network meetings, as shown in Figure 4.3.

Training for mentees includes:

- personal development (communication, conflict management, presentation, etc.);
- gender competence;
- application competence;
- project management;
- team and leadership competencies.

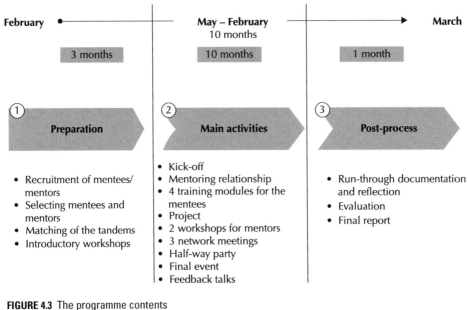

FIGURE 4.3 The programme contents

Assessment

In the eight rounds since 2005, 210 mentees have participated. To ensure quality and to keep improving on the concept, each round has been evaluated internally. In 2009, the project was evaluated externally by Dr Astrid Franzke looking at mentees' development process. This included answering a questionnaire before the start and half-way through the programme – questionnaires were also answered by a control group of non-participants. The questionnaire asked about their:

- definition of a career;
- evaluation of their career possibilities;
- wishes and fears in regard to starting their career after graduation;
- self-assessment of their self-esteem, attitude towards teamwork, performance motivation, leadership motivation, action motivation, and work–life balance sensibility.

In addition, a number of mentees and mentors were interviewed during the programme.

The evaluation concluded: 'Mentoring for Women' is a professional and fitting offer to support female students in their transition from student life to work life with documented effects.

In 2010, a job-entry survey was taken externally of the 157 mentees, who had passed through the programme at that time. The combination of the one-to-one-mentoring relationship, the interdisciplinary training module and inter-disciplinary networking was seen as the endorsed value of the programme.

Within three months of graduation, almost 75 per cent of the mentees had found a position relevant to their degree and 77 per cent had started careers in the region. Combining these data with the high satisfaction of the entrants with their workplace (74 per cent), we can extrapolate that we have contributed to preventing outward migration of talent.

Another gratifying result is that two-thirds of the mentees, who entered the labour market, achieved degrees in humanities and social sciences and one-third in science and technology. This corresponds to the proportion of the fields of studies of all mentees, who took part in the programme. Usually, those who graduate in humanities and social sciences have more difficulty finding jobs.

In retrospect, 72 per cent of the mentees said the programme facilitated their labour market entry at least partially. One reflected that the encounter with her mentor was the best thing that had ever happened to her. Another former mentee said she is often asked from where she gets her courage and self-confidence from, and she ascribes it to the mentoring programme. All participants valued the interdisciplinary groups and the networking opportunities.

Lessons learned

The project team needs to understand and deal with the diverse expectations of all the stakeholders – mentors, mentees, and involved universities, the ministry, those funding the programme, etc. In this process, important factors are: clear communi-cation of the project goals, adjusting expectations of stakeholders, and accuracy in selecting mentees and mentors. The more time and energy we invest in the starting phase, and the more we focus on quality instead of quantity, the more successful the programme is.

Of course, we are aware of the limitations of this programme. It can only have a small effect on the migration problem and on wider cultural change. It depends on many factors we cannot influence directly. So we focus on factors we can influence.

We see the mentoring relationship as working across hierarchy and generations, as being voluntary, as transferring knowledge from mentor to mentee and as a mutual learning process where mentors also reflect and gain new insight into their own knowledge. It is like a tandem: two people sitting on a bike sharing specific tasks to reach their goal. The mentor is sitting behind and gives power and stability. The mentee is sitting at the front deciding in which direction the tandem is going. Mentoring works through giving and taking, learning and reflecting. Knowledge, new ideas and feedback are created in this process.

Reflection questions

1. Why do we still need a mentoring programme supporting young well-qualified women in preparing their career paths?
2. In this project you have to be aware of diversity in gender, age, organisational background, working experiences and different locations. How can you cope with all these kinds of diversity?

Notes

1 STEM – an abbreviation for Sciences, Technics, Engineering, Mathematics. In Germany, the abbreviation is MINT – Mathematik, Ingenieurswissenschaften, Naturwissenschaften, Technik.

Case study 9: Canada

Group mentoring for mid-career women Associate Professors

Merridee Bujaki, Jenepher Lennox Terrion, Catherine Mavriplis and Françoise Moreau-Johnson

Introduction

Women professors have long felt an accumulation of disadvantage that has negatively impacted their careers (e.g. Valian 1998) and promotion. Even though women earn a greater share of the doctorates and occupy a greater share of the assistant and non-tenure track positions at universities, their emergence into the highest rank of Full Professor is still limited (Perna 2005; Bonawitz and Andel 2009; Zinovyeva and Bagues 2010). Time in the Associate Professor intermediate rank has been shown to be greater for women than men across disciplines in several countries, even when accounting for leave and greater outside responsibilities (e.g. Ornstein et al. 2007; Stout et al. 2007).

According to McKeen and Bujaki:

> [The research on gender and mentoring] contains a great deal of information about why mentoring relationships are essential (not just important) for the success of women in organizations. A trusted guide,

sponsor, and interpreter – a mentor – is critical to (a) assisting women in decoding the masculine culture in organizations, (b) promoting women's successful functioning and advancement in organizations, and (c) enhancing women's feelings of safety and belonging in such an environment.

(2007: 198)

Gibson reviewed research looking at women in academic careers and concluded that 'In higher education, mentoring has been suggested as a vehicle to improve the socialization, orientation, and career outcomes of faculty as well as to promote increased equity for women faculty' (2004: 173–4). Gibson identified five themes that reflected the experience of being mentored for women faculty members: (1) having someone who truly cares and acts in one's best interest; (2) a feeling of connection; (3) being affirmed of one's worth; (4) not being alone; and (5) recognizing that politics are part of one's experience.

While universities are starting to adopt formal mentoring programmes for new hires, especially in relation to obtaining tenure (e.g. Wasserstein et al. 2007), little mentoring is available for mid-career Associate Professors. Women overwhelmingly say they would like to have a mentor, but find few available, capable or willing (e.g. Mavriplis et al. 2009; Smith 2000). Furthermore, the lack of female role models or mentors, especially in the sciences and engineering, further limits the availability of mentors when women seek a female mentor. This dearth of female mentors is all the more detrimental because female role models are better able to address issues women mention as barriers to their success: work–life balance, timidity for self-promotion, burdensome administrative assignments, gendered communication styles and expectations of behaviour (Mavriplis et al. 2009).

With this backdrop, the University of Ottawa's Centre for Academic Leadership (CAL) decided to pilot a group mentoring programme for women Associate Professors (the Mentoring Group) from all the non-medical faculties of the university.

Beginnings

The university is located in Ottawa, Ontario – Canada's capital city. It is North America's largest bilingual university, has approximately 38,000 undergraduate and graduate students (full- and part-time) and approximately 1,200 full-time faculty members organized in nine faculties (including a Faculty of Medicine). Female students make up approximately 60 per cent of both undergraduate (60.8 per cent) and graduate students (57.3 per cent). In contrast, women comprise 37.6 per cent of full-time faculty.

In 2005, the university established the CAL in response to concerns that faculty members were either not ready or not willing to take on leadership roles within the university. An early programme was a traditional formal mentoring programme, under which junior faculty members with a self-declared interest in being mentored were paired up with more senior faculty members.

In 2009, the university President appointed a task force on women in academia to investigate and report on the status of women faculty at the university. This task force noted both the importance of mentors for women academics and their scarcity. In Fall 2009, two female full professors who had been members of the task force approached CAL to propose a mentoring group for women and volunteer to facilitate the group. The programme focused on women Associate Professors since many of CAL's other activities targeted Assistant Professors. The objectives were: (1) to encourage female Associate Professors to apply for promotion to full professor; (2) to lower the stress experienced by women Associate Professors; (3) to provide an opportunity for women known to the CAL to get together and network; and (4) to provide a forum for the transfer and exchange of knowledge and expertise.

Implementation

CAL organized the Mentoring Group to follow principles similar to the traditional mentoring programme for faculty: the relationship would span an academic year; meetings would take place approximately monthly; and each meeting was to have a specific agenda item or topic for discussion. The CAL coordinator decided to invite one woman Associate Professor from each of the eight non-medical faculties to participate. She selected women based on her personal knowledge of women across campus. While some of the women had participated in more traditional mentoring through the CAL (either as mentors, mentees, or both), the CAL did not offer any formal mentoring training or preparation. Once invited, all the women enthusiastically accepted the invitation, including one who was on sabbatical and would not otherwise have been on campus.

The structure of the group was a hybrid of traditional mentoring by two senior mentors and peer mentoring by the participants themselves. No known one-on-one meetings between the mentors and the mentees took place. The group held six two-hour meetings between November 2009 and May 2010, on campus. The CAL contributed the support of the coordinator and refreshments for each of the meetings. The first meeting focused on the group members getting to know each other and on identifying topics for future sessions. Subsequent meetings addressed: demystifying the application for promotion to full professor, including strategies for managing academic curricula vitae; navigating the 'old boys' network'; engaging in self-promotion, strategic planning and outreach; juggling research, teaching and academic service; and, finally, the work–life balance. Through this agenda, the programme provided an opportunity to discuss career and personal concerns that might not have had a forum elsewhere. Both Full Professors and the coordinator attended each of the meetings, along with at least six members of the group. No one missed more than two meetings. The quality of the conversations and the relaxed atmosphere of each meeting fostered high commitment to the group.

The group relied mainly on the considerable experience of the two mentors but a rich set of experiences also emerged from the participants, especially as they compared practices in the different disciplines and faculties of the university. The group brought in one external speaker to address strategies for the application for promotion from the point of view of the university level committee that reviews applications.

Evaluation

Early in the programme the group considered how its insights could be communicated to other women academics at the university and more broadly. The group decided the coordinator should take detailed notes of each meeting for later use by the Centre and as a reference for the participants.

To assess the impact of the programme on the eight mentees, each participant responded, in writing, to the following questions:

1 Describe the top three impacts of participating in the group on any aspect of your work or yourself.

2 Name three concrete actions that you undertook or plan to undertake as a result of your participation.

3 Identify one thing that you would recommend to other group mentoring leaders.

The main positive impacts of the programme, as perceived by the participants, emerged from a thematic qualitative assessment of the responses identifying the following themes:

Impacts of participating

1 *Personal growth*: Positive changes experienced by the participants lay in the areas of confidence, self-esteem, empowerment or motivation, along with better understanding of one's own style, strengths and weaknesses, and motivation to change. One participant wrote, 'I was reassured to see that other women faculty members were going through experiences similar to mine and that I could develop the confidence to push my career forward.' Another commented, 'I am more confident I am on the right track – even if it is a rather circuitous track.' The mentors also found the programme enriching, with one of them commenting: 'I found this experience with a mentoring group one of the most positive of my career.'

2 *Creation of a community*: Establishing connections with colleagues from different faculties and the sense of support experienced by the participants was another theme. One mentee commented, '[I] . . . developed a network of women from whom I have already benefitted in a number of ways (along with

the camaraderie and sense of connection).' Another commented, 'I realize that women from all across campus encounter similar challenges and difficulties in their careers and lives.' Participants also signalled a desire to 'give back' to the community by becoming mentors themselves.

3 *Acquisition of practical skills*: Participants spoke of learning skills to help build reputation, to promote themselves and to present their accomplishments more effectively: Comments included, 'I learned some practical skills to advance my research dossier' and 'A better sense of organization for presenting my accomplishments.'

4 *Career strategy*: Several comments indicated people refined career plans to include actions to enhance professional reputation and more strategic approaches to academic activities. One mentee commented, 'The meetings helped me to see that I had to develop a career plan and stay focused.' Another indicated she would be 'hopefully forcing myself to be more strategic (and less "nice") about my own career advancement'.

Concrete actions

In terms of concrete actions that participants indicated they had undertaken, or would undertake, three main themes emerged:

1 *Self-promotion*: They identified more attention to self-promotion (e.g. enhancement of one's webpage, development of a statement of research, continuous updating of one's CV). One commented, 'I took steps to get myself on the university web page banner via my Faculty media people.' Another indicated she would 'work on language and ways to describe and promote my work to show its worth' and a third indicated she 'updated [her] webpage and CV to provide a stronger research presence and a clearer statement synthesizing [her] work'.

2 *A strategic approach*: Participants committed to a more strategic approach (e.g. to projects, career, priorities, writing, promotion, graduate students, referees, citations and advice). One woman said, 'I learned how to be strategic in taking on new projects'; another indicated, 'I am now planning concretely my career, especially setting a timeline for asking for promotion.'

3 *Focus on research*: This theme reflected an increased focus on research (new initiatives, grant applications, proposals, reduced administrative involvement). One indicated, 'The first action that I undertook as a result of my participation was to refuse to take on an administrative position within my faculty when it was offered to me.' Another commented, 'I now "schedule" my writing time', while a third indicated she 'began working on a grant application and book proposal'.

In addition to the qualitative assessment of the impact of the programme, participants also completed a formal evaluation. Given the small number of participants, we present no quantitative data. However, the survey results echo those reported above. The participants reported a number of positive psychosocial outcomes, including greater confidence, reduced levels of stress, improved job satisfaction, and a lessened sense of isolation. At the task level, the programme helped them identify their strengths, enhance their research productivity, and improve their job performance. From a career perspective, they reported the programme had sharpened their strategic focus on their careers and aided them in identifying professional priorities.

Lessons learned

Outcomes identified include that group mentoring:

1 is more economical than traditional mentoring in that it reaches more people, with a lesser investment of time and human resources.

2 offers the opportunity for a more structured and controlled mentoring experience, compared to individual mentoring.

3 allows for the transfer of knowledge within the organization.

4 is a more efficient way for participants to expand their networks, compared to traditional one-on-one mentoring.

5 permits the training of mentors through the twinning of an experienced mentor with a more junior mentor as mentors for the group. (At the same time, the mentees from a mentoring group can be added to the pool of future mentors – either individual or group.)

6 should not replace individual mentoring. Rather, a range of programme types should be offered to serve diverse organizational members.

7 needs a mechanism for follow-up to be built into each mentoring session's agenda so participants can report back on action items arising from earlier sessions.

8 presents topics arising during meetings that may serve as indicators of emerging concerns, giving CAL an opportunity to update and adapt their programmes and workshops on a timely basis and assist CAL in its annual planning of activities.

All of the mentees indicated they would choose the same mentors if they were to do it again and that they would recommend the programme to their colleagues. Participants suggested a number of recommendations to enhance future programmes. These included: (1) encouraging a diverse representation of mentees in the group; (2) continuing to allow each group to set its own agenda for the sessions; (3) inviting experts or third parties to address some topics; (4) extending the life of the programme to eight sessions; (5) including a follow-up component to the programme; and (6) promoting healthy and balanced approaches to work–life integration.

As a whole, this hybrid of traditional hierarchical mentoring and peer mentoring has proved beneficial, and may be especially useful for women in male-dominated environments, who seek mentors but find few available, especially female ones.

Reflection questions

1. What differences are there between a mentoring group and a support group? What characteristics made this relationship a mentoring group?
2. What are the advantages and disadvantages of using a hybrid (hierarchical and peer) mentoring model? Would this work equally well in all types of organizations?
3. The programme described in this case was for women only. Would the outcomes have been the same if the programme was for men only? If the programme included both women and men? Why or why not?

References

Bonawitz, M. and Andel, N. (2009) The glass ceiling is made of concrete: the barriers to promotion and tenure of women in American academia, *Forum on Public Policy Online*, Summer 2009.

Gibson, S.K. (2004) Being mentored: the experience of women faculty, *Journal of Career Development*, 30(3): 173–88.

Mavriplis, C., Bédard, C. and Cloutier, N. (2009) Grooming women's leadership in the aerospace industry: the scientific and technological careers of women and men, in Second PROMETEA International Conference, forthcoming.

McKeen, C. and Bujaki, M. (2007) Gender and mentoring: issues, effects, and opportunities, in B.R. Ragins and K.E. Kram (eds) *The Handbook of Mentoring at Work: Theory, Research, and Practice.* Thousand Oaks, CA: Sage Publications, pp. 197–222.

Ornstein, M., Stewart, P. and Drakich, J. (2007) Promotion at Canadian universities: the intersection of gender, discipline and institution, *Canadian Journal of Higher Education*, 37(3): 1–25.

Perna, L.W. (2005) Sex differences in faculty tenure and promotion: the contribution of family ties, *Research in Higher Education*, 46(3): 277–307.

Smith, P.J. (2000) Failing to mentor Sapphire: the actionability of blocking black women from initiating mentoring relationships, *UCLA Women's Law Journal*, 10(2): 701.

Stout, P.A., Staiger, J. and Jennings, N.A. (2007) Affective stories: understanding the lack of progress of women faculty, *NWSA (National Women's Studies Association) Journal*, 19(3): 124–44.

Valian, V. (1998) *Why So Slow? The Advancement of Women.* Cambridge, MA: MIT Press.

Wasserstein, A.G., Quistberg, D.A. and Shea, J.A. (2007) Mentoring at the University of Pennsylvania: results of a faculty survey, *Journal of General Internal Medicine*, 22(2): 210–14.

Zinovyeva, N. and Bagues, M. (2010) Does gender matter for academic promotion? Evidence from a randomized natural experiment, paper presented at Third World Conference of the European Association of Labour Economists (EALE) and the Society of Labor Economists (SOLE). Available at: http://www.eale.nl/Conference2010/Programme/PaperscontributedsessionsA/add127253_mGJBfX5wSf.pdf.

Case study 10: the USA

Mentoring adult learners to engage in conversations about sexuality and heterosexual privilege

James W. Koschoreck and Cynthia Miller Veraldo

Introduction

Every educator who works to assist adults develop has a set of preferences, ideals and desired directions regarding development informing their practice, even if these are beneath the surface of practice and even if the educator professes to be value-neutral and only student-centered (Brookfield 2009: 41). Mentoring adult learners on their journeys to develop into harbingers of political and social change steeped in the philosophical principles of social justice is a daunting task even in the best of circumstances. It becomes even more challenging when the objective of the transformational learning experience turns towards embracing non-normative sexualities.

This case study explores a particularly effective way in which the professor of a doctoral program in Urban Educational Leadership at the University of Cincinnati mentored a first-year cohort of future educational leaders to interrogate the notions of heterosexual privilege and to work through their individual and collective discomfort of seeking the relevance of sexuality in educational environments. It reflects on the experience from the perspectives of the professor (Koschoreck) and of one of the students (Veraldo).

Mentor reflections

During their first year in the doctoral cohort, students take a sequence of seminars, the last of which is designed to introduce them to the various social, political, economic, and legal contexts surrounding the practice of urban educational leadership. Students were required to read and reflect on a collection of materials edited by Koschoreck and Tooms (2009) entitled *Sexuality Matters: Paradigms and Policies for Educational Leaders*.

As an Associate Professor in my then tenth year in the doctoral program, I was well aware of the multiple 'forces of resistance in schools and other educational institutions that maintain the heteronormative status quo' (Koschoreck and Slattery 2010: 157). As products of these educational institutions, many doctoral students resist critical discussions around sexuality that might lead towards significant social transformation. As I endeavored to develop a curriculum that would gently guide these students along 'a path of least resistance', as it were, I purposely left discussions of sexuality and heterosexual privilege for the end of the course. I surmised that by this point, having already had many opportunities to engage in difficult conversations about race, class, ability, and gender, students might be slightly less reluctant to broach the more uncomfortable issues of sexuality. This was indeed the case.

Noting that the students were both willing and enthusiastic to explore the relationships between sexuality, heteronormativity, and leadership, I wondered why my experience with this particular cohort was so different from previous ones. It might be due to the peculiar collection of individual personalities that happened to come together that year; however, my sense was that there was more going on. This was the first time I was using the text *Sexuality Matters* (Koschoreck and Tooms 2009). Some have argued that one of the strengths of this text is that the authors focus on solutions as well as problems.

The enthusiastic engagement of the cohort in discussing issues of sexuality caused me to think that I might provide a different sort of experience for them, changing the nature of our relationship from that of professor/students to mentor/ mentees. Thinking of the career development and the psychosocial support provided by the mentor (Kram 1985), I tried to seek new ways to provide 'sponsorship, exposure and visibility, coaching, protection, and challenging assignments' (Greiman 2007: 156). Additionally, I tried to provide 'acceptance, counseling, friendship, and role modeling' (Greiman 2007: 156). I decided, therefore, to invite them to take on the responsibility of carrying this conversation to a larger audience beyond the classroom (i.e., at a scholarly conference) in order that they might indeed view themselves both as agentic[1] and as transformative leaders. As we stated in the co-created proposal for that symposium:

> One of the goals of this conversation is for educational leaders to 'continue the arduous task of incorporating the notions of equality, democracy, and justice within the educational leadership discourse that embraces all of the identifiers' (Dantley, 2009, p. ix) . . . Secondly, the conversation would act as a blueprint for high school administrators, district level administrators, and university level administrators as they struggle with the political complexities of gay–straight alliance clubs, events, harassment, and sex education. This conversation will provide opportunities for all participants that are still wrestling with their own dispositions to learn from their peers effective strategies and communication processes to allow difficult conversations to take place.
>
> (Koschoreck et al. 2010)

Mentee reflections

In our curriculum for the doctorate in Urban Educational Leadership, my cohort and I learned about extreme societal, educational, and economic inequities as well as the racial re-segregation of America's urban schools. Additionally, we engaged in reading and discussions about the social, legal, and political climate for students, teachers, and administrators who identify as lesbian, gay, bisexual, transgender, or queer (LGBTQ). As acting and aspiring urban educational leaders, we were encouraged to think about leading overwhelmingly heteronormative institutions where bullying and harassment of LGBTQ students and teachers is far too common. We learned about our responsibilities for fostering environments where Gay–Straight Alliances are embraced, where the curriculum engages rather than isolates LGBTQ students, and where teachers feel comfortable to affirm rather than conceal their identities.

Throughout the readings and discussions, our professor challenged us to reflect upon the concept of heterosexual privilege, for a deeper understanding of the multi-dimensional aspects of the LGBTQ experience. At the end of that segment of the course, he invited us to continue the discussion by developing a conference presentation. He wanted to provide a forum for us to continue to think about the impact our leadership can have on creating an inclusive atmosphere for LGBTQ students, staff, and teachers. Having learned of a regional diversity conference, he guided us through writing a proposal. Together we developed a format and design for the presentation that would engage all the presenters in a substantive dialogue about their responsibilities as educational leaders around issues of sexuality. The result of this collaboration was the presentation of Conversations on sexual identity and P-20[2] educational leadership at the 2010 Diversity Research and Teaching Symposium at Indiana State University. The presentation was so meaningful to all of us, that we decided to do a similar presentation with additional members from the cohort at the Diversity Conference on our own campus.

The mentoring experience was particularly beneficial to me because I was able to deepen my knowledge and leadership in an aspect of diversity on which I previously would not have considered doing an academic presentation. I remember raising an issue at the second presentation about a previous experience I had where a student refused to attend a presentation on sexuality, because it was adverse to her religion. At that time, I decided it was acceptable to excuse her from the presentation. I was challenged on that decision by someone from the audience who responded 'Would you have let a student out of a presentation about ethnic diversity?' I was almost speechless because I did not know how to respond. I had not previously thought about how my decision may marginalize a whole group of people. My participation in that conference presentation furthered my thinking about how LGBTQ issues are different from other aspects of diversity; about how the intersection of sexuality and religion can interfere with how some people view social justice. Through multiple individual meetings, my professor/mentor helped me work through that particular challenge by discussing the difficulty of the decision making process of leaders when it comes to social justice issues and diversity. Grappling with the intersection of sexual, racial, religious, and other diversities will be a continuous process for me as a leader in the field of education.

The conversations between me and my professor/mentor led me to enroll in his LGBTQ Issues in Educational Leadership course. In the course, we were required to construct a transgressive art project and reflect on that project in the form of a paper. I decided to look at my own sexuality and how I have transgressed across my life. The atmosphere my professor/mentor created both in the class and in our individual meetings was so comfortable that I was able to share these personal and private ideas about my own sexuality with him and the rest of my classmates. In fact, I have now suggested to my professor that we present the transgressive art project assignment at another conference.

The mentoring relationship I have with my professor has helped me continue to grow my knowledge of LGBTQ issues. My career aspirations are to go into the professoriate or higher education administration, and I am particularly interested in all aspects of diversity and educational leadership. My professor asked me if I would feel awkward or worried about discrimination for including a citation on my curriculum vitae for a presentation on LGBTQ matters. It does not concern me at all; in fact, I would not want to work at an institution that would discriminate against me for presenting on LGBTQ issues in the first place.

Lessons learned

The success of a mentoring experience can be assessed in many ways. Certainly, a successful result occurs where the mentor has provided the opportunities for students and/or mentees to develop positive dispositions as a result of the experience. Moreover, with difficult conversations concerning sexuality and heterosexual privilege, mere movement away from resistance might signal successful engagement with the topic. In the current case, however, not only did the mentees enthusiastically participate in the fullness of the discourse, they expressed eagerness to take the conversation to other arenas in order to influence the thinking of more individuals.

The warm, positive reception we received from those attending the Diversity Research and Teaching Symposium at Indiana State University encouraged us to submit yet another proposal to our own Diversity Conference at the University of Cincinnati. With over 50 persons in attendance at this session – ranging from secondary school students to professors at advanced levels in their careers – one senior faculty member remarked towards the end of the session that she was quite impressed by the ability of our group to create an environment that allowed the secondary school students to feel sufficiently comfortable to participate in the conversation.

Reflection questions

1. How might a professor move from being merely a tutor to becoming a proper mentor of his/her protégés as they seek to explore the complexities of sexuality?
2. Recognizing that mentees have agency and responsibility to effect social change, what responsibilities do they have in the dyadic relationship?
3. What is needed to prepare mentors for mentoring leaders around LGBTQ issues – and when is mentoring not the right tool anymore?

Notes

1 My hope in this experience was that the students would not merely be passive recipients of knowledge about sexuality, but would actually exercise agency by owning the responsibility of finding new ways to effect social change.
2 In the context of the American educational system, 'P-20' refers to the integrated system that extends from pre-school through tertiary education.

References

Brookfield, S. (2009) Understanding development, in G.I.E. Strohschen (ed.) *Handbook of Blended Shore Education*. New York: Springer Science+Business Media, LLC, pp. 27–43.

Greiman, B.C. (2007) Influence of mentoring on dyad satisfaction: is there agreement between matched pairs of novice teachers and their formal mentors? *Journal of Career and Technical Education*, 23(1): 153–66.

Koschoreck, J.W., Finke, G., Martin, R., Mayo, N., Powell, J., Veraldo, C. and Watkins, P. (2010) Conversations on sexual identity and P-20 educational leadership, conversation conducted at the 2010 Diversity Research and Teaching Symposium at Indiana State University, Terre Haute, IN, November.

Koschoreck, J.W. and Slattery, P. (2010) Meeting all students' needs: transforming the unjust normativity of heterosexism, in C. Marshall and M. Oliva (eds) *Leadership for Social Justice: Making Revolutions in Education*, 2nd edn. Boston, MA: Allyn & Bacon, pp. 156–74.

Koschoreck, J.W. and Tooms, A.K. (eds) (2009) *Sexuality Matters: Paradigms and Policies for Educational Leaders*. Lanham, MD: Rowman & Littlefield.

Kram, K.E. (1985) *Mentoring at Work*. Boston, MA: Scott, Foresman and Company.

Case study 11: Great Britain

Mentoring for gay and lesbian professionals: a personal story

Helen Worrall

Introduction

When starting to look at the area of mentoring for gay and lesbian (G&L) professionals within the workplace, I assumed that I would find a plethora of reviews, studies and cases of best practice. It seems, however, that, although the challenges facing G&L employees are well documented with the key areas of discrimination and disclosure, the area of targeted mentoring programmes is lacking in data. On further investigation, it seems that the area is lacking in research, full stop (Russell and Horne 2009), and surprisingly there is hardly any G&L research within the hugely popular arena of leadership (Fassinger et al. 2010).

Of those resources available to me, I did find a few noteworthy themes within existing research that could extrapolate to enhance formal mentoring programmes. There seemed to be far more research conducted within the sectors of adolescent and higher education than in business. This is understandable given that, in the 2009 Gay, Lesbian and Straight Education Network (GLSEN) National School Climate Survey found over 80 per cent of G&L adolescents had experienced some kind of homophobic discrimination or taunts by classmates and another, more disturbingly found a presence of discriminatory remarks by teachers too.

The majority of searches for G&L mentoring programmes brought up many university sites with advice and guidance for LGBT students and a blanket statement on respect and the realistic expectations of work rather than a staid policy statement on their Diversity policy. The presence of mentoring or positive role modelling within education can only be a positive step as younger generations grow up with a different perspective on what it is to be openly out at work. Younger generations, who have developed to enter a workplace where the Equality Act and Sexual Orientation Act is in force, feel that to hide their identity short-changes their careers and potential relationships with colleagues at work, according to a recent Reuters article. Older G&L employees often have differing opinions, taking the perspective that work is work and personal life is personal. This possibly originates from the most common reason to remain in the closet; a fear of disclosure ending career aspirations, promotions or discrimination. It is therefore reassuring that programmes focusing on younger G&L individuals build on realistic expectations and confidence to approach working life as they wish.

The majority of studies originated from the US. Recent high profile suicides and the 'It Gets Better' campaign have raised awareness of the need to protect a population at risk at an early stage.

The research provided interesting findings on the mechanics and practicalities of a mentoring programme. A review of a targeted programme with PhD students and faculty members by McAllister et al. (2009) emphasised the positive experiences of those who responded (although a limited sample) but questioned its longevity as a useful programme. For example, there was little emphasis on training or indeed matching of the mentors to mentees. This possibly led to the small sample size and sporadic nature of the mentoring relationships. As within various other observations on G&L mentoring, 'giving something back to the community' is a primary objective of the mentors within the relationship. However, the mentee was primarily looking for psychosocial support, so the experience of participants was mixed.

The big gaps in research are around where the most effective source of psychosocial support will come from. Although Lin (2001) found that G&L mentees found more perceived support from G&L mentors than heterosexual, there have been no published reports as to the utility of programmes, which match-based on sexual orientation (McAllister et al. 2009). Brighton and Hove Council placed training at the core of their LGBT mentoring scheme, but make no mention of whether the mentors are of similar dynamic to the mentee. It seems from the research that this is usually the case with G&L mentoring. As disclosure is the most common concern to G&L professionals for fear of discrimination in recruitment, promotions and general policy and practice, I find it difficult to believe that a mentoring programme based on G&L employees with a heterosexual colleague would be as effective as that of a G&L dyad.

As formal research into mentoring within a business context was rather limited, I progressed down a more informal route. In searching for a practical answer, I approached the organisation, Jake, founded by Ivan Massow in 1999. Coined as the world's largest professional G&L community, Jake is an inclusive network for individuals, groups and organisations. The mentoring scheme within its vast membership defines mentors as more experienced. The aim of the scheme is to provide relaxed, flexible relationships. Jake offers no training to their mentor/mentee population and allows the programme to evolve organically. Maintaining the relationship falls to the participants – regular events and suppers bring them together. For me as a lesbian in a professional environment, I can see how putting social elements with mentoring together would be attractive as a scheme. But what if I wasn't as confident? Would I feel comfortable with this proactive approach? The literature suggests that mentors and mentees require more involvement of the mentoring coordinator with their programme (McAllister et al. 2009).

I attempted to contact Jake to explore this further; to understand the particular challenges found in the programme and perhaps to start to uncover some tangible success stories of how mentoring has benefited professionals. My attempts to make contact were only successful after calling the founder himself but my follow-up to interview someone within the organisation ground to a halt after countless attempts. As a result, I feel quite isolated from a group that I would hope to relate to.

My final route to discover mentoring programmes in real-world organisations was through an even more informal route of starting a discussion on LinkedIn under the group LGBT Professional Network. With over 10,000 members, I thought this would provide me with some practical positive experiences of mentoring within business. Once again, I found a lack of examples of formal programmes. I had responses on individuals mentoring other individuals, but could not access any programmes within organisations that I could glean insight from.

It is with surprise that I can summarise this article with a call for research on gay and lesbian mentoring programmes within professional environments. It seems that, although legislation is changing and becoming more inclusive, research on mentoring in this space is exceptionally limited.

References

Fassinger, R.E., Shullmen, S.L. and Stevenson, M.R. (2010) Toward an affirmative lesbian, gay, bisexual and transgender leadership paradigm, *American Psychologist*, 65(3): 201–15.

Lin, J.J. (2001) Are all mentors equal? The impact of diversity on mentoring relationships, unpublished Master's thesis, Rice University, Houston, TX.

McAllister, C.A, Harold, R.D., Ahmedani, B.K. and Cramer, E.P. (2009) Targeted mentoring: an evaluation of a program, *Journal of Social Work Education*, 45(1): 89–104.

Russell, G.M. and Horne, S.G. (2009) Finding equilibrium: mentoring, sexual orientation, and gender identity, *Professional Psychology: Research and Practice*, 40(2): 194–200.

Case study 12: Denmark

Mentoring immigrant women into employment and into society

Elisabeth Møller-Jensen

Introduction

More than 6500 mentors and mentees have taken part in KVINFO's mentoring project since 2002. According to David Clutterbuck, KVINFO's Mentor Network is the largest of its kind in the world – and it is also one of the most successful integration projects ever conducted in Denmark. 'How has KVINFO attracted so many mentors and mentees?' I have been asked. 'Why are so many women eager to volunteer and be part of this mentoring programme?' Because KVINFO's approach to mentoring is simple, straightforward and it works!

The idea

'If I'm going to be a part of this, there are two words you mustn't use,' said an Iraqi woman who had been invited to discuss the idea of a mentoring network for ethnic minority and refugee women back in 2002. 'Which two words?' I asked with some trepidation. The response was prompt: 'Equality and integration.' I had to be honest and explain that it would be difficult to avoid using those words. But it gave me something to think about – such everyday words and terms are so overused that they can seem highly provocative to a refugee woman.

The sad consequence is that integration is often viewed as something forced upon immigrants, requiring them to relinquish any form of personal identity and brush aside individual views. Participants in the Mentor Network, however, see integration as a way to find their place in the community. For them, the integration process cannot move fast enough.

In KVINFO's Mentor Network, we use the word 'integration' in its most positive sense, where the aspiration for a unified community is shared by mentors and mentees. And 'equality' is the cornerstone of the entire mentoring relationship; the core principle being that what we have in common with one another is greater than that which divides us.

We therefore take it as a given that the mentee who volunteers to work with a mentor genuinely wants to become part of the unified community. Danish mentors happily open up their networks to immigrant women looking for a first foothold in the job market. Every day we see the creation of trust, tangible results and positive new connections.

Practice

Günes was born and raised in Turkey. She came to Denmark with her mother, brothers and sisters to join her father, who was already working here, when she was only 17. During her first four years in Denmark, Günes thought that one day she would return to live in Turkey. However, she went to college to train as a dental technician, did very well and reached the point where all she needed in order to graduate was a period of work experience. She sent many applications, but did not receive any offers of a placement and had to abandon her career plans.

She decided to change track and try to qualify as a laboratory technician instead, taking extra classes in physics and mathematics. Once offered a place to study at her new college, Günes decided to look for a mentor to help her find a work experience placement.

Günes was matched with Christine. Christine had studied microbiology and has a PhD in food science. She was working for a large pharmaceutical company and expecting her second child. Christine had a good professional network and she was willing to use it to help someone else. They met regularly while Christine was on maternity leave, and also kept in contact via email, telephone and text messaging.

They worked on Günes's college projects, focusing on structure and language. Günes finished the theoretical part with top marks, and they were both very pleased. Next, they worked on finding a work placement for Günes – and a few weeks later she had indeed found one. They later practised job-seeking techniques, which resulted in Günes being hired to work at a laboratory in a Copenhagen hospital.

Günes is one of the 3400 mentees in Copenhagen who have found a mentor through the KVINFO Mentor Network.

Beginnings

Good ideas are often very simple. In 2002, I presented a new integration project to Bertel Haarder, Denmark's first Minister for Refugee, Immigration and Integration Affairs: a mentoring network for ethnic minority and refugee women. It was the perfect platform for KVINFO – a research library and leading centre for information on gender, equality and ethnicity – to utilise the institution's unique network and resources. I told him that by imagining Denmark as one large company we could create a professional one-to-one relationship between mentors and mentees. Haarder immediately saw the potential.

For our pilot project, we needed mentors for an initial group of 12 mentees. The response was overwhelming: more than 300 Danish professional women volunteered to participate as mentors. The solution was to set up a 'mentor bank', from which we could select the mentors as mentees signed up.

The first big challenge was to make contact with mentees and then to generate confidence in the project. KVINFO is well known and commands strong support among Danish women, but back in 2002 it was an unknown entity among immigrant women. So, the first group of women had to be found and convinced to give the project a chance. Luckily the pilot project went so well that the story immediately spread from the participating women to friends and family members.

The breakthrough came in October 2004 when the Mentor Network received two awards in the same month: the Annual Award from the Danish women's magazine *Alt for Damerne*, and the official Public Sector Integration Award. Since then, the flow of mentors and mentees has continued to grow – so fast, in fact that at times we have had to set up waiting lists.

The challenge

If you come to Denmark with high qualifications, you soon find out that you cannot use them, and then you are not privileged and most likely you will experience social isolation and depression. The Mentor Network was the first programme to address the problems faced by highly educated immigrant women in Denmark. However, the network is for everyone, regardless of education and work experience.

The immigrant women define their own needs as individuals. They set the agenda. Mentors and mentees (from 133 countries), both learn to put their 'cultural spectacles' aside. Where a mentee comes from, what she believes, the food she eats and the clothes she wears are not relevant. What is important is how we can support her in achieving a good life in Denmark. And this dream can, for the majority, be translated into a job corresponding to the qualifications she either arrived with or has acquired in Denmark.

The success of the network is not only the result of this conscious focus on the wishes and needs of the individual, but also of the way in which the project links two so very different spheres: the business world and the world seen from the women's movement perspective. The KVINFO model is distinguished from other mentoring programmes by combining professional business methods developed in the HR departments of large international corporations with the fundamental principles of the women's movement, defined as the belief that it is in women's interests to help one another, acknowledge and respect one another.

The strength of the mentoring situation is that it is a one-to-one. Finding a mentor who matches the mentee in professional interests, will often lead to finding the door into the right professional field. After seven months in the Mentor Network database, a Russian doctor, who was working as a cleaning assistant at a residential home for elderly people, was matched with a mentor – and thanks to their collabo-ration, she got a job as a doctor at a Danish hospital. A grateful email concluded with the words: 'Thank you so much, KVINFO. You are helping me fulfil my dream.'

The mentoring network also offers purely social matches. It is not unknown for a mentee to feel so isolated that she weeps throughout her interview. If the over-riding need is to establish contact on a personal level with a Danish woman, then she is matched with a social mentor. If this goes well, we subsequently supplement the mentoring arrangement with a vocational match.

The prime focus of the majority of the matches is to get a job. However, there are also procedural hurdles to be cleared. Many immigrants are 'on hold' – getting their qualifications officially recognised is sometimes very time-consuming. Often a degree is judged to be of less merit than in its country of origin. A Pakistani woman discovered that her MA from Scotland was apparently the equivalent of a BA in Denmark, and a Russian woman had to take extra university courses in order to have her degree validated (and a Danish language test to be admitted to the course). A mentee might well spend a year with a mentor during this period when a job is perhaps not yet an option.

Bearing this in mind, it makes sense to emphasise the 'softer' goals, those that are of paramount importance in finding and opening the doors to Danish society and gaining a permanent foothold: improving Danish language skills, having qualifications evaluated and specified to build up a CV and broaden the job search, establishing a network of people in the target trade or profession, and so on. Furthermore, many mentees are not ready for the job market because of personal challenges.

Some mentees battle with depression due to their prolonged social isolation. A number of women have been in abusive relationships and find themselves stranded as single mothers. They often have no family or other significant social circle in Denmark, so they cannot get out of the house and forge a new support network and create social ties. Thus, some mentees are matched with two mentors from the start of entering the programme – one for social needs and one for professional requirements.

Slowly their hope in life returns by having someone who will listen, who will support and help them to build social relations. It is often a long and painstaking process in which the prospect of a job might be three years down the line. It is important to keep a two-fold focus in the network: mapping the 'soft goals' of what goes on in the mentoring process and the partial goals achieved, as well as documenting the rate of employment among the women.

From the beginning of the project, the official rate of success was defined as the number of matches made per year – not the employment rate achieved by mentees. The Ministry sanctioned this yardstick. The media and, in particular, the local authorities are understandably most interested in how many jobs result from the programme. The good news is that successful matching leads to far more than a job. For some mentees, the mentor is the first Danish person with whom they have had a positive relationship.

And when the job is found, the need for a mentor does not stop – because how do you navigate a Danish workplace? What does it actually mean to be encouraged to speak one's mind and claim one's rights? Social conventions among colleagues and seemingly flat organisational structures require invisible knowledge that is difficult to access, if you are not an insider. The mentoring situation puts words to this invisible knowledge, the codes can be learned and both parties become wiser en route. It was not, for example, an unmitigated triumph when a nurse from abroad said to a social and health care assistant at a busy hospital: 'You're just sitting there drinking coffee – why don't you get your finger out and give a hand?' At a Danish workplace it is quite acceptable to speak your mind, but when and how it is appropriate to do so is quite another matter.

Resources

Between 2002 and 2010, KVINFO's Mentor Network opened branches in three other Danish cities. As of 2010, the network comprises departments in Copenhagen and Odense, while the branches in Århus and Esbjerg have acquired independent status and independent funding. A contract between the divisions ensures continued collaboration, idea development and sharing of expertise. At the end of 2010, the Copenhagen and Odense offices had eight full-time employees and an annual budget of DKK 5 million. When the project involved all the branches, the total number of employees was 16 and the overall budget was DKK 10 million.

Since 2004, the project has maintained a mentor database designed to facilitate appropriate mentor–mentee matches. With the most recent redevelopment of the database we can register and evaluate in relation to mentees' origins and migration history, marital status, age, education, occupation and postal code. Mentees are ensured full anonymity, and evaluation is made in accordance with the feedback from both parties at the end of the mentoring process.

Expansion

In celebration of the 2008 centenary of Danish women's voting rights, the then Mayor of Copenhagen, Ritt Bjerregaard, encouraged KVINFO to set up a mentoring network designed for immigrant women, who wanted to become involved in politics or in some other way influence Danish society. Fifteen high-profile politicians – variously from the national Danish parliament, the local Municipality of Copenhagen authority and the EU parliament – agreed to be mentors. The project resulted in five out of the fifteen mentees standing in the 2009 local elections – three were elected.

Another target group is talented daughters from immigrant families. In 2010, The Egmont Foundation funded a two-year project in the Vollsmose branch of the network, targeted at young women between the ages of 16 and 24. The title of the project, 'My Own Way', indicates that it is not a question of following a parental way of doing things or a specifically Danish one. Jamal Elobari, project coordinator at Vollsmose, has herself experienced the pull of two cultures and two generations.

The future

In November 2009, KVINFO held an international conference in Copenhagen: 'Mentoring and Networking: Women Building Trust and Social Capital in Our Cities'. Since 2010, concrete collaborations have been set up with partners in Portugal, Spain, Germany, Finland and Norway. Our vision is to spread the concept of the Mentor Network to the other European countries with large groups of immigrants struggling to gain a foothold in the workplace.

Lessons learned

In the course of establishing and running the network we have learned that perhaps the most difficult time for a mentoring programme comes when it proves successful in practice and can then be grown, replicated and adapted. Scaling-up a mentoring initiative requires not only strategy, coherent vision and ability to manage resources, but also clear frames for collaboration and cooperation across geographical borders. Proper funding is decisive in helping a mentor initiative through this phase.

Reflection questions

1. Learning and adaptation turn mentoring initiatives into forms that may be different from the expectations at the starting point. Why do so few mentoring programmes register/document this learning experience properly?
2. How would you go about doing so?

Case study 13: Canada

Integrated women's mentorship program

Patricia Pedraza Cruz

Introduction

The Immigrant Services Calgary (ISC) began in 1977 and to date, with 34 years of experience ISC has served more than 20,327 clients. ISC is an organization built by immigrants and Canadians working together for diversity, equity, accountability, and inclusion to ensure that immigrants and their families become full participants both as beneficiaries of and contributors to Canadian society.

The Integrated Women's Mentorship Program (IWMP) was created in 2008 and was funded initially by Status of Women Canada, Nexen Inc. and TD Canada Trust Bank. The first phase of the program ran in 2009 with funding from Citizenship and Immigration Canada and United Way of Calgary. It has served more than 650 mentees from all over the world, including individuals from Latin America, Asia, Europe, and Africa.

Says mentee Rosa Elias: 'When I arrived in Canada I was very confident that I would pretty soon find a job in my field but the reality was quite different; I thought that I had everything to be successful until I realized that the companies were looking for Canadian experience; that changed everything in my plans.'

Says mentor Raj Dhaliwal: 'My mother and aunt immigrated to Canada in the late 1970s. After hearing their stories of how difficult it can be to set up your life in a new country I have been helping women in my family who have immigrated here to find jobs, learn how to create a cover letter, edit their résumés and how to adapt to the Canadian culture. When I saw the ad of the IWMP I thought that it would be the perfect way to apply what I have done with my family in a formal atmosphere.'

Purpose

The IWMP creates partnerships between established professional women and new immigrant and refugee women, assisting the latter to overcome barriers to employment and to realize their full potential in Canada as individuals and professionals. This program serves those who have the ability to effectively communicate in English, but have experienced difficulties when looking for a professional job. Participants increase their pre-employment knowledge and improve their life skills. They are provided with mentoring support by professionals already established in positions that are in line with their educational background, career field or area of interest.

Mentors are volunteers who share their time, knowledge and experience, and provide peer support to the mentees. Some mentors are Canadian-born women – among these are first generation immigrants, who are educated and well integrated in the community. They carry with them the background of their immigrant parents and their memories of the struggle and frustration of that first generation.

Program components

1 *Training*: Weekly workshops open for all invited guest speakers from community partners and educational institutions to discuss life and employability skills. Topics include: Parenting, Health and Wellness, Personal Development, Healthy Relationships, Life Styles, Stress Management, Career Action Plan and Goal Setting, Résumé Writing and Cover Letters, Interview Skills, Job Searching Techniques, and Work and Life Balance. Mentor training focuses on identifying areas of interest and improving their skills in leadership, cross-cultural communication, and personal development.

2 *The mentoring process*: This is the soul of the program. Often mentees have to wait for the right mentor in terms of similar experience, education, and

personality. This is vital to build a relationship that starts with seeking specific goals in their personal or professional areas and often finishes in a long-lasting friendship. The most important success criteria of this phase are the willingness of the mentor and mentee to learn and be flexible when required. Program staff provide one-to-one counseling to support relationships.

3 *Work Links*: For phase two in 2010, a new service called Work Links started, offering internship opportunities for mentees where they can gain Canadian experience in their field of work. The organizations learn the value of a diverse and integrated workforce and it gives them the opportunity to develop educational programs to counter discrimination and racism and fully embrace diversity and inclusion.

In April 2009, the Resource Centre was opened with the one-off funding by the United Way of Calgary and Shell Immigrant Employment Project. It offers participants a computer lab and internet access for job research; opportunities to work on their résumés; interactive mock interviews in an employment lab; and the facilitation of meetings with mentors. It also creates a safe environment to have a conversation. Here, they feel free to express the frustrations and emotions that they cannot reveal at home or in public spaces, where they feel obliged to maintain their professionalism and conserve the image of being strong.

The mentee

The typical mentee is an immigrant or refugee woman, unemployed or underemployed, pursuing employment directly aligned to her educational or professional background and with the ability to communicate in English. The program's expectation by the end of the process is to increase participants' employability and marketability, equipping them with skills that enable them to effectively perform in the workplace. In addition, it keeps participants well informed about how to tap into their targeted job market, facilitates the development of a great network of professional contacts, and provides opportunities to gain first-hand information on targeted companies within their fields. Also, the participants learn about the Canadian workplace culture, improve their knowledge of relevant industry-specific terminology and about how to access education and training opportunities as well as being provided with the information about the International Education Accreditation process.

The mentor

The mentor is a professional woman with a minimum of two years' experience in her field and passionate about guiding others to develop and succeed. She has strong interpersonal and communication skills, is culturally sensitive, supportive and encouraging. She is keen to learn from different cultures and enthusiastic about getting involved in the community. She benefits from new understanding of settlement issues of immigrants and refugee women, from developing their communication, coaching and leadership skills, from meeting people from different cultures – and from personal satisfaction from helping others succeed.

Evaluation

The model for the mentoring program is framed on 24 hours mentoring over four months, where mentors and mentees discuss topics including: the Canadian workplace culture, job-search skills, professional terminology, and targeted labor market, academic skills up-grading and professional accreditation. Monthly follow-up services for mentors and mentees have been available since the beginning. However, the monthly record of the mentor–mentee partnership was not sufficient to show the evolution of the relationship. So a new tool – a blog – was integrated into the program by Patricia Pedraza, the program developer. This encourages participants to write journals to document their individual experiences at every stage of the process. Both mentors and mentees follow guidelines and preliminary questions that help them explore their feelings and experiences. It has been a successful process, and is currently on its second phase, in which participants interact in a blog community to exchange experiences and suggestions. Even though, for some people, it has not been easy to write about their problems or learning experiences, it has proved to be very successful in most cases. Three editions of successful stories have been published.

Support services

Before being assigned a mentor, mentees are assessed to determine their job-readiness, and they are matched with mentors who have comparable educational backgrounds or career interests. Progress is monitored and evaluated before, during and after mentoring and employment and personal status are followed up two months after program completion. Participants provide ongoing feedback on the topics treated and the guest speakers. Overall, program staff can follow the process with a mentee for a total of eight months.

A mentoring guide gives information on how to conduct mentoring meetings and suggests topics for discussion. A Mentorship Agreement outlines roles and responsibilities and gives guidelines for length and structure of meetings. Career-related resources and materials are available for workshops held to increase participants' effectiveness in managing their professional and personal lives.

The learning experience

For participants, the program has provided a great learning experience, not only because they have achieved their career goals, but also because they have become active protagonists of this program. Some of the first mentees are now part of the mentor pool.

Says Lissell Himede, one of the first generation of mentees and second generation of mentors: 'When I received the invitation from the program to participate as mentor, I hesitated a little bit. I could not see that I would be able to help others. However, now that I meet my first mentee, I can feel the strong desire to dedicate my time and share all my experience like I received from my mentors before.' In addition, some of the mentors have become 'senior mentors', who continuously help and provide peer support to new mentees.

Lessons learned

- Whatever your motives to become a mentor, be open to learn. Success is not only about achieving career goals; it also comes from learning from mistakes; and from seeing oneself in different work scenarios.

Reflection questions

1. What are you waiting for to embrace the opportunity to mentor someone in your life?
2. What could you learn from helping new skilled immigrants to make the transition for new life and career development in the new culture?

Case study 14: Great Britain

Mentoring women entrepreneurs in Africa, South Asia and the Middle East

Giulia Corinaldi

Introduction

The Mentoring Women in Business programme is a push in the right direction to help you reach your goals, especially if you are operating in a challenging and unstable business environment. Mentoring by someone who has insight and expertise in your business area gives you the comfort that you are on the right path and it also has a positive effect on your project.

(Suhair, mentee from Palestine)

The aim of the Cherie Blair Foundation for Women is to strengthen the capacity of women entrepreneurs in countries where they lack equal opportunities so they can start or grow their businesses and become greater contributors to their economies. It works in partnership with local organisations in Africa, South Asia and the Middle East to provide women entrepreneurs with support in business development, access to finance, technology, and network opportunities.

Studies reveal that increases in women's economic activity have a positive impact on the well-being of their families and communities. On average, women reinvest 90 per cent of their income into their families and communities.[1] Fostering entrepreneurship among women improves their livelihoods, creates wealth and strengthens economies, enabling societies to prosper.

The Foundation targets women who have the potential to become successful entrepreneurs or already own their own businesses, but are struggling to sustain their position or expand. The focus is on small and growing businesses in developing and transition countries.

In line with the Foundation's mission, the Mentoring Women in Business programme combines ICT (information, communication and technology) training with mentor and peer networks to support women who want to develop their businesses and achieve financial independence. The e-mentoring platform offers these women an interactive space where they can seek practical support to help them gain the confidence and knowledge they need.

Research on e-mentoring demonstrates that electronic communication enables honest feedback, develops trust and facilitates connections across cultures and genders (Petridou 2009). E-mentoring provides many of the same benefits associated with face-to-face mentoring, such as psycho-social support and information sharing, and also offers advantages that face-to-face mentoring cannot (Single and Single 2005). Universal access, an egalitarian virtual environment and flexibility with regard to time, space and cost, all make it easy for women entrepreneurs to acquire new knowledge, skills and networks from their mentors (Petridou 2009).

Objectives

The Mentoring Women in Business programme aims to build capacity, confidence and ultimately capital through virtual mentoring. The mentoring process is defined as a supportive and inspirational relationship based on trust and mutual respect, where the mentor helps the mentee become what she aspires to be. This is a two-way learning process, where mentors and mentees learn from each other's experiences and benefits accrue to both parties in the mentoring relationship.

In its first three years, the programme's objectives are to do the following:

- enhance the entrepreneurial success of the mentees' businesses;
- improve the mentees' self-confidence;
- strengthen the mentees' business skills and ICT skills;
- expand the mentees' market opportunities;
- boost the mentees' access to financing.

The primary beneficiaries are the mentees; however, the programme is designed to benefit both mentor and mentee. Mentors have the opportunity to enhance their personal and professional skills and to positively contribute to the mentees' lives. Both benefit from customised training materials developed by the Foundation and have the opportunity to learn how to use the relevant Google tools to engage with each other.

Implementation

The programme is based on 12-month one-to-one e-mentoring relationships between mentees in developing and transition countries and mentors worldwide.

Mentees are women with talent, entrepreneurial skills and innovative ideas who struggle to access support. They are selected through an application process and are recruited with the support of local partners. They must meet the following criteria:

- be female;
- be an entrepreneur or have the capacity to take the next step towards running a business;
- be highly motivated to develop ICT and business skills;
- be willing to prepare before and follow up after the mentoring meetings;
- have sufficient availability (one hour every two weeks minimum);
- be committed to participating in the programme for a period of 12 months;
- be committed to completing the periodic programme feedback;
- have access to a computer and the internet;
- be proficient in written and spoken English.

Mentors are skilled professionals and entrepreneurs (mid-career), committed to giving women a chance to fully contribute to their economies. Mentors are vetted through a rigorous application process and must meet the following criteria:

- adequate ICT literacy;

- proven business and professional skills relevant to the mentees' needs;
- sufficient availability for their mentoring role (one hour every two weeks minimum);
- dedicated to supporting a woman entrepreneur over a period of 12 months;
- committed to completing the periodic programme feedback;
- access to a computer and the internet;
- proficiency in written and spoken English.

More mentors than mentees are provided to fulfil the role of 'group mentors'. Group mentors are responsible for moderating group discussions, maintaining a vibrant and engaging mentoring community and providing responses to queries posted on the forums.

For the pilot phase, the Foundation selected 27 mentees with the support of project partners in the Middle East and South Asia:

- seven women from the Western Galilee College, Israel;
- five women from the Nablus Women Entrepreneurs project, West Bank;
- three women from the Business Development Centre, Ramallah, West Bank;
- five women from the Asian University for Women, Dhaka, Bangladesh;
- two women who participated in the Foundation's 'Women Mean Business' Conference, Mumbai, India;
- five women from the National Entrepreneurship Network, India.

The pool of mentors was on this occasion limited to the United Kingdom, to foster a community where the Foundation could ensure frequent communication, feedback and updates during the crucial first few months of the programme. Mentors for the pilot were recruited using the Foundation's networks and relationships with organisations such as Google and Astia.[2]

Programme partners

The programme relies on the continued support of partners who contribute to its implementation, development and quality control. All mentees are selected by programme partners in their respective countries as they are best placed to identify who will benefit most from the programme. Partners also facilitate all communication and feedback between the Foundation and programme participants to ensure that they are benefiting from the mentoring relationship.

The programme encourages the support of corporate partners in the form of pro bono services, mentors and/or funding. Mentoring provides a means for mentors to cultivate their existing knowledge, while developing new skills, and gives them a unique insight into the challenges and opportunities in developing and emerging markets. For example, thanks to her mentee, one of the pilot mentors felt more energised in her job: 'The bond I have formed with my mentee . . . has inspired me to be a better, more grateful and harder-working woman. It's been great to interact with someone who has overcome completely different barriers to myself, and has a very different attitude to the world and to life.'

Training

Training is an essential component of the programme, ensuring that mentors and mentees have a framework to guide them through the various stages of their relationship. It includes: (1) how to use the platform and Google applications to engage with each other; and (2) how to develop a strong and effective mentoring relationship. Overcoming cultural differences, identifying and setting tangible goals and maintaining a proactive attitude are also essential elements. During the pilot phase, training was carried out face-to-face; however, as the programme grows, the Foundation now facilitates training on-line.

A customised on-line training course, consisting of podcasts, video modules and downloads has been created in collaboration with mentoring and on-line training experts. All successful programme applicants receive a link to the on-line training platform via email, and are required to complete all the training sessions within seven days of their admission to the programme. At the end of the training they are required to take a test based on the materials covered in the training and upon successful completion, are admitted to the platform. This is to ensure that participants have digested information and can apply it practically when interacting in their mentoring relationships and on the platform.

The mentoring platform

The mentoring platform offers resources to support the participants and makes use of Google applications such as Sites, Docs, Chat and Gmail[3] enabling mentees and mentors to communicate and share documents through a password login system. Operating as a secure information database for mentees and mentors, forums serve as a marketplace whereby programme participants are able to freely share and promote ideas and business opportunities. They can also access the e-library, which provides business information and tool-kits.

The platform also facilitates the process of matching mentees with appropriate mentors. A rules-based system generates matching scores for each participant, based on a gadget embedded in the platform. This gadget analyses responses to each applicant's questionnaire, and, accordingly, suggests mentoring compatibility. It is then the responsibility of the programme coordinator to manually pair all participants. This matching system, which still leaves space for the irreplaceable 'human touch', has been tested extensively throughout the pilot and refined to ensure efficiency and accuracy as the programme enlarges.

To stimulate a sense of competition among participants as well as to measure the progress of the mentees' business goals, the platform creates league tables. Mentees provide bi-monthly updates about their business and mentoring relationships via an on-line questionnaire. League tables log information gathered from the mentees' updates and are posted on to the platform for members to view freely. For existing businesses, the rating is based on progress in revenue and frequency of mentoring meetings, while for mentees who have not yet launched their businesses, the rating is based solely on the number of mentoring meetings. Failure to provide the bi-monthly update results in termination of the mentoring relationship after two warnings.

Through the platform all mentors and mentees also have access to CAMEO,[4] an on-line supplementary support system where programme participants are able to raise concerns and problematic issues regarding their mentoring relationship. Cross-cultural mentoring can occasionally raise communication barriers between participants and while the programme team is on hand to provide support, it is important to have external mentoring expertise to mediate if necessary.

The on-line mentoring community

The platform hosts a range of media including forums, webinars and an e-library – all of which are designed to foster a strong and actively engaged on-line community. Each mentor and mentee has an on-line profile they can edit, visible to all programme participants, that enables network members to make contact should they require specific advice, or want to discuss business partnership opportunities.

The platform comprises three virtual forums where participants can post questions and network: one exclusively for mentors, the other exclusively for mentees and the third open to both mentors and mentees. Group mentors are on hand to respond to enquiries and engage in group discussions, with the aim of maintaining a dynamic on-line mentoring community. Through the forums the programme advertises upcoming group events and posts relevant links to organisations, sites and publications, which widens the network of knowledge and support. One group mentor recounts her view of the forums as an empowering tool for mentees: 'They offer a space for mentees to interact with one another, share their business challenges and ideas and to overcome them together.'

During the pilot, the programme team organised a series of webinars for mentors and mentees to interact collectively. A pilot webinar, hosted by Cherie Blair, gave mentors and mentees a unique opportunity to share experiences about personal and professional challenges with the founder. Based on the positive feedback received from participants, the programme will continue to feature similar events, enabling mentees and mentors to connect with inspirational speakers, network and come forward with their business ideas.

The power of networks and sharing information resonated well with one of our pilot mentees: 'Thanks for providing us with a platform to share and discuss our learning from business providing such a great community of empowered women, just a click away.'

Evaluation

The mentor–mentee relationship is monitored regularly and the programme team arranges feedback sessions in order to assess the mentoring method, address glitches in the platform and tackle any particular challenges that arise. Published on the platform and updated bi-monthly, the league tables assist with monitoring the programme's progress and impact on the mentees' businesses.

The programme manager provides progress reports to partner organisations, the Foundation CEO and the programme's international steering committee, who all share their expert knowledge to further support programme development.

A pilot phase determined the viability of the programme and identified opportunities and challenges to be addressed in subsequent phases. As a first step a mid-point evaluation was carried out, with documentation of case studies.

Mid-point evaluation

The mid-point evaluation was completed by Clutterbuck Associates in March 2011. Its aim was: (1) to review the programme's processes and the platform features; and (2) to assess the impact mentoring was having on the mentees and mentors. The evaluation was conducted through on-line questionnaires to mentors and mentees, a review and brainstorming session for mentors only and solicited feedback from partner organisations working with the mentees.

Lessons learned

The lessons learned from the mid-point evaluation included the following:

- All pilot participants felt well supported by the Foundation throughout their participation in the programme.
- Some 95 per cent of mentees and 87 per cent of mentors were satisfied with the platform's Google support tools.
- Most participants were using email and Gchat as their preferred method of communication.
- The majority of participants were more than satisfied with their match and their relationship but would have liked to know more about the matching process.
- Mentees' confidence and public-speaking skills had improved significantly.
- Some 94 per cent of mentees and 93 per cent of mentors were either satisfied, more than satisfied or very satisfied with their relationship.
- Some mentors expressed the need for additional training in building rapport and cultural awareness.

- Some mentors found it difficult to achieve meaningful results with mentees who lacked focus and commitment to a business idea or project.
- Some of the mentees and mentors encountered difficulties finding convenient times to meet, given the different time zones.
- The majority of the mentors and mentees agreed on the benefits of a mentoring relationship lasting more than nine months.

One mentor evaluates his mentoring experience: 'I've learned to be more open to the creative process – to accept that failure is an inherent element of that process and important too! My mentee has been very flexible with herself – especially when things did not work the way she imagined.' Another cites the advantages of remote mentoring and the ICT skills gained in the process as the main benefits of her mentoring experience.

The mid-point evaluation report included a list of recommendations to further enhance the mentoring experience, to build on the current platform and strengthen the community. On-going improvements will continue to be made to the programme, taking on board the feedback and advice from the mentoring experts conducting the final evaluation. The phase following the pilot will reflect these changes, including, among others, enhanced cultural awareness training, more transparency in the matching process, targeting mentees with a defined business idea or plan and a longer mentoring period of 12 months. The aim is for the programme to expand and reach out to 1000 women entrepreneurs by 2014.

Pilot case studies

During its pilot phase, the programme connected mentors in the United Kingdom with mentees in Bangladesh, India, Israel and Palestine. In many cases this has led to positive results for the mentees' businesses and it has given the mentees confidence in achieving their goals.

A sample of pilot mentee success stories:

Jane and Anna

In 2009, Jane launched a website marketing opportunities for Palestinians to study and work abroad, while exploring other business ideas in the field of education and training. As a mentee, Jane sought advice on finding the right entrepreneurial opportunity, on how to build a successful business and marketing plan and on potential sources of funding. Ideally, Jane wanted to set up relationships and learn how to network with international educational institutes. Jane's mentor, Anna, was interested in learning from Jane about the challenges and opportunities women entrepreneurs face in Palestine.

Jane and Anna first of all identified the website's target groups to help Jane market it towards specific groups within the Palestinian and expat community. This helped Jane to increase traffic to her website. Jane and Anna also discussed how to communicate with these groups. Next, they discussed obstacles faced by Palestinian women, particularly those who attempt to try innovative business ideas. Jane decided to focus her business on teaching Arabic to foreigners living in Palestine and business/management skills training; Anna helped her complete her marketing plan and business approach.

With Anna's guidance, Jane obtained a loan of US$8,000 from Caritas that allowed her to purchase furniture for two of her training rooms.

Using the plan she had formulated with Anna, Jane was able to apply for a licence from the Ministry of Higher Education. In October 2010, she received approval for a first licence for Educational Services from the Ministry of Higher Education. She is now working to get another two licences from the Ministry of Labour and the Ministry of Education to provide language and business/management skills training services.

Nehaya and Giles

Nehaya, a Palestinian food and wine entrepreneur, owns a company, Bait Alaileh, which specialises in traditional Palestinian foods. She needed help devising a financial plan for her business, but she only had limited ICT experience. Nehaya also needed advice on how to source funding and improve her networking skills.

Nehaya and Giles, her mentor, held several on-line meetings to discuss marketing and financial planning. Giles helped Nehaya identify the YMCA's small business start-up fund as a potential source of funding, then assisted her in preparing marketing, financial and business goals for her pitch to YMCA. Nehaya was awarded US$5,000 from the YMCA. Lastly, Giles helped Nehaya to allocate the funding she was awarded. With Giles' support, Nehaya successfully developed a marketing strategy, received funding and set up a viable budget. As a result, she has been able to launch her restaurant and develop a more lucrative business.

Reflection questions

1. How can technology be used as a tool to bridge the gender gap in both developed and developing countries?
2. In what ways can mentoring empower women in developing and transition countries?
3. How can global connectivity foster entrepreneurship and stimulate innovation?

Notes

1 The Organisation for Economic Co-operation and Development, available at: http://www.oecd.org/dataoecd/14/27/423310124.pdf.
2 Astia (www.astia.org) is a community of experts committed to building women leaders and accelerating the funding and growth of high potential, high-growth, women-led companies.
3 For additional information about the Google on-line applications, see: http://www.google.com/sites/help/intl/en/overview.html; http://www.google.com/google-d-s/documents/; http://www.google.com/talk/; and https://www.google.com/accounts/.
4 For additional information about CAMEO, see: http://cameo.clutterbuckassociates.co.uk/.

Case study 15: Argentina

Global virtual mentoring programs

Silvia Inés Monserrat

Introduction

Formal mentoring programs are quite new in Argentina. Andrea, a participant in the program being presented, described the situation like this, 'I believe people in general in Argentina have not discovered yet the benefits of mentoring programs. Many consider this kind of activity a waste of time, or don't understand the real value. While many companies invest in training programs for employees, a complement with a mentoring program can expedite the ramp and learning curve as well as develop leadership skills.' This case describes the benefits and challenges for mentors and mentees in a program in a global IT industry where dyadic relationships match people from different cultures, across the world.

Context

- *The macro-level*: Argentineans share with general Latin American culture a set of values that the most important goals in life are taking care of family and having close companionships and friendships. Yet the tendency is for smaller families because of the drop in the fertility rate, the drop in marriage rates and increasing divorce rates. At the same time, Argentina's feminine work force has expanded greatly from 27.4 per cent in 1990 to 48.5 per cent in 2004.

- *The micro-level*: In Argentina, women engineers are rare. Some 73 per cent of students in public universities and 83 per cent in private ones are male, and women at ITC multinational corporations are even rarer. The higher the position, the fewer women are to be found there.

● *The corporation*: Intel Argentina is less than five years old in Argentina and employs 220 people, 30 per cent of whom are women. Only 18 per cent of top management positions are held by women. Facing a career in a male-dominated corporation is always difficult, but it is even more difficult if the society stills remains 'machista'.[1] Working in a predominantly male environment can be especially intimidating for Argentinean women.

Recognizing the need to make the workplace more welcoming for women, Intel Argentina began a mentoring program in 2008. It is a non-bureaucratic and open-style program and 10 per cent of the local employees participate.

Alejandro Fernandez, HR Manager at Intel Argentina, says:

> Being a mentor is considered something that everyone, and especially managers are expected to do. Being a mentee is voluntary, and as Intel promotes egalitarianism among the staff, anyone is free to contact someone in the organization and ask that person to become his/her mentor. People willing to mentor others are included on a list, and can easily be contacted all over the world.

At Intel, anyone can be a mentor, since people are matched not by job title or by years of service but by specific skills needed. Those willing to be mentored only need to log in to an internal web page, where they can search for the mentor that he or she feels will meet his or her goals. Mentors can come from any Intel location around the world, and the choice only depends on what the mentee is looking for (career development, special skills, balancing work and family issues, etc.). Intel's program allows relationships to be as flexible as possible; they only ask for six months commitment (for both mentor and mentee), and results are assessed by satisfaction questionnaires.

Participant motivation

A previous positive experience related to mentoring caused Andrea, a 38-year-old engineer, to take part in the mentoring program. She states, 'My main goal as a mentee was to receive guidance in aspects like career development, and how to overcome some other difficulties/challenges in my day-to-day work by exchanging thoughts and experiences in an open and trusted communication channel.'

Andrea was surprised at her range of mentor choice.

> When I saw the extensive list of all people volunteering as mentors
> . . . There was one that immediately caught my attention. It was a
> woman mentor with over 15 years working with Intel, and the way
> she openly wrote her profile I knew she was my choice. She had

written something like 'Over the years at Intel I have not been very career oriented but rather life oriented and have always found the way of work in things that made me happy.' I also liked the fact that she was interested in mentoring people from cross-cultural teams, so I presumed she would be interested in having me (being from Argentina) as a mentee.

Molly, an American, who had been mentoring others for 20 years explains: 'Learning without the benefit of another's experience is painful and slow. Helping people understand how to move forward to become more effective in the area they are interested in is a very rewarding thing to do . . . if I can help the company to grow stronger leaders – that makes me happy.'

Mentoring purpose

Andrea describes her mentor's role thus,

> My mentor as a woman was also a counselor on work–life balance. She would often use real life examples from women's daily life. She openly shared her experiences of being a working mom and how best to maximize the use of our time and avoid taking work home (due to inefficient use of work hours). This led to very hands-on mentoring sessions. We would work on something that I could re-use: on a topic that I was interested in learning about; on a presentation that could be shared with my broader team. This way we created concrete results out of the learning experience. Having a female mentor was very important to me and for the success of this mentoring experience. I felt in many ways identified with the experiences and knowledge my mentor shared.
>
> Measuring the results is closely related to having clear goals and expectations agreed between mentor–mentee. This provides a framework to work with. In the very first session my mentor asked me about my interests, about the areas I wanted to develop or improve (business, planning, strategic thinking). Then she considered whether she could help me or could point me to other people in her network.

Marina, a Russian employee, who became a mentor four years ago, describes her role:

> It is mostly career development support. I'm not an expert in psychology and would not dare to dive too deep into psychological issues. Though there were cases when I shared how I deal with emotions, how to manage stress and how to deal with difficult people based on my own experience and limited knowledge which I gained

from classes, books and articles I've read. Some people found my BKMs (an acronym for 'Best Known Methods') useful and applied successfully.

As a condition of a mentoring engagement, I require the mentee to focus on a specific work achievement. [I believe this] gives us a non-arbitrary way to measure success. The mentee has a focus area they want to work on that is relevant to their current assignment.

Cross-cultural mentoring

Good communication is essential in mentoring. Because Intel Argentina is still a young organization, local mentors are scarce, so Argentinean employees were often forced to choose a mentor from another culture. Mentoring literature points out how cultural differences can affect the mentoring relationship. Marina, speaking from her experiences agree, 'Some people coming from China or India have very strong respect for management hierarchy and may perceive their mentor as a big boss, which can make it difficult to build trust and true openness between mentor and mentee.'

Maxfield (2005) has theorized (in absence of empirical studies) that social distance, hierarchy, and power characteristics could have relevance concerning mentoring in Latin America, but Andrea's vision when choosing a mentor from another country was that cross-cultural mentoring could be an advantage. 'I really wanted to exchange experiences with someone who could have a fresh and objective view, without being immersed in local culture.' Molly adds,

> My value is helping them understand what is expected as normal in the company – across a wide range of behavioral topics – from communication styles to values. The real work is then to help them find out how to meet that norm while retaining their personal style, or recognizing when they are not willing to do so and understanding when it is not a good fit. There are some common 'fit' issues that emerge in working across cultures – so helping them understand these issues can help them move forward.

Assessment

Intel's mentoring program is assessed annually through a satisfaction questionnaire. However, according to Alejandro, the local HR manager, the response rate is always very low – normally around 50 per cent, because Argentineans do not like answering questionnaires. This makes it difficult to determine program outcomes. However, in the following we offer some reflections about how the program might be improved from our observations and feedback.

Lessons learned

Scarcity of previous research and literature on mentoring in Latin America means that there is little knowledge about how best to use mentoring in this environment. However, difficulties in getting mentors might decrease as more formal mentoring programs are developed.

Benefits from the positive results of mentoring need to be communicated. Participants point to the need to share their own experiences and for the company to prioritize mentoring as an important personal and professional development activity; and emphasize to the value of success stories.

A mentor's gender appears to be directly related to mentoring functions, and mentees should consider their goals when choosing a mentor. As Andrea says, 'Through the experience with a woman as mentor, I realize gender helped us establish better rapport and open communication. Gender was very important to me and to the success of our relationship.'

Molly thinks that, 'There is no different approach if it is a man or a woman.' Marina states, 'I build rapport more quickly with women, almost from the very first moment. With men it takes a while – two or three meetings to build trust. Women are generally better listeners. In many cases men would approach me with a strong opinion on an issue already and everything they want from me is to confirm they are right, while women are more open to challenge their own thinking.'

It also appears imperative that cultural issues be considered. Our experience indicates that in terms of becoming more global, cross-cultural dyadic relationships are an advantage.

Reflection questions

1. What barriers do you see in implementing mentoring programs in very 'machista' cultures?
2. How would you recommend that the women in this program approach their immediate superiors to support their mentoring experience?
3. Some people still feel it is more difficult to build virtual relationships. What advice would you give for developing on-line mentoring programs in order to overcome difficulties and be successful?

Note

1 According to Duque and Montoya:

> Machismo is a form of masculinity used to describe an attitude of superiority and domination by men, which is stimulated by the practices of education and upbringing of patriarchal societies in Latin America, it seems that begins with the introduction of Hispanic culture during the Conquest. It is an expression of hyper-masculinity.
>
> (2010: 3)

References

Duque, L.F. and Montoya, N.E. (2010) Características de las personas, actitudes machistas. Documento para la prevención de la violencia y otras conductas de riesgo. Universidad de Antioquía. Available at: http://previva.udea.edu.co/Archivos/Publicaciones%20relacionadas/Doc%203%20PERSONA%20Actitudes%20Machistas%2004.02.2010.pdf.

Maxfield, S. (2005) Modifying best practices in women's advancements for the Latin American context, *Women in Management Review*, 20(4): 249–61.

Case study 16: USA

Mentoring women and minorities in computer science

Norma T. Mertz and Shari Lawrence Pfleeger

Introduction

It is no secret that women and minorities are underrepresented in the hard sciences and engineering (Kulis et al. 2002; Babco 2003; National Action Council for Minorities in Education 2008). This is particularly true of computer science (information technology), one of the younger science disciplines, where their underrepresentation has been a persistent characteristic, in spite of continuing calls for action programs to change the demographics of the profession (Grant and Ward 1992; Gunn 1995; Bierma 1996; National Science Foundation 2000).

Mentoring Women and Minorities in Computer Science, a project and study initiated by the Association for Computing Machinery and funded by the National Science Foundation and others, was a response to repeated calls to enhance the representation of women and minorities at senior corporate levels in computer science by establishing mentoring programs. The aim was to learn what and how to make an arranged mentoring process effective in helping women and minorities advance in settings where cross-race, cross-gender relationships are the norm, in three major computer corporations, which agreed to participate in the project.

The participating corporations agreed to do the following: (1) select women and minorities with promise for upward mobility; and (2) choose mentors high enough in the administrative chain to influence the promotion of junior people. The pairing of mentors and protégés was left to the individual corporation.

Corporation A had three pairs; Corporation B, two pairs; and Corporation C, five pairs. The gender and racial composition of mentors included 6 white males, 2 white females, 1 Black male, and 1 Black female; of protégés, 4 white females, 4 Black males, and 2 black females. The gender and racial composition of the pairs included: 2 white male–white females pairs; 2 white male–Black male pairs; 2 white male–Black female pairs; 1 Black female–Black male pair; 1 Black male–Black male pair; and 2 white female–white female pairs.

The project began with a one-day workshop for mentors and protégés to explore the nature of mentoring and what it required of mentors and protégés, and to initiate the relationship. It provided an opportunity for the pairs to get to know one another, to set goals, to determine how they would operate once back in the office as well as when separated, and to give them an opportunity to express their expectations, fears, and concerns, which were then aggregated and shared with the other group. We administered a researcher-developed attitudinal survey about mentoring, and about mentoring women and minorities for advancement. It was also administered post-project to determine any attitudinal difference changes after 18 months of mentoring.

Mentors and protégés were individually interviewed near the beginning, at the mid-point, and near the end of the program. The interviews were open-ended, revolving around questions of perceptions of the experience, how it was progressing, how comfortable the individuals were with their counterparts, and what problems or impediments they were facing. Feedback was used to try to improve the relationship if there were concerns or problems identified that could reasonably be addressed with the other party, with the permission of the one identifying a concern.

Findings

Three success criteria were established *a priori* for the success of relationship: (1) the mentor and protégé would both perceive the experience to be successful or at least positive; (2) the experience involved activities and content designed to help the protégé advance in the organization; and (3) the professional relationship that developed went beyond the formal boundaries of the project and was likely to continue after its conclusion. Three of the ten pairs met all three criteria; their relationship could be reasonably termed successful. These pairs involved different configurations of race and gender (a white male mentor and white female protégé; a white male mentor and a Black female protégé; and a Black female mentor and a Black male protégé), in three different corporations. One pair met the first two criteria, but not the third. Beyond these pairs, two pairs were judged to be spectacularly unsuccessful, having met none of the criteria and both mentor and protégé having seen the experience as unsatisfactory and disappointing. That left four pairs who failed to meet at least two of the three criteria, or all three, and perceived the experience to have been inconsequential or irrelevant.

For those pairs that were successful, the experience was affirming and energizing. For those that were unsuccessful, the experience tended to be embittering. Protégés in unsuccessful experiences saw the lack of success as an affirmation of their marginal status in the organization and their mentors as obstacles to their advancement. Conversely, mentors in unsuccessful experiences saw their protégés as ungrateful and unworthy of their efforts, thus calling into question the value or need for mentoring. For those pairs for which the experience was inconsequential, they were less certain than they had been in the beginning about whether or not mentoring was a good thing, they suggested they did not know what was expected of them, and questioned the legitimacy of devoting time to mentoring since there was no project code to which to assign mentoring activities.

It was not possible to disaggregate attitudinal data by pairs. Overall, mentor–protégé responses were similar pre and post with respect to the importance of the project, the importance of mentoring for advancement in the field, and the importance of special efforts to recruit women and minorities in the field. However, after the experience, while mentors still agreed it was harder for women and minorities to advance in organizations, they were less convinced about the necessity for mentoring them. In contrast, protégés were more convinced of the difficulty and became stronger in their belief of the necessity of mentoring for advancement.

Lessons learned

The multi-site case study yielded important lessons for maximizing the success of arranged mentoring for the advancement of women and minorities in corporate settings:

1 The organization must be committed to enhancing the success of women and minorities in the corporation – in deed, not just in word. Many organizations give lip service to the idea of increasing diversity in the executive ranks and are all too ready to agree to a program that seeks to achieve that. They can then point to the program as evidence of their commitment. The findings of our case study suggest that this is insufficient to achieve the ends, and may lead to attitudes and behaviors that actually make achieving the results less likely.

   To be successful, the organization – and the top level executives – must demonstrate they value the activity and make it an integral part of the institution. This means they must recognize and reward mentors for undertaking the responsibility; publicly discuss and legitimate the activity, enhance the visibility and credibility of the project; and to the extent possible, participate as mentors themselves ('do as I do'). The key lesson learned is that what executives and senior staff do signals to others in the organization what is important and valued. In the absence of such clear signals, the message sent to the organization is that the activity is 'for show' only.

2 The organization cannot just set the project in motion and assume it will go well. Someone within the organization must be charged with supervising and monitoring the process and progress of the relationships. Mentors and protégés in the study repeatedly talked about the need for someone on-site to whom they could turn with questions about their responsibilities; about how to approach or deal with one another; to remind them about what they were supposed to be doing and to keep them doing it; and to call them together periodically to share what they were doing and to clarify expectations. In the absence of someone 'right there', that both could 'trust', they suggested it was 'all too easy to let mentoring-related activities slide'.

3 Not everyone can or should be a mentor. Of all the lessons learned, this one is perhaps the most important. There appears to be an assumption that anyone can, and more than that, wants to mentor a junior person; indeed, that it is part of the developmental life cycle (Levinson et al. 1978). There is no evidence to support this assumption, and much to suggest that not everyone feels either a commitment or an interest in helping others – particularly those who are non-traditional applicants for the position. To be a good mentor requires a person committed to the welfare and success of the protégé, particularly if the protégé is a women or minority. They must believe that mentoring – and the mentoring they can provide – can honestly help the protégé advance in the organization (or like organizations), and they must be willing to devote themselves to the actions and activities that lead to such success. That does not mean mentors must be selfless. Our experience suggests that mentors benefit from association with promising protégés; that the protégé's success becomes associated with the mentor's skill in choosing and nurturing talent, but that cannot be the primary motivation. Becoming a mentor should be an honor only few can attain.

4 Not everyone should be a protégé. If the organization is truly committed to equity, then it recognizes that not everyone, thus not every woman or minority, should advance in the organization. Protégés should be chosen because they show promise and potential for upward mobility, not merely because they fit some demographic. They should be easily recognizable as 'comers' and thus deserving of special attention and nurturing. Their recognition does not guarantee they advance, but rather that they are being 'fast-tracked' for consideration and training.

5 Mentors and protégés should be purposefully matched. Whether or not the pairs 'clicked' was the single most important precursor for establishing trust, and thus a meaningful relationship. It was the single differentiating condition

between successful and unsuccessful (and even indifferent) pairs. By 'clicked', the pairs spoke about liking, respecting, and wanting to be involved with each other. Most striking for us, this compatibility did not appear to relate to race or gender; all of the successful pairs were mixed race, mixed gender, or both. Nor did it relate to the particular job in which they were involved and whether or not they did the same kind of work. Nor, even, if they had the same preferences. (We did examine the Meyers-Briggs Type Indicator for each of the mentors and protégés, and found no relation to success or lack thereof.) Indeed, the successful pairs defied all of the assumptions about what makes for a good relationship. Nevertheless, both parties recognized a compatibility that allowed them to trust and communicate honestly and effectively.

In truth, it is not clear how this matching might be achieved. One possibility might be to have potential mentors identify the junior people they feel have promise, give them a chance to get to know one another, and then allow them to decide if they are a good match. Another might be to arrange activities in which proposed pairs might be matched to accomplish some organizational task and then consider whether they are a good match. In the case study, the successful pairs were well matched, but it was more a matter of chance than choice.

A few final words

If it is true that everyone who makes it has a mentor, then it is equally true, and unrecognized, that not everyone who is mentored makes it. Indeed, the failure to consider the implications of mentoring everyone may lead to undermining the very thing being sought in establishing mentoring programs. We found that unsuccessful mentoring led to negative attitudes about mentoring and the need for mentoring women and minorities. In the very act of trying to enhance diversity, we may inadvertently subvert it with unexamined assumptions such as: everyone should be mentored; everyone can and should be a mentor; and mentoring is the cure-all for the ills and deficits of almost everyone.

Reflection questions

1. How can you motivate highly placed business executives to mentor women in advancing up the leadership career ladder?
2. What would you set as measures of success before engaging the mentoring process?
3. How will you monitor the process to ensure the achievement of the program goals?

References

Babco, E. (2003) *Trends in African-American and Native American Participation in STEM Higher Education*. Commission on Professionals in Science and Technology. Retrieved from http://www.cpst.org/STEM.pdf.

Bierma, L.L. (1996) How executive women learn corporate culture, *Human Resources Development Quarterly*, 7(2), 145–64.

Grant, L. and Ward, K. (1992) *Mentoring, Gender, and Publication among Social, Natural and Physical Scientists*. Washington, DC: US Department of Education.

Gunn, E. (1995) Mentoring: the democratic version. *Training*, 32(8), 64–7.

Kulis, S., Sicotte, D. and Collins, S. (2002) More than a pipeline problems: labor supply constraints and gender stratification across different disciplines. *Research in Higher Education*, 43: 657–91.

Levinson, D.J., Darrow, C.N., Klein, E.B., Levinson, M.A. and McKee, B. (1978) *The Season's of a Man's Life*. New York: Ballantine Books.

National Action Council for Minorities in Education, Inc. (2008) *Confronting the 'New' American Dilemma: Underrepresented Minorities in Engineeering*. Retrieved from http://www.nacme.org/user/docs/NACME%2008%20Research Report.pdf.

National Science Foundation (2000) *Women, Minorities and Persons with Disabilities in Science and Engineering, 2000*. Arlington, VA: National Science Foundation.

Case study 17: Great Britain

South East Mentoring Network for Women

Christina Hartshorn

Introduction

The South East Mentoring Network for Women (SEEDA) is one of nine Regional Development Agencies in England and has responsibility for the economic development of South East England, an area with a population of 8.1 million people that covers Kent, East and West Sussex, Hampshire, Surrey, Berkshire, Buckinghamshire and Oxfordshire. One of the primary foci has been to encourage talent from all sections of the community, including women who are underrepresented at senior levels in many occupations and sectors in the South East and tend not to benefit from as many career progression opportunities as their male counterparts (University of Greenwich 2006).

As a co-financing organisation managing a European Social Fund (ESF) Programme, SEEDA was able to work with one of the objectives of the ESF 2004–2006 programme, 'Gender discrimination in the workplace'. The ESF Team devised a pilot project aimed at releasing the untapped potential of women in the region, helping them to progress to more senior positions.

Mentors were individuals who had worked in senior positions for private sector small and medium-sized enterprises (SMEs, i.e. those with 1–249 employees) based within the South East Region; who had experience of leadership roles; and who had a desire to share their expertise to assist women into leadership positions. Mentees were women in management positions in private sector SMEs who faced barriers to progression into senior management and leadership positions and who wished to progress their careers.

Objectives

The specific objectives of the SEEDA ESF project were to do the following:

- Recruit 100 women aspiring to more senior positions (the mentees), to receive mentoring and coaching.
- Recruit 50 mentors and train them for a minimum of 14 hours face-to-face training, plus 24 hours equivalent of additional self-directed learning.
- Mentor or coach 100 mentees for at least 12 hours each.
- Give the 100 mentees an additional minimum of 21 hours face-to-face training, plus 24 hours equivalent of self-directed learning.
- Create 100 Individual Development Plans agreed with mentees.
- Develop a training course for mentors/coaches.
- Develop a training course for mentees.
- Organise and hold a dissemination event.
- Evaluate the project and produce a report with recommendations.

In this project, mentors acted with no personal agenda, having self-selected to be part of the project. Their focus was on the individual mentee's career, supporting their individual growth. The mentor specification included an ability to act as a role model for the mentee, sharing their own knowledge and experience and to act as facilitators, enabling mentees to discover their own direction. Mentors also had a coaching function that was client-centred, helping mentees to achieve the goals of their individual development plan. This plan was regularly updated to redefine SMART (Specific, Measurable, Achievable, Realistic, Timebound) objectives and the resources needed to achieve them, along with review dates and progress milestones. The mentors worked with mentees in a variety of ways to support their progression, including sourcing training opportunities, addressing confidence issues and improving interview skills. They also brokered access to other services, where appropriate, including to Further/Higher Education providers.

The programme

The project ran in 2007–08. Project specification was designed by Dorothy Grobler from SEEDA's ESF Team, informed by results from a previous ESF project (University of Greenwich 2006) and with advice from key colleagues with specialist knowledge in the field of women's development in the workplace. Business Link Solutions led the delivery of the project, now entitled South East Women's Mentoring Network (SEWMN), and the project covered the entire South East region. Its approach was to do the following:

- Establish a dispersed regional network of trained and qualified mentors and coaches, supported by efficient centralised processes.
- Provide a comprehensive and tailored portfolio of high quality mentoring/coaching services for aspiring women managers.
- Support a cohort of women employed in businesses to progress into senior management and leadership roles by providing them with mentoring/coaching.
- Identify barriers to women's career progression – particularly within the South East labour market, through direct engagement with the mentors and mentees.
- Encourage more women to progress into senior management and leadership roles through the development and wider promotion of a pool of positive role models and case studies.
- Disseminate successes of stakeholders, mentors and mentees by hosting a celebratory conference at the end of the project.

At the outset, a Steering Group was formed to arrange how the project would develop, how to recruit mentors and mentees, how to handle geographic considerations, and how to manage partners. It comprised the contracting partners including the six Business Link organisations in the region: Apex Business Solutions, Clutterbuck Associates, Oxford and Cherwell Valley College/JIVE South East; SEEDA ESF, and the Economic Partnerships representing Buckinghamshire, Brighton and Hove, and Surrey.

Recruitment to the project for mentors and mentees was primarily through a specially designed website 'Breaking Barriers', which also provided a platform for, and was in itself, a support resource for the participants and for the Steering Group. Additionally, the contractors contacted Managing Directors of SMEs in the South East to alert them to the project. Potential participants were registered through the site, which later helped when matching mentors with mentees.

A 'cascade' approach to training was used. First, mentors received a minimum of 14 hours of face-to-face training including the distribution of a mentor's CD, 'The Effective Mentor'. Although the mentors were all experienced individuals, one project objective was to enhance their skills and capabilities, thus increasing capacity within the South East region with a cohort of high performing mentors for future progress. Each mentor also had access to 24 hours of self-directed learning material. This ensured that mentees had access to highly skilled mentors. Using the website, mentees were matched with mentors, based on compatibilities, similarities, and geography.

Mentee training was also delivered in workshop format, with each participant receiving seven hours minimum training. Initial training equipped them with confidence and competence to benefit from a mentoring relationship. Each mentor committed to deliver 12 hours of mentoring time and a minimum of 10 mentors would participate in the Women into Leadership conference.

The Steering Group quarterly meetings were a major communication channel. An online newsletter provided frequent updates on the progress of the project. The final conference, Women into Leadership, communicated lessons of the project. Mentees were living case studies of how the project had impacted their lives, and the advances they had made in their careers.

Assessment

The headline targets were indeed met. Just over 100 women were mentored, with 91 of them completing the initial training. Each mentee had a personal development plan, with 21 hours of face-to-face training and access to 24 hours of self-directed learning material. Seventy-two mentees received ongoing support after completing the training and 35 of them opted for additional review meetings. A greater number of mentors were recruited (76, of which 63 completed the training) to cover the large geographic area of the region and to assist in matching.

Objectives in the specification to tender were designed to be achieved over a period of 15 months. Progress reports were submitted quarterly. An evaluator observed training sessions, reviewed feedback from those sessions, attended quarterly Steering Group meetings and reviewed a final participant questionnaire.

This report used an on-line data-gathering questionnaire to verify three specific measures, namely the performance, achievement and satisfaction levels of mentees and mentors. A comparison was made with average programme performances of all the organisations engaged with Clutterbuck Associates and the SEWMN was found to have exceeded on these three measures, in 23 out of 28 key areas.

Results from the questionnaire also show that many obviously successful women managers appear to have barriers that they subdue or otherwise 'control'. This project created a trusting environment where women were able to put any setbacks behind them and focus on their future with confidence.

The impact of mentoring on the individual mentees was overwhelmingly positive. Case studies were gathered to demonstrate the beneficial changes that mentees were able to make to their work situations, including promotions and salary raises. Both mentees and mentors were optimistic about future economic benefits and future opportunities for themselves and their organisations. Social impact was also considered. In the on-line questionnaire, mentees and mentors were asked how many people, including themselves, had been positively affected by the project. The average answer was 4 for the mentees and 3.5 for the mentors, so the evaluation concluded that when factored against the 100 mentoring relationships, some 350 people may well have been positively impacted by the project. Unfortunately post-project career tracing was not possible.

Outcomes

The mentors acquired higher levels of mentoring skills. In the initial training they were given new tools and techniques to augment their existing competencies, which they put into practice with their mentees. Mentors also learned how to use a variety of media – face-to-face, by telephone and through email. Their confidence increased through the success of the relationship.

Mentees learned how to use a mentor effectively. Initial training showed what a mentor was, and was not, dispelling myths or false preconceptions. Training boosted their confidence and proactivity from the start. Mentees co-created a personal development plan with their mentors. This laid the foundation for self-directed goal setting and identified any learning needed (on the job or off line). Workshops enabled mentees to learn with and from each other's experiences. They learned it was possible to be in control of their future career destiny.

The final conference, 'Women into Leadership', demonstrated to a wide audience how mentoring has a powerful impact on women's lives and economic futures.

Lessons learned

This was a high profile, highly justified and successful project that went far beyond simply 'upskilling beneficiaries'. The business capacity of the South East region has been raised by improving the confidence and skills of 100 women managers. This will have further impact as they themselves become inspiring role models and proactive mentors for future generations of aspiring women managers.

The close support given to the project by SEEDA's ESF team maximised positive outcomes, including the production of case studies highlighting success stories of the women mentees. This is important for use in any future projects that target diversity in the workforce, to have living testament, role models from 'near peers' to encourage others.

All of the stakeholders were enthusiastic about continuing in some way. Unfortunately, however, this was the final project under the 'Gender discrimination in the workforce programme' objectives.

The final event, the Women into Leadership conference, gave everyone involved in the project the opportunity to celebrate, and share the celebrations with a wider audience. Every project should similarly recognise and honour the achievements of all those concerned.

Reflection questions

1. What arguments could you use in your organisation to promote mentoring for women?
2. Are there specific benefits for mentees (male or female) to have access to/ choice of a male or female mentor?

Reference

University of Greenwich (2006) *Gender and the Labour Market in the South East*. London: University of Greenwich.

Case study 18: Luxembourg

The International Cross-Mentoring Program

Rita Knott and Kirsten M. Poulsen

Introduction

Luxembourg is an ideal place for diversity – and not only in leadership. It is one of the smallest nations in the world with a population of just over 500,000, comprised of 57 per cent Luxembourger and approximately 16 per cent Portuguese, 6 per cent French, followed by Italian, Belgian and German and others (2010 census). In addition, Luxembourg has approximately 170,000 cross-border workers who daily come in from other countries.

The first International Cross-Mentoring Program (ICMP) was initiated as a local activity in Luxembourg by program manager Rita Knott, then HR Director and member of the board of management of a financial corporation in Luxembourg. The Ministry of Equal Opportunity funded several companies to participate. The Ministry continues to supply partial funding; and the Minister has participated as a speaker in all conferences held until now.

In the first program, 12 female mentees from six different companies participated. The second program had 24, the third had 20 and the fourth had 14 mentees. The fifth program is scheduled to start in the beginning of 2012.

Since 2007, when the ambition to become an international program took form, the number of business partners has grown and now includes partners in Belgium,

Denmark, France, Germany, Great Britain, Israel, Portugal, Serbia, Sweden, and Switzerland. All are working to initiate programs in their countries. The goal is to have national cross-mentoring programs in all the countries and thus add even more of an international dimension to the annual conference.

Purpose and design

The aim of ICMP is to develop ambitious and competent women leaders into even higher leadership positions – and to impact the mentors' perception and understanding of women and of women as leaders, thereby developing ambassadors in thought and action for more women leaders.

Each program includes matching of mentors and mentees, four or five reflection workshops for mentees – some of them together with the mentors – master classes for mentors, coaching as needed for all participants to ensure a good mentoring process, and an annual conference. And, of course, the 10–12 mentor/mentee meetings that are recommended over the 12-month timeframe.

Mentees are matched with mentors on a cross-company, cross-sector, cross-culture and cross-gender basis to achieve the fullest potential for learning. Company representatives participate in matching meetings where they look at the candidates together and work to achieve the best possible match and avoid problems with competition and confidentiality. Surprisingly, it has never been a problem to find enough high level mentors, because mentors are proposed and selected carefully by each company representative – and mentors can be both men and women (until now there has been a 50/50 proportion). Often the mentors are quite proud to be selected and interested in learning from a mentee from another corporation. By inviting at least one mentor and one mentee from each participating corporation into the program, and matching them with mentors and mentees from other corporations, confidentiality is ensured in the relationships and many corporate-internal political barriers are avoided.

At the kick-off, mentees meet for a half-day interactive workshop about their role and to explore best practice in mentoring. At the end of the workshop, they meet their mentors for the first time during an informal lunch to facilitate their getting to know each other and to plan their individual meetings. The company representatives also join the lunch to meet all the mentors and mentees.

In the following workshops for the mentees the focus is on their mentoring relationships, sharing experiences and developing strategies for learning with the mentor. Here we meet the mentee, who is frustrated with a mentor, who keeps cancelling meetings, but who is fantastic in his support and knowledge sharing and helping to develop career strategies and build alliances with influential people when the meetings actually take place. Here we meet the mentee who is frustrated because the mentor keeps suggesting that to become a top manager you must compromise and find ways to deal with work–life balance. We meet the mentee who is blossoming and growing exponentially simply because of the attention and because another person has shown a belief in her potential and positively encourages new actions. And we meet the mentee who has encountered a mentor who will probably become a friend for life. The reflection workshops become a place for learning how to be a great mentee and finding inspiration in each other's experiences.

The workshops also include training in topics such as active listening and effective communication, feedback giving and receiving, assertive leadership, business networking, career planning, self-branding, etc. The last workshop is an integral part of the annual conference in Luxembourg, organised in cooperation with the business partners and with international guests and speakers. All mentees, mentors and company representatives are invited.

Mentors join a two-hour mentor master class a couple of days before the kickoff and a follow-up after six months. On average, only about two-thirds of the mentors participate. However, those mentors really do appreciate the master classes and the networking.

Outcomes

Mentees and mentors both value the experience. An example is the mentee who was very surprised that already after two or three meetings she and her mentor had achieved an extremely close relationship and were able to exchange really confidential and personal concerns. And her mentor had the same reflection including surprise over how little he knew about women's challenges and concerns in their leadership careers. He was very touched by the mentee's openness and confidence in him – and became even more motivated to support and help her. Rita has heard similar stories many times during the years and we strongly believe that the cross-mentoring principle is important in achieving this openness.

Since the start of the first program, the same evaluation form has been used to document the outcomes of the program (Table 4.1).

TABLE 4.1 Selected questions from the program evaluation

	1st program	4th program
Mentees: who said they had already achieved positive changes in their career at the end of the program	Yes – 36% Partly – 9%	Yes – 53% Partly – 34%
Mentees: who said that existing and near future career development would be significantly based on their participation in the program	Yes – 55% Partly – 45%	Yes – 53% Partly – 40%
Mentors: who had identified at least one female colleague in his/her own area who was worth promoting	14%	18%

There is no doubt that the program has had an effect on the careers of the mentees and had an eye-opening effect on the mentors. However, other results of a more personal character include mentees reporting greater clarity in their ambitions as leaders, better understanding of internal politics and how to assert themselves, more self-confidence and understanding of their own competencies – and thus more readiness to market themselves and communicate their ambitions and their strengths.

Lessons learned

Assumptions about stereotypical gender roles in business are difficult to influence and take time to change. Some corporations are really not ready to engage in cross-mentoring programs, since their top management, their working conditions and their corporate culture are not prepared to accept women in higher leadership positions, no matter how positively they phrase their views on women and leadership in official communications. However, when you have high-level managers genuinely interested in learning more about women and leadership, who really wish to make a difference in their corporation for a better balance of men and women, they can make a huge difference.

Another challenge is ensuring that mentees have the buy-in of their immediate superiors. In the best cases, the immediate superior is attentive and interested in helping, gives advice on internal career opportunities and feedback on the mentee's learning and development. In the worst cases, the immediate superior is hardly aware of the mentee's participation.

Coaching sessions were not included in the first program. However, it quickly became clear that they were needed. Today, the coaching sessions serve as both quality assurance and supervision to help the mentors in their role and support the mentees' learning.

The challenge of time

While it is reasonably easy to find willing and relevant mentor candidates, it is much more difficult to find mentors, who can prioritise and take the time for mentoring. This issue must be addressed at the beginning of a program. In the cross-mentoring program, the program manager several times had to compensate for unavailable mentors by giving more coaching time to the mentees. Likewise, training mentors to ensure they understand their role and responsibility is a challenge for two reasons: (1) time; and (2) because there is a widespread opinion that a manager is automatically a good mentor. However, what we see when the mentors actually meet is that they do not have the same understanding of what mentoring is, so this makes it even more important to ensure they attend training.

The future of the program

In March 2011, the 4th International Cross-Mentoring conference took place also marking the end of the fourth edition of the program in Luxembourg and the first program in Switzerland (managed by Ricarda Harris). As new programs are established in more countries, it will add new dimensions to the program, as new experiences are gained and shared. We have already seen that the program design has to be adapted to each country, as the maturity and readiness for 'women and leadership' are very different depending on national history, politics and culture.

Reflection questions

1. How can the existing perceptions and culture regarding women and leadership in a country influence the implementation of mentoring programs? And what implications will that have for the design of the program?
2. How can a mentoring program help female leaders to achieve a sustainable work–life balance?
3. What do you believe is the most valuable lesson that a woman can gain from a mentoring program – and how?

Case study 19: Norway

Mentoring and gender diversity in Norway

Jennybeth Ekeland

> A society which does not educate and train its women is like a person who just trains the right arm.
>
> (Plato, 427–347 BC)

Introduction

Norway is a pioneer in terms of placing women into management positions and involving them in board work. There are many possible reasons for this. Norway elected their first female prime minister in 1981, Gro Harlem Brundtland. On the

9th of May in 1986, she introduced during her second period a cabinet that was unheard of at the time: 8 of 18 cabinet members were women. This was a strong sign that Norway was leading in terms of equal opportunities for women in politics. And if it was possible in politics, it had to be possible within private enterprise and the public sector.

In 1996, the NHO (the Norwegian Federation of Business and Industry) started the mentoring programme Oppdagelsesreise (Discovery) with the goal of placing more women in management and board positions. This was the first official programme with this aim.

In 1999, when AFF, a consulting company at the Norwegian School of Economics took over Oppdagelsesreise, the NHO insisted that they put together a steering committee to follow the programme's development and results. In addition to NHO and AFF, the steering committee was made up of representatives from Norwegian private enterprises and SND (later Innovation Norway). As a result of the steering committee's work, Innovation Norway started a programme in 2001, the Ledermentor Programme (Leader mentor), to mentor female managers of small and medium-sized companies all over Norway.

Oppdagelsesreise and Ledermentor were influential in initiating a trend where private businesses, industries and the public sector initiated their own similar mentoring programmes. All in all, these programmes have contributed considerably to placing more women in management positions and as members of boards. Now, in 2011, mentoring is an accepted method in Norway to increase the number of women in management positions, but also to cultivate leadership potential in general, therefore developing both female and male mentees, as well as mentors.

AFF and mentoring

In all the mentoring programmes AFF's approach is very similar. We use David Clutterbuck's definition of a business mentor: 'A business mentor is someone who makes you think about yourself and your business.' Mentoring, in our case, is a process of development, where not only the person but also the company or the entity that the mentee is leading is the focus of the development.

Mentoring is seen as a mutually beneficial partnership where both partners, the mentor and mentee, will learn and develop. David Clutterbuck's 'The behavioural matrix', described most recently in the book *Learning Alliances* (1998) is used to define roles and behaviour for the mentor and mentee. Therefore, we focus on the roles of guardian, counsellor, coach and networker/facilitator in the mentoring relationship.

The matching process

For AFF, matching is one of the crucial factors in ensuring the success of mentoring. In most of the programmes each mentee is interviewed to identify development goals, ambitions, values, and challenges both personally and vocationally; as well as to inform the participant about the programme, the opportunities available, and to gain commitment to the programme. Prior to the interview, each mentee meet with their direct line manager to discuss and gain commitment for the mentee's participation. The meeting is summarised in a document that is signed by the mentee and his/her manager. Using information gained in the interviews, mentors are handpicked to match each mentee.

In open mentoring programmes such as Oppdagelsesreise and Ledermentor, mentors are found within AFF's large network of senior executives. Previously, it was common for mentors to be men as there were few female senior executives. Today, many more women hold senior executive positions and it is not unusual for two out of three mentors to be women. Often the female mentors are former mentees who have now progressed to senior executive positions.

Innovation Norway undertook an interesting study in 2008.[1] The results showed that women mentees were in general more satisfied with the Ledermentor programme when they were mentored by a woman – according to the report, this is supported by international best practice.

Two cases of mentoring and gender diversity

Ledermentor

The first Ledermentor programme started in 2001. The programme is for women primarily in small and medium-sized companies. Today the programme runs in Eastern Norway, Western Norway, and Northern Norway with an additional programme specifically for the tourism industry. The programme is strongly subsidised by Innovation Norway. Without their support it would not be possible for women from small and medium-sized companies to participate in such a comprehensive programme.

The programme aims to do the following:

- place more women in senior management positions and on boards by supporting them in their career development;
- contribute to the development of management culture and quality of management at the companies of the mentors and mentees.

Each programme includes 16 mentor–mentee pairs. The average age of the mentees is about 42.

Structure of the programme

The Ledermentor programme runs over 12 months, plus the time for the interviewing process, the matching, and the mentor master class prior to the first seminar. The mentee's commitment is six seminars – a total of 14 seminar days. For mentors, it is mandatory to attend six of the days, however, they are welcome to attend the entire programme, something many mentors do.

Content

Most women in the programme have no previous leadership training. Therefore, the programme also includes: leadership and personal development, career development, networking and relationship building, strategy work, board work and community responsibility. It is the intention that topics covered during seminars will be discussed at meetings between mentees and mentors.

Additional tasks between seminars are:

- 360-degree evaluation;
- role analysis, with a focus on increasing understanding of their own management role;
- personality testing;
- two reflective tasks: one at the beginning in relation to their own role as a manager and a summary of experiences at the end.

In this programme, the mentor role is especially important. A mentor will not only support the mentee in taking on management responsibilities, but also assist her with the management challenges.

Benefits

Innovation Norway undertook an extensive evaluation of the programme in 2008 which showed very meaningful learning benefits, and that the programme gave 'particularly positive results' for both mentor and mentees especially in relation to the following:

- management issues
- personal development
- business-oriented challenges
- marketing and sales
- challenges within own branch
- access to a useful network.

Evaluation further showed that mentees were very satisfied in terms of increased awareness and confidence in the role as manager and in the career development that resulted from participation. And nearly 50 per cent of mentees had been placed in a management position with more responsibility. Also, the more time that passes since the women had participated, the higher the percentage of those who had been promoted to more senior management positions or given greater responsibility. We can therefore conclude that the programme meets the goal of increasing women's presence in Norwegian enterprise.

The evaluation also put forward the following improvement ideas:

- strategy as a topic;
- more focus on leadership and leadership development;
- a need for mentors who understand the issues in small and medium-sized businesses;
- more individual follow-up.

As a result of the evaluation, it was made a priority to find appropriate mentors who could understand the issues arising in a small and medium-sized business, and a mentor master class was implemented prior to the first seminar. This resulted in mentees reporting greater benefits from the experience with their mentor. Having a mentor is now identified as the most worthwhile component of the programme.

The police force

In 2007, Søndre Buskerud and Vestfold police district took the initiative to establish a mentoring programme together. Both of the districts involved had female Chief Commissioners. From their point of view, the lack of women in key management positions was unfortunate for the culture of the police stations.

The first programme, the pilot, was thoroughly evaluated. The evaluation resulted in implementing important changes before starting the second programme in 2009. The second programme also included a third police district, Telemark, which had a new female Chief Commissioner.

Programme aim

The aim of the programme was:

- to place more women in management positions;
- to develop and motivate women with leadership abilities to take on manage-ment positions;
- to support new managers with their management issues and help them to succeed.

The last point provided an opportunity for men to participate as mentees.

Selection and matching

The programme was advertised internally so that interested women could choose to apply. In addition, the management team of each district encouraged the right candidates to apply. A total of 15 mentees and 15 mentors from the three districts participated in each programme.

Each mentee was interviewed. Two tasks were set prior to the interview:

1 The participants were to meet with their direct manager to discuss their learning goals for the programme. The aim was not only to prepare the mentee but also to gain the commitment of the manager.

2 Prepare for the interview. They received questions in advance to assist them in their preparation.

The aim of the interview was to make the mentee aware of how they could use the programme and to identify their ambitions. A safe and confidential atmosphere was created during the interviews so that the women could speak openly about their experiences in a male-dominated field and the challenges they faced because of this and their ambitions. This was something that few people or nobody in the police force had previously encouraged them to do. Thus the process to motivate and support women in their management career had already begun!

Chief Commissioners selected mentors from their own police district. All were members of the Chief Commissioner's management team or persons in key senior management roles. They were selected because they were seen to be role models for good management and motivated to take on the role as mentor. Mentors and mentees were matched across the police districts based on interviews and observation of the mentors in the master class.

Structure and content

The programme ran over 12 months and had four seminars of one to two days. In addition, there was a one-day workshop for mentors and one for the mentees. The following tasks were assigned between seminars:

- Role analysis: to increase understanding of their current role and expectations of good management within the police force.
- Application process preparation: creating an application and CV for a tentative management position, and training for a job interview.
- As a summary of the programme, mentees were to document their values and viewpoints as manager and co-worker.

The main point of the evaluation was that the programme had initiated a process towards its goal but that there was still a long way to go to change the culture of the workplace – and that other initiatives also were needed.

Mentoring meetings

Mentees and mentors had between 8 and 15 face-to-face meetings during the year and contact via phone or email. The mentees reported that the number of meetings was important for them and they applauded their mentors for their involvement and willingness to spend the time.

In the experience of AFF, we saw that preparation and follow-up increased the benefits of mentoring. Careful re-evaluation of each evaluation survey confirmed this.

Mentees' learning outcomes

All the mentees wrote in the evaluation that they had benefited greatly from the programme and that their motivation in their current job had increased. Those who were not currently managers had gained confidence and would like to apply for a management position.

The mentees also gained the following benefits:

● motivation and desire to contribute further to the police force;
● personal development and self-awareness;
● valuable networking within the police force;
● clear career goals for the future;
● increased motivation to take on new tasks and management responsibility in the future.

Some comments from the evaluation: 'I have been made aware that I will one day seek challenges in a management position.' 'To see how our senior managers are, think and prioritise, has strengthened my loyalty to the organisation and I wish to be a good co-worker and manager in the future.' 'The most important thing that I learned was that it is important to dare, to take a risk, and the importance to be aware of how one appears to others.'

When we asked what mentees had learned about the police force, answers included: 'It is actually possible to be a manager, even though you might not have been in the organisation for a long time.' 'There are many good, serious, talented managers. I have a better understanding of the culture and what kind of employee I should be. We are an organisation that is "modern" and future oriented.'

All mentees were very satisfied with their mentor. They used descriptions such as 'perfect match' and 'good chemistry'. Despite being very satisfied, some mentioned that their mentor could have challenged them even more, while others felt they were challenged more than enough.

Mentors' learning outcomes

It is obvious that the programme was very beneficial for the mentors too. Mentors gained awareness of and increased focus on their management role. One mentor wrote:

> I now see the role as manager from another perspective . . . the mentoring role contributed to development of my leadership skills. I was also humbled by the role. It is a great experience to make a

difference for another person . . . I am more aware of how I am as a manager, what my strengths and weaknesses are.

Another mentor wrote, 'For me it was important to reflect on my role as manager. I have worked on my listening skills, something I know that I need to work on. The programme has contributed to me maintaining and developing my understanding of employee's expectations of their managers.' Another positive outcome was seeing the mentee develop during the programme.

When asking mentors what they had learned about the police force as a workplace, mentors answered that they now had greater belief in women as managers in the organisation and the value of diversity. Many of the mentors also reported that they now actively supported and encouraged women to apply for management positions!

Challenges within the programme

Some 80 per cent of mentees found that colleagues and their direct manager showed little or no interest in the programme. The direct report did not follow up on their participation in the programme. This must be seen as a challenge, not only for the programme but also for the culture of the police force.

In terms of topics for future programmes, there was a need for more focus on how the mentees should react when they were unsuccessful in applying for a management position. What is the tactically smart thing to do when they are in such a situation? Some experienced that it was not always smart to be angry and spread the dissatisfaction over the entire organisation!

Information

In future programmes it is necessary to disseminate more information about the programme and make it better known internally in the organisation. The top level management initially felt that this was done sufficiently but it always seems to be a challenge.

The programme was met with disinterest from those not participating in it. It will be a challenge for the next programme to see how units/unit managers can be more involved to support the mentees, both during the programme and in terms of their further development. To aid in remedying any resistance or disinterest in the programme, it is now discussed if it could be strategically smart to include more male mentees. Perhaps this will reduce the resistance and remove the perception of the programme as a 'woman's thing' as one of the mentors described the response from various parts of the organisation.

Implementation and commitment

For such a programme to succeed, it is critically important that the programme is well implemented within the organisation and has commitment from top management. The importance of this was discussed initially with the police force and the Chief Commissioners took this very seriously. The Chief Commissioners were passionate about the idea of placing more women in management positions. Therefore, they followed the programme closely:

1 The project manager and Chief Commissioners met several times during the programme to plan, evaluate and discuss the effect of the initiative.

2 Chief Commissioners met with each mentee from their district to encourage them to take on management responsibility.

3 One or more of the Chief Commissioners attended multiple seminars, either to present the challenges faced in the police force or just to observe the seminars and what they involved.

4 Chief Commissioners focused on the programme at a couple of their senior management meetings. Mentors were followed up and they monitored the mentees' involvement in terms of applying for management positions.

5 The project manager followed up on the participants continuously during the programme.

Mentors and mentees also praised the Chief Commissioners and the project manager for their focus and interest, and they highlighted the importance of their role in the programme.

The culture of the police districts

The direct line managers did not follow up their mentees as planned. The mentees were faced with jealousy and ignored by many of their colleagues. There are many possible reasons for this. One of the reasons might be that the three districts of the police force involved were reasonably weak in resources for internal leadership development. There were a lot of resources for management education, but there appeared to be relatively few for leadership development training. Leadership development was something that few received, and therefore those who participated in the leadership and mentoring programme encountered jealousy and ignorance. The resistance can also be explained as a power game.

Selection of mentees

The programme was advertised internally and in addition, managers encouraged the right candidates to apply. Experience showed that the police force had reasonable success with this, however, the conclusion after the second programme was that it was still a challenge to involve middle management more actively in the process. Numerous mentors mentioned in their evaluation that they had become aware that talent scouting was an important part of being a manager. Therefore, talent scouting is now an issue that they focus actively on in their units.

Lessons learned

The matching process

Even though the matching process used by AFF required a lot of time and resources, our experience and evaluation results have convinced us that this is the best practice – not least in challenging programmes for women in leadership – and in very male-dominated organisations.

The mentor master class

In later years, AFF introduced a mentor master class before the first seminar in some of our mentoring programmes. Here, the mentors receive an introduction to the mentor role, training and the opportunity to network. As a result, the mentors feel well prepared when they meet their mentees at the first seminar. It also ensures a common approach to the mentoring process – and evaluation confirms this.

Professional consultants

Managers and internal HR managers in Norway often see mentoring as an easy initiative to implement. They couldn't be more wrong! Professionalism is just as important in implementing a mentoring programme as in an ordinary leadership development programme. AFF's success in mentoring programmes is down to the experienced consultants who have a thorough knowledge of management and leadership, organisational challenges and process work. Mentors greatly appreciate this professionalism when they participate in the programmes.

Development takes time

Managers with responsibility for the development process can be very impatient to see results. It is important to remember that 'Rome wasn't built in a day.' The evaluation of Innovation Norway confirms this; the longer it is since participation in the programme, the more management responsibility the women achieved. This shows the importance of not looking for results too early. Unfortunately, we have seen women's mentoring programmes cancelled as they did not produce results early enough.

Note

1 Evaluering av Kvinner i Fokus og Nettverkskreditt, by Rambøll Management, 2008 (An external evaluation report of the initiatives of Innovation Norway).

Reference

Clutterbuck, D. (1998) *Learning Alliances*. CIPD Publishing.

Case study 20: the USA

Return on Mentoring™: Developing leaders and advancing diversity and inclusion within the organization

Pamela M. Dixon, Dellroy O. Birch, Lynn P. Sontag and Kimberly Vappie

Introduction

In 2011, the Menttium Corporation, based in Minneapolis, MN, USA, celebrated 20 years of successfully implementing formal, structured mentoring. Two programs support our clients' commitment to diversity and inclusion: The Menttium 100® program which focuses on developing high-performing female leaders in predominantly male environments and the Momentum® program which focuses on developing high-performing professionals of color, and was designed for emerging leaders of color from predominately Caucasian work environments.

These 12-month programs were originally launched in Chicago, IL, Dallas, TX, and Minneapolis, MN, United States. Since their inception (Menttium 100® in 1991, and Momentum® in 2008) both have expanded to become global, cross-company programs operating through face-to-face and virtual partnerships and supporting development of mentees' leadership and performance capabilities.

This case study describes and integrates outcomes and lessons learned from the Menttium 100® and Momentum® programs across the 2008–09 program year. We weave in the voices of mentees and mentors who, through their hard work and dedication, achieved tremendous personal and professional growth, and strong enduring relationships.

The mentees in this case include Shoaib and Muna. Shoaib is a Marketing Sr. Analyst with a large energy company and Muna is an international manager with a global skin care and cosmetics company, both based in the southwest United States. The mentor is Rick, who is a long-term Menttium 100® mentor and a senior executive at a Fortune 500 business-to-business distributor based in the Midwestern United States.

Program design

> The program success is due to a very well planned program that keeps mentors and mentees clearly informed along the way and well ahead of time, and equally well execution of all the group sessions, tools, and publications.
>
> (Shoaib)

Both programs are formal, structured and year-long, combining experiential learning (on and off the job) and connection to the wisdom of others. Mentees are high performing women and professionals of color with at least three years of business experience. Mentors are successful mid to senior level executives with ten or more years of experience, from a variety of industries and functional areas, and from all races and genders.

Program components consist of one-to-one mentoring, small group peer learning and connection, large group forums, and goal setting and measurement.

One-to-one mentoring

Through regular interactions (face-to-face, on the phone, email, or web forum), a mentee receives guidance and feedback resulting in increased self-awareness, broadened perspective, and deeper insight into their challenges.

According to Shoaib, the mentoring experience was a success in large part because the 'mentor followed through on a commitment to keep all of our 1-on-1 meetings and made himself accessible by phone or in person in between those scheduled conversations. He also made himself available to meet on weekends for breakfast or afternoon coffee as we both juggled responsibilities for work and family.'

Similarly, Muna stated that her mentor contributed to the success of the partnership by 'constantly challenging me to reframe experiences. I drove the schedule, but she pushed and challenged me. She acknowledged everything I said, probed constantly and related with what I was saying. Also, it wasn't one-way. It was a conversation and we shared experiences.'

Rick acknowledges that the process is mentee-driven; however, after six years of serving as a mentor, says that in the beginning of the partnership, he drives some aspects of the partnership. For instance, his assistant sets up a meeting schedule that will work for the mentee (versus having the mentee take on this responsibility). He finds this to be most effective due to busy schedules. Further, he provides a template for mentees to use that documents actions taken (homework) in between one-on-one meetings. 'Getting this to me a day ahead of the meeting is their ticket to the meeting.' Finally, Rick says that he's able to build a strong relationship with mentees by 'building trust, which is more important than building ego. I have found that the more I give, the more capacity I have to give. Also, listening is more important than speaking.'

Matching

Menttium creates a customized match based on a mentee's development goals. Technology is used to collect professional background information in an online profile, which becomes the basis for an in-depth phone interview conducted by a Menttium Interview and Match Specialist. Questions asked during the mentor interview probe into their background and professional experience, as well as their level of cultural competence. A Match team consisting of no less than three specialists then convenes. Less than 4 percent of matches fail. When they do, a rematch is done using results of mentee and mentor profiles and interviews saved in a database. Menttium strongly believes that the high rate of successful partnerships is due to the human intensive match process.

Small group peer learning and connections

Small peer groups are formed based on similarities in their development goals and diversity in terms of ethnicity, background, and professional experience. Structured sessions are designed to promote experiential learning and accountability through input and insights gained from the group experience. These meetings occur bi-monthly and consist of an online dialogue using WebEx, a web-based tool that incorporates voice, visuals, and the ability to move from large to small groups virtually.

According to Muna:

> Peer group sessions were a great vehicle for pushing back and discussing tough issues, but in a supportive and meaningful way. The outcome was self-awareness. Regardless of gender or culture, there were so many similarities within my group. All of us talked about a lack of opportunities, not knowing how to operate in the work environment, not having a clear vision for a career . . . and most

importantly how we hold ourselves back. Many of us acknowledged that we could be a hindrance to our own success based on how we reacted to our work environment. It's not about the color of my skin, but it is how I speak up, how I feel, and how I carry myself. This was an eye opener for me.

Large group forums

There are two types of large group forums in a Menttium program. First, each program has a 'Launch', which is the official start. Second, six times during the year, Menttium conducts virtual web-based forums facilitated by subject matter experts, including our mentors. The forums focus on core leadership and business topics regarding capabilities associated with high-performing organizations. These sessions also provide opportunities to share wisdom and professional insights by connecting with participants from across the globe. Mentees and mentors from both programs are invited to participate.

Shoaib states that the forums enabled him

to walk away with a different perspective toward things that I would normally not notice or think about. They helped me renew my thoughts around self and career development and lit the fire to focus on the important things in life. I walked away knowing it was OK to take time and challenge myself to maximize my potential, which in turn has a ripple effect on my performance at work every day.

Goal setting and measurement

Goal setting and measurement are two important contributions to an impactful mentoring experience. Mentees use Menttium's goal setting framework to establish development goals and take action during the program. The model consists of five steps: setting goals, taking action, reflection and dialogue (with a mentor and/or peer group), tracking progress toward goal achievement, and measuring results.

Pre-post assessments are used to measure leadership performance capabilities associated with high-performing organizations. The pre-partnership assessment is completed by the mentee and his/her direct manager. The result is compared to a benchmark average to identify the mentee's strengths and opportunities for development. The results are used to establish development goals for the mentee.

Check-in surveys are conducted at months three, six, nine and at the end of the program. The check-in survey at month three is used primarily to determine the extent of engagement and satisfaction with the partnership. It also documents the mentee's goals. Both mentees and mentors complete this survey. If there is low satisfaction or engagement on the part of the mentee or mentor, a Menttium staff member intervenes and works with the partnership to resolve any issues.

At the mid-point of the program (month six) and at month nine, check-in surveys measure level of engagement and satisfaction, the extent of trust within the partnership, progress toward goal achievement, applied learning, and impact on the mentee's job, team/unit and organization. Mentees, their direct manager, and mentors complete these surveys.

At the end of the program year, a final check-in survey is completed by the mentee, the mentor, and the mentee's direct manager. Measures are similar to the month six and nine check-ins, however, a post-partnership assessment is included. This assessment is used to determine the extent of change in leadership performance capabilities on the part of the mentee.

Implementation

Five milestones underpin the mentoring relationship and navigating the program (Table 4.2).

TABLE 4.2 Momentum® milestones

Program launch (full-day session for mentees, half-day session for mentors)
- Program overview
- One-to-one mentoring philosophy, orientation and tools
- Group mentoring philosophy, orientation and tools
- Learn about program structure, curriculum, learning objectives and structure for small group work
- Positive and motivating experience to build energy and excitement for the year ahead

One-to-one mentoring partnership meetings (90 minutes to 3 hours)
- Provide individual development time for mentees
- Focus on program goals and action learning opportunities
- Increase mentees' business knowledge/acumen, and skill sets
- Enhance mentees' confidence
- Provide mentee with a different perspective on business and work-related issues

Peer learning groups (half-day session for mentees only)
- Improve mentees' ability to examine their experiences and circumstances effectively
- Increase ability to communicate and improve conflict management skills
- Enhance ability to ask powerful questions of oneself and others
- Promote action learning and accountability through insights gained from the group experience

Mid-point session (half-day session for mentees and mentors)
- Focus on a relevant leadership development topic
- Share best practices, successes and challenges, group mentoring process and level of engagement

Program close and celebration (half-day session for mentees and mentors)
- Hear from a featured speaker on a leadership development topic
- Share success stories and best practices
- Provide closure to the Momentum experience
- Recognize mentors and client sponsors

Outcomes

> As a result of my participation, I had some 'ah-has' about my own biases. I had to acknowledge it and deal with it versus blocking it out.

> My ability to view situations through different culturally diverse 'points of view' in the workplace instantly improved. I became more aware of how I viewed other cultures and identified ways to increase my intercultural competence.

Shoaib's and Muna's personal achievements included increased self-awareness, broadened perspectives, and increased confidence to challenge assumptions and the status quo. Shoaib indicated that he 'is able to handle changes at work more effectively and focus on what is best for his team'. He has built trust with his team, which in turn has positively impacted the teamwork within his department. Muna stated that she is able to 're-frame situations with colleagues and achieve better results'. Further, she has also begun to mentor others based on her experience.

Aggregate results of the mentees across four programs (two Menttium 100® and two Momentum® programs) during 2008 and 2009 mid-point check-in surveys indicated that:

- 96 percent applied new learning from their mentoring partnerships in their current job;
- 96 percent agreed the program positively impacted their achievement of development goals;
- 85 percent agreed the program positively impacted their enthusiasm to seek career opportunities within their current company;
- 91 percent agreed the program positively impacted their readiness to take on roles with greater complexity, authority, or scope.

Results from mentor's and the mentee's direct manager check-in surveys support these results.

Mentors who responded to the check-in surveys about their own learning acknowledged that their mentoring partnership was reciprocal. In some instances, white mentors learned lessons about cultural differences and the challenges facing professionals of color. They applied these lessons to interactions with their own employees.

According to Rick, the work–life balance is a typical issue raised by his female mentees, but less so for his male mentees. He states:

> I think this is largely because women still carry most of the burden of managing home responsibilities, while also having a full-time management role at work. Another difference I've noticed is that female mentees feel guilty about doing things for themselves, like

their own development. I tell them it is like the oxygen mask on a plane, you have to take care of yourself first in order to take care of others. Other than these differences, my experience mentoring males and females suggests they have the same needs: relationship building, strategic thinking/planning, and managing their communication style.

Lessons learned

Menttium has gained significant insights into what makes structured mentoring focused on diversity and inclusion effective. These lessons are based on three observed outcomes:

1 Structured one-to-one mentoring partnerships and peer group meetings/connections drive effective mentoring experiences and accelerate development.

2 'Paying it forward' became a collective mindset stemming from the commitment made by mentees in the Momentum peer groups. The concept of being a role model and mentoring other professionals of color was an expectation fervently set forth and acted upon by a large majority of participants.

3 Training is an imperative component to a successful structured mentoring experience.

Structured programming

Menttium's participants are high-performing leaders and key contributors to their organizations; therefore, carving out the time to meet is always a challenge. Menttium 100® and Momentum® include pre-scheduled mentor/mentee one-on-one meetings and peer group meetings/connections. Successful mentoring partnerships set and maintain regularly scheduled meetings.

The peer group meetings and connections provide a safe environment to discuss difficult professional issues facing women and professionals of color. The groups foster an authentic, transparent dialogue about approaches to overcome challenges, while promoting critical thinking and challenging underlying assumptions and expectations. These dialogues create the platform for collective thought leadership.

Paying it forward: becoming a mentor

Mentees consistently tell us they take on the role of mentor within their own organizations. Further, mentees are selected from successful mentor/mentee partnerships to become mentors in successive Menttium 100® and Momentum® programs. The outcomes include: (1) a more robust diverse mentor pool; (2) continuance of the deliberate and intentional spark that ensures the core values of communication, trust and authenticity; and (3) a positive impact on client organizations in terms of increased leadership and performance capabilities.

Training

Mentee and mentor training places emphasis on their roles, which establishes clear expectations for the partnership. Mentors complete additional training that focuses on active listening, asking probing questions, and sharing experiences. We have found that clearly articulating roles and expectations up-front and ensuring mentors have a strong skill-set support enduring and successful partnerships.

Conclusion

To appreciate the success achieved by Menttium's structured mentoring programs for women and professionals of color is to gain a glimpse of the power of human interaction. Technology is useful to support the partnerships and knowledge sharing; however, human interaction is the key to ensuring growth and development as well as enduring relationships – beginning with the intensive matching process and continuing with the one-to-one relationship and peer group interactions.

Reflection questions

1. How can your company leverage the power of formal mentoring programs to drive increased productivity and a strong bench of internal diverse talent?
2. How can structured mentoring programs targeting diversity benefit your company as you expand and conduct business globally?
3. How can the knowledge creation and the knowledge-sharing session in peer learning groups enhance the output of your diverse talent?

Mentoring in the context of race and culture

David Clutterbuck

Introduction

The case studies presented in this chapter reflect two levels of difference. Racial difference is frequently (though not always) obvious. Colour, facial features, accent, and sometimes dress define an individual both to themselves and to others. Cultural difference can be expressed through dress, but is otherwise normally only apparent through conversation.

There is a positive side to both of these factors when it comes to mentoring. Because racial difference is largely obvious, it is relatively easy for two people, who have goodwill towards each other and a willingness to confront their prejudices, to work their way up the diversity awareness ladder as they gradually learn more about themselves and each other. And because cultural difference is not so obvious, conversations can begin and develop initial bridges between people, before the differences emerge in the way they think and what they value.

On the downside, racial stereotypes can be so ingrained that they reduce people's willingness to engage and experiment with diverse relationships. The instinctive reactions of fear or caution inhibit conversation, so the participants struggle to make the relationship authentic and open. And cultural stereotypes can create rapport-busting feelings of disappointment, when the other person turns out to be 'less like me than I thought'.

Our case studies recognise the complexity of human reactions to race and culture and attempt, in a variety of ways, to ensure that participants are both aware of the issues, equipped to manage them and supported in terms of having a resource to turn to, when difficulties arise. They cover all ages, from schoolchildren to mature adults; the world of education (school and university), employment and entrepreneurship; and a wide mix of races – both specific target groups, such as Australian Aboriginals and Hispanic Americans, and the heterogenous groups formed by immigrants from numerous countries and regions.

Case study 21: Great Britain

Transport for London Mentoring Programme
Clive Saunders

Introduction

Transport for London (TfL) was established under the Greater London Authority Act 1999 with a remit to coordinate and deliver public transport in the capital. Within that remit, TfL also had a remit to promote equality. TfL started work officially in July 2000 and comprised a number of elements, some of which, like London Underground, with a history that extended over 100 years.

In 2005, the Equality and Inclusion Directorate was restructured and a number of new staff were appointed with a remit to support the delivery of equality and inclusion outcomes across TfL. A number of priority areas were identified for action including re-establishing a number of staff network groups covering disability, ethnicity, gender, faith/belief and sexual orientation. New programmes were also set up to provide equality and inclusion training for all staff, particularly managers. TfL also launched a London Chapter of the Women Transportation Seminar (WTS) to promote the engagement of women in the transport industry. Mentoring was another key area identified for action.

As a part of their early work, both the Women and Black, Asian and Minority Ethnic (BAME) Staff Network Groups identified that mentoring was an important developmental requirement for their members. WTS London also identified mentoring as a key area for development for women in transport.

At this time, TfL had been operating a mentoring scheme located in the Finance and Planning (F&P) Directorate for over six months. Mentoring was also embedded in the graduate programmes operating in both the Surface Transport and London Underground modes. However, there was no mentoring initiative that was accessible to staff from all parts of the organisation.

In summer 2005, TfL invited Clutterbuck Associates to complete a review of the F&P mentoring scheme against the requirements of the International Standards for Mentoring Programmes in Employment. The scheme scored 61 per cent overall against the international standard which was not enough, unfortunately, to secure the bronze award (the lowest award) which required a score of 80 per cent or above. Nevertheless the review found the F&P scheme to be very well regarded and positive. The review report stated: 'This mentoring scheme has created the foundations of an excellent platform for delivering mentoring across the organisation.'

Following the review, TfL decided to establish the Mentoring Programme located in the Equality and Inclusion Directorate, but working closely with the Human Resources Directorate and in particular the Learning and Development

Team. A Mentoring Co-ordinating Group was established, made up of representatives from all sections of TfL.

The TfL Mentoring Programme

The programme's purpose was stated as 'to contribute to the development of an effective, diverse and inclusive organisation that is equipped to deliver an excellent transport system for London'. A Mentoring Programme Co-ordinator worked with the Equality and Inclusion Delivery Manager. Both completed a two-day mentoring programme co-ordinator workshop, covering the basics of mentoring and the core requirements for the operation of a successful mentoring programme.

Early consultation indicated that, although the wish to engage with those staff from under-represented diversity target groups was supported, no group wished the programme to be specific to them. Both the Women and BAME Staff Network Groups indicated that they would not support an initiative that was not inclusive. It was therefore decided to open up the programme to all staff. However, the mentoring team worked very closely with staff network groups to ensure that women, disabled, BAME, lesbian, gay, bisexual and transgendered staff were given particular encouragement to participate.

The programme was officially launched in April 2005. The launch was attended by a number of Managing Directors and had the support of the entire senior management team and sponsorship from the TfL Board.

The key objectives were:

- to enable mutual learning and development;
- to help employees realise their own potential;
- to increase the confidence of staff;
- to encourage reflective practice.

TfL defined mentoring as: 'Off-line help by one person to another in making significant transition, in knowledge, work, or thinking.' It was important to the organisation that the focus be on the development of the person so mentors and mentees were not in the reporting line or from the same areas of the organisation.

Potential mentors and mentees were invited to apply by completing an application form. TfL employed over 20,000 people at the time and a target of 100 mentors and 100 mentees was set for the first intake. In fact, over 230 applications were received. Approximately 100 were mentors and the rest mentees. All those deemed to be suitable, who had completed the form were sent on the training programme.

For mentees, it was agreed that priority would be given in the first instance to staff who fulfilled the following criteria:

- able to demonstrate that they would gain most from the experience consistent with building a diverse organisation;

- be willing to complete a mentoring dynamic survey and other programme evaluation exercises;
- be willing to undertake mentoring skills development training; and
- demonstrate some value to TfL through their participation. They were required to indicate what benefit TfL would gain from their successful participation.

Mentors were required to demonstrate that they had the attributes to meet the needs of mentees, were willing to undertake appropriate mentoring skills development and were able to identify personal benefits from a mentoring relationship.

Core requirements were devised to create clarity for participants:

- It would be a formal programme that would last up to 12 months.
- Mentors and mentees would require line managers' support.
- Both mentors and mentees would be required to attend the training programme to ensure quality and consistency.
- There would be a recognition event at the end of 12 months.
- Mentors and mentees would be supported throughout the process.

TfL wanted a programme that would provide staff with a real challenge and was of the highest standard. A Mentoring Programme Manual was developed to accompany the training; it provided mentors and mentees with an overview of TfL's expectations, informed them about the training and the areas to be covered, and also provided access to a range of resources.

A DVD complemented the training and was used in all training sessions. This included an introduction by the TfL Board Champion and statement of encouragement from the TfL Commissioner and other senior managers.

The Programme Co-ordinator and the key trainer from Clutterbuck Associates matched mentors and mentees using information from the application form alongside intelligence gained through the training sessions. All 100 matches were completed. Participants were then informed of the matches made and asked to meet for the first time. As it was anticipated that the mentee would possibly have less flexibility, it was agreed that the mentor should initiate the first meeting. Future meetings were expected to be primarily initiated by the mentee.

A Mentoring Support Group of 20 people was established to support the programme participants. The support group members were either mentors, mentees or members of the Programme Co-ordinating Group, plus some mentors who were not matched, but had undertaken the mentoring training and were willing to support others. Each member of the group took responsibility for engaging with 10 mentors and mentees. They made contact with participants on a regular basis and gave feedback at monthly meetings on any issues relevant to the programme. Feedback included frequency of meetings between mentors and mentees and indications of the quality and value of the mentoring relationships.

A Mentoring Newsletter was published online quarterly to keep participants informed of developments, to share good practice, and to keep the organisation updated. This included case studies of mentor and mentee experiences. It proved a good way to keep stakeholders engaged.

Programme assessment and outcomes

Several assessment tools were used throughout to gauge programme operations, outcomes and success. The Mentoring Dynamic Survey from Clutterbuck Associates provided an objective assessment of the overall impact of the programme and was conducted at the beginning before mentors and mentees met, at the midpoint, and at the end. It showed a much clearer understanding by participants as they progressed; and it provided some benchmarks with other mentoring organisations.

In addition to the survey, the line managers of both mentors and mentees were sent a briefing at the beginning of each mentoring intake, on what mentoring is about and how they could engage with the programme. After each 12-month cycle, each line manager was asked to indicate changes over the period and any impact they could tie to engagement with the programme.

Each Mentoring Programme intake is subject to a half-day midterm review to identify what has gone well and identify any areas for improvement. This was initially attended by both mentors and mentees but later the sessions were for mentors only and this enables mentors to explore additional mentoring techniques. At the end of each cycle there is also an end-of-programme review for all participants, to help them reflect on and indicate what they have learned from the experience and to identify areas for programme improvement.

To end each intake, all participants and their line managers are invited to a recognition event, hosted by a Managing Director, where mentors and mentees are given a certificate of recognition for their participation. Members of the Support Group are also recognised with a certificate.

The programme was extended to other sections of the Greater London Authority (GLA) from 2007 onwards, and to the Metropolitan Police Authority. Their participation enabled TfL staff to have access to mentors still further detached from their immediate working environment.

In spite of the difficulty of measuring the impact, a number of success indicators were identified:

- successful establishment of a network of mentors;
- high level of participation by staff from E&I target groups such as women, Black, Asian and minority ethnic, disabled and lesbian, gay, transgendered and bisexual staff;
- staff progression within and outside TfL to higher positions;
- positive external validation of the scheme;
- increasing staff satisfaction with the programme and with TfL;

- the development of a positive organisational culture;
- attraction of outsiders to work at TfL.

Results also indicated that the Mentoring Programme was particularly effective in engaging women and other underrepresented groups of staff. Although women constituted less than 24 per cent of the employees over a three-year period from 2006, they constituted at least 46 per cent of participants. This position was also broadly reflected for disabled, BAME and LGBT staff.

Lessons learned

Effective ownership at the top is critical. The programme gained most recognition and support in those areas where senior managers recognised and valued the contribution of mentoring. Equally essential is communication across many dimensions. It should not be presumed that colleagues will read their e-mails or open a newsletter!

A successful mentoring programme must be owned and resourced, so it should be located in a directorate with adequate people and financial resources. The TfL Mentoring Programme gained significantly from the presence of dedicated staffing support and access to the communication resources of the organisation.

The programme team learned that mentors and mentees do not need the same training, particularly if resources are limited. While mentors receive the maximum training, mentees still need to learn the basics, so they can understand and perform their role effectively.

Not all senior managers are suitable mentors. A few managers were fixed in their view that they should tell the mentee what to do. While occasionally a mentor would have and share expert knowledge, this was not the norm in this programme.

Reflection questions

1. How can you effectively measure the contribution that mentoring makes to an organisation?
2. How can you ensure that mentoring is effectively resourced?
3. How can the ownership be secured at the highest levels in an organisation?
4. How do you measure the intangibles that arise from a mentoring relationship?

Case study 22: Great Britain

100 Black Men of London

Olu Alake and Kolarele Sonaike

Introduction

This is the story of the 100 Black Men of London (100BMOL) and its Community Mentoring Programme. This is also the story of Siobhan, whose experience as a mentee in our programme exemplifies the potential of passionate mentoring to inspire young people to fulfil their potential.

The 100BMOL is a chapter of the 100 Black Men International Inc., which consists of 116 chapters around the world delivering programmes and events focused on mentoring, education, economic empowerment, and health and well-being. The 100BMOL runs a wide range of programmes and events, including its Community Mentoring Programme, Black History Challenge, Education Through Film, 100 Book Club (*Real Black Men Read*), Youth Debate, Fathers' Day Quality Time, Family Fun Day, Schools Programme, Black Heroes Walk, and more. We are primarily self-funded through a combination of membership dues (all members pay annual membership dues), fundraising activities, standing order contributions from supporters and some grants.

The Community Mentoring Programme

The 100BMOL runs its 'life-skills' 'Community Mentoring Programme' targeted at children and parents in the Black community, and consisting of:

- *'Me I Can Be' Programme*: A 13-module life skills programme for Black boys and girls, covering self-identity (including self-esteem); family roles and re-sponsibilities; effective expression; guns, knives and violence; drugs and substance abuse; goal-setting; peer relations; and health and well-being.
- *Youth Leadership Academy*: The YLA builds on the 'Me I Can Be' pro-gramme with sessions themed around leadership in home life, school life and street life, covering career development, conflict resolution and money management.
- *Peer Mentoring Programme*: This programme guides Diamonds (mentees) to become mentors to their own peers. Public speaking, researching, project management, team building and leadership are the main skills learned. The culmination of the programme is that the peer mentors then deliver one of the sessions in our 'Me I Can Be' programme to the younger Diamonds.

- *'Parents in Partnership' Programme*: A community support and discussion forum for parents to discuss pressing issues of child upbringing, including social networking, gang involvement, successful single parenting, raising boys vs. raising girls, and proactive parenting.

All four programmes run concurrently in line with the school year (from September to June) with a graduation ceremony in July.

Our mentors are Black men and women from a range of backgrounds and professions including geologists, urban designers, economists, social workers, IT consultants, fundraisers, civil engineers, HR managers, policemen, financial analysts, community safety officers, life consultants, barristers, and property developers. The primary qualification of a mentor is to have a passion to guide and inspire young people.

Our mentees are Black boys and girls between the ages of 10 and 17 and we call them our 'Diamonds', signifying the central premise of our entire programme, that they are precious individuals to be treasured. Diamonds come to us from varied circumstances and for different reasons: single parents seeking support with the upbringing of their children, local authorities looking to augment their services, schools that see the benefits of mentoring to inspire their pupils.

Throughout the programme, parents and guardians are routinely briefed with parents' notes about the session topics, calls from the mentor assigned to their child and performance reports at the end of the programme year. All learning points are further reinforced through the Parents in Partnership programme.

Siobhan's story

Siobhan joined the 'Me I Can Be' programme at the age of 14. Her mum, Carole, had perceived that Siobhan was at that difficult point in life with many competing, negative influences. She searched for a mentoring programme to help with her own efforts to give Siobhan some direction. But of course, from Siobhan's point of view, she joined the programme for one reason only: 'My Mum dragged me here!'

At the onset of her involvement, Siobhan described herself as having no self-esteem, and being unable to voice her opinions. Her school performance was average. 'I didn't think I was very smart so I concentrated on socialising.' She hung out with similarly disaffected friends who were 'feisty' including their attitude towards teachers. She didn't really know what she wanted to be and had no particular idea or plan as to how to achieve any goals or ambitions she secretly harboured.

Olu, her assigned mentor observed: 'When she came on the programme she was sullen, quite petulant, and so disengaged it was hard work even getting her to lift her head to look at either me or the other mentors and Diamonds.' Siobhan found the experience very 'full on', with Diamonds expected to stand when speaking. Her stubbornness made her initially shut herself off.

Siobhan's journey over the next few years is a testament to her own character, the support of her family and the transformative impact of passionate mentoring.

Objectives and mentoring the 100 Way

Our aim is to help our Diamonds become positive contributors to the community, not only by steering them away from negativity, such as that expressed by Siobhan, but also by actively encouraging them to make dramatic improvements to their lives, education and health and well-being.

We deliver our programme on a 'group-mentoring' basis with bi-weekly sessions in a classroom setting with a facilitator leading the session, supported by other mentors sitting with the Diamonds at tables. Diamonds are assessed for punctuality, participation and behaviour. They also receive assignments for each session.

Each session incorporates audio, visual and kinetic elements to keep Diamonds engaged, and they are encouraged to contribute their views and opinions in a respectful manner, providing a safe and positive environment. Training is delivered by internal and external trainers on an ongoing basis including weekend training days, provision of training materials and facilitated practical experience. All new mentors are paired with more experienced mentors.

This year our training capabilities were recognised as we delivered training to the mentors, registered in the Mayor's new mentoring programme. The evaluation of this training showed that 95 per cent of the participants found all aspects of the training programme used and relevant, and 82 per cent definitely intend to continue the process to become a mentor.

Our aim is to help our Diamonds to come up with their own answers, find their own paths and understand the impact and consequences of their thoughts and actions. We call our approach, 'Mentoring the 100 Way Across a Lifetime'.

History of the Community Mentoring Programme (CMP)

The CMP started with the 'Me I Can Be' programme in North London and over the following 10 years, it has grown to cover North and South London. An East London programme begins in November 2011, as well as the Youth Leadership Academy, Peer Mentoring Programme and Parents in Partnership programme.

The resources required to deliver the programme are minimal – an adequately sized room with good audio-visual equipment. However, delivery has been enhanced by incorporating enrichment experiences such as films, museum and theatre trips, sponsored walks, debates and conferences, office visits, guest speakers, etc. We have graduated over 350 Diamonds and this year we expect to graduate up to 50 Diamonds and Parents. Our stakeholders are primarily the Black community, particularly parents and young Black boys and girls, who we directly impact through our mentoring. The outcomes are often astonishing.

Siobhan's story continued

Siobhan continued with the programme at her mother's insistence, but still showing little interest. However, something stirred in her during the 'Effective Expression' session, when she witnessed the respect her own cousin received when he spoke up and expressed his opinion. Siobhan said, 'It made me want to step up.' Slowly, Siobhan began to come out of her shell so that by the time she graduated through the first year on the 'Me I Can Be' programme, she felt she had learned a lot about herself. Though still unconvinced about her own abilities and the programme, she could at least state: 'Graduation felt good. I had a real sense of achievement.'

When Siobhan moved on to the Youth Leadership Academy (YLA) she appreciated the fact that debates were freer with more 'grown-up' topics discussed. But it was really in her second year on the YLA when having been nominated as leader of the group to deliver on a particular session, that she really felt engaged. She had never taken leadership seriously before, especially at school, but really enjoyed the experience of teamwork and delivering on a project. 'Graduating from the YLA was really good. I didn't think of myself as a loser any more.'

Siobhan won the YLA's 'Young Leader of the Year' award. Her prize – a trip to the annual conference of the 100 Black Men International in Miami. Olu, her mentor, observed, 'Siobhan was a certainty for Young Leader of the Year. Her growth over the year had been phenomenal.'

Miami was a real eye-opener for Siobhan. Meeting other young people going through the same experience was energising. Siobhan gave a presentation at the main event, talking about her life and experiences and received a standing ovation. 'The trip was wicked!' she exclaimed.

She returned the following year to join the Peer Mentoring Programme. She stated:

> I wasn't optimistic about it at first. I didn't like the thought of delivering a session to younger Diamonds where I would be the authority figure. But it was good in the end. Planning was really good, learning how to deliver to an audience and skills of teamwork.
>
> Graduation was great. It was my peak, the highest point. I felt I had gone through the whole programme and really achieved.

Assessing the programme

Measuring the impact of our programme has probably been our greatest challenge so far. While we have lots of anecdotal evidence (years of feedback commentary from grateful parents, school heads and others, including a number of previous Diamonds graduating from college and university, and dramatically improved school performance), we have only this year introduced a more formal evaluation system, with a pre and post programme questionnaire, measuring:

- self-esteem levels
- school performance
- truancy levels
- exercise levels
- fruit and vegetable intake
- reading levels.

The early indications are that the programme has resulted in a positive impact on each of these areas, particularly school performance and self-esteem levels. A detailed evaluation of the programme is also currently being undertaken by the Black Training and Enterprise Group (BTEG).

Siobhan's story continued

Siobhan is now 18 years old and considers that she has great self-esteem and confidence. She is very confident speaking in front of people and expressing her opinions. Her family life and school performance have improved dramatically. She got As and Bs in her exams and is now at college. 'I thought about getting into finance. I had never considered that before.'

Siobhan has just applied for a programme at Goldman Sachs and an internship at the Bank of America. 'I want to be a financial adviser and I have a plan now.' Siobhan was clear about the value of the programme:

> Any chance to get into the 100BMOL is a chance to better your life. No matter how much you doubt what it can do for you, the best thing is to try it and you won't be disappointed. All the mentors really affected my life. I will always remember each one. Really. The 100 has a legacy.

Siobhan's Mum, Carole, was equally clear:

> It gave us stability and made Siobhan so much more confident, giving her understanding and without a doubt has helped her find her self-identity. Her friends have dropped out but she is now so determined to succeed. She is able to speak more openly and correspondingly we can listen to her as a young person. She teaches me as much as I teach her. It has really made our family life so much better and I am always now referring other parents and children to the programme.

Siobhan states, 'You've got to target the problem at the root, not just punish people. Take the pressure off single mums, show positive male role models, break down stereotypes and present men and women who actually listen. Help the young people get back respect.'

The present and the future

The recent disturbances in London in which many young people were involved and were caught up in the anti-social and damaging actions of a riotous crowd served as a clear signal of the disassociation that many young people feel with society and their community. While the immediate political focus concentrated on the importance of meting out severe punishment, the more urgent question has to be, why did it happen?, and what do we as a community and society need to do, to help young people develop more of a stake in our society so that such behaviour feels as wrong to them as it did to those watching in shock? Mentoring has to be a major part of the solution. Mentoring done properly and seriously has an immense capacity to unlock potential and challenge even the most disengaged young person to explore greater possibilities. That is why the 100 Black Men of London has been mentoring for 10 years and will continue to do so for many more years to come.

Lessons learned

As an organisation delivering these programmes, we have learned over a period of 10 years the importance of the following:

- planning for the medium and long term;
- a holistic approach to addressing challenges confronting our youth;
- the critical importance of involving parents and schools in the mentoring process to reinforce learning;
- involving young people in programme design and evaluation;
- regularly updating the programme content to keep it relevant.

Reflection questions

1. What does it take to help make not just a difference, but a real change in a young person's life? The kind of change that smashes through inhibiting mind-sets and expands horizons?
2. How much do we as a community suffer if our young people do not get the benefit of the kind of positive influence that strong mentoring can bring?
3. At what age does mentoring need to be introduced to have a proper chance of positively affecting the life circumstances of a young person? Is 15 too late, for instance?

Case study 23: South Africa

Mentoring engineering graduates in the mines in South Africa

Penny Abbott

Introduction

In the second decade since the end of apartheid and the advent of democratic government, skills shortages and the legacy of enforced racial discrimination have created great challenges for talent management and career development in South African companies. In particular this has affected the mining industry, which needs to attract, retain and develop engineers and other skilled categories of staff to meet targets for racial and gender transformation. The mines are generally far from urban centres, while the young engineering students are usually urban born and educated. One mining company used a mentoring programme to overcome the inevitable clash of cultures and expectations. Unfortunately, it did not refer to mentoring best practices, and to date, little success has been achieved. The case offers reflection and learning on some very difficult issues in diversity mentoring.

The mentoring programme

The company operates through joint ventures in many different types of mining throughout Africa. It was founded in the early 1990s and is one of the leading examples of a Black-owned entrepreneurial mining venture. Its joint-venture business model means it directly employs only a handful of head office people – the mines are run by joint-venture partners, within an agreed framework of strategy. In this model, the company can place its employees in the mines, by agreement with the partner. It adopts a strategic approach to sustainability and is proud of its transformation and empowerment record. It employs 10,000 permanent employees and a further 7,000 people on contract.

The Board decided in 2006 that, to ensure its future supply of high-level skilled people, it would start a graduate development programme, recruiting up to 15 graduates each year and deploying them to the mining operations for two years. The programme involves rotations around operating departments and mines. At the end of the programme, each graduate may be offered permanent employment, depending on performance. The programme is supervised by a Team of Experts – head office senior technical managers recruited by HR and led by the HR Superintendent at head office. HR practitioners on the mines ensure that graduates' Portfolios of Evidence (required for their technical qualifications) are built up, while one of the Team of Experts supervises each graduate to ensure that the right exposures are obtained (the term mentor is used for this role). Most of these mentors ended up delegating their mentoring tasks to other people based in the mines, whom the mentors thought would be suitable.

After initial success in developing and retaining graduates, the Board asked for more diversity in the recruitment of graduates, particularly women – 17 of the 27 graduates who have been through the programme are female. With the advent of greater diversity, new issues arose, and the mentors found themselves unable to cope with the difficulties encountered by the graduates. At first, the HR practitioners attempted to provide additional supportive mentoring themselves, but this could not substitute for help from people 'at the rock face'.

While the male graduates 'could fight their own battles', the females grew up in a post-apartheid South Africa and find it very hard to understand the attitudes and behaviours of 'old-style' managers in the rural mines – they have simply not encountered such attitudes in their city upbringing and are not skilled at constructive confrontation. They hesitate to raise their issues with the hierarchy and thus then bottle up their resentment and frustration.

Programme objectives

The programme aimed to help bridge many gaps between the mentees and the mine environment – gaps in gender, age, social and racial backgrounds. In order to retain these 'different people', the company wanted to make their workplace congenial and accommodating. It was hoped the graduates could clarify what they valued in terms of work and life, learn how to manoeuvre in the workplace, become more integrated at work, develop their career and be grounded and confident in themselves as young adults.

A huge structural gap, not untypical of many workplaces, exists between the university world and the world of work. At the university, the young people are encouraged to argue and debate, to experiment and to innovate. On the mines, 'It's not about strategy implementation, it's results-driven.' Safety is key, so innovation is discouraged. In such an environment, young graduates feel they cannot afford – and are not allowed – to experiment.

A simple example of the difficulties which the mentoring programme should help overcome is the dress code/safety code. Clearly, as a potentially unsafe working environment, mines have strict protective clothing regulations – including hats and overalls. The girls find these highly restrictive in terms of self-expression; they are used to being able to braid their hair and wear all sorts of individualised fashion items.

At the mines, many people speak Afrikaans rather than English, which is the language the graduates are used to as a social and work language. The mining communities have a lot of unwritten social rules, such as which levels of seniority socialise together and who sits where on the bus to work, whereas in Johannesburg, for example, there are few rules.

Other problems in accommodating these different young people include their request for living accommodation, which allows their family to visit; their need for social networking in café-type facilities; and their need for access to 3G connections for mobile phones and the internet. The mines' traditions of hierarchy-based accommodation and transport (car) allocations are seen as discriminatory on the grounds of age and level.

Perceptions of mentoring

HR expected mentoring to act as an acculturation process, explaining the mining culture to the graduates and acting as a vehicle within which accommodations could be negotiated between the expectations of the mining community and the expectations of the graduates. Mentors were to act as role models.

Mentoring was also expected to help the graduates develop interpersonal skills needed to interact with the wide variety of people within a mining workplace – illiterate lower-level workers, other professionals, contractors, and families living within the community.

The way the programme defined the word mentor was as senior technical specialists from head office, who would visit each graduate regularly and monitor their progress against their technical skills development plan. These mentors therefore have a performance management role and are seen by the graduates as holding power over promotions and job rotations. Thus it was difficult to combine this role with supporting acculturation and personal difficulties. This problem was never resolved.

How the programme was managed

HR at head office realised in 2009 that the female graduates in particular needed some sort of 'shoulder to lean on' with regard to lots of practical living issues and also their career development. The graduates were on rotation, spending a few months in a series of the mine's departments, and therefore did not have continuity of line management who could have assumed the 'sponsor' role. Head office then involved the HR practitioners in the mines. They started with one-on-one induction sessions followed by circulating useful information such as books and articles on women at work. They encouraged the graduates to join women's forums and career groups such as Women in Mining.

HR then realised that the issues the graduates were raising required more support from line people, for example, job assignments, where black graduates perceived that white graduates were assigned to meaningful strategic projects while they were assigned to menial support tasks in production. The programme manager therefore asked the mentors already supervising the graduates to take on an additional role and have intensive personal discussions with the graduates, rather than, as previously, limiting discussions to technical development issues. These expanded mentoring relationships never progressed beyond the early stages, as both mentors and mentees failed to find common ground. One of the ideas was to get the mentors to facilitate group discussions with the mentees, but these deteriorated into emotional sessions with frustrated mentees, e.g.:

Mentee: What's the point in discussing career development? You promote who you like and if you don't like me, I won't get promoted.

Mentor: What do you mean, you want recognition? Why should you get recognition when you can't even dress properly?

[. . .]

Mentor: How can they take you seriously when you drag yourself around, you don't pitch on time, you don't speak up?

At the time of writing, the HR people are considering recruiting external mentors because 'the mentees won't listen to internal people, they want a safe space to talk in'.

One of the important issues with internal mentoring programmes is to ensure that the mentoring is integrated with support, and is supported by other human resource programmes such as succession management and career development. In this company, these processes are complicated by the joint-venture structure and in practice, there are few formal agreed development plans. Succession management is not transparent and the processes are little understood by the graduates.

Practical issues

The senior manager mentors have some understanding of mentoring, but have not fully grasped the 'softer' issues, which may require different approaches to the purely technical career development they have been supporting. Where these mentors delegated their tasks, the replacement mentors were identified through informal networks and informally briefed by the HR practitioners. No training was provided. Mentees were also briefed informally and again, no training was provided.

A big difficulty in providing mentors has been to find technically skilled senior Black managers to act as mentors and so mentees have struggled to use their white mentor as a role model.

Outcomes

Despite the many problems, some male graduates have integrated well into the company, but it would appear that such success stories have come about because these graduates survived well on the limited amount of supportive mentoring that they have received. The key factor in achieving satisfied employees and satisfied managers in this company's experience was whether the workplace was innovating technologically – in these situations, the graduate's greater level of up-to-date technical expertise has been appreciated and sought; the graduate receives positive feedback on his efforts, and in turn responds to this appreciation with a greater sense of self-worth and job satisfaction. However, not all the mines are in this situation and in these more old-fashioned workplaces the graduates have battled to integrate and to progress. These Black graduates joined the company because it is a leading example of a Black-owned company – and the graduates are shocked and disappointed when they reach the mines, which are managed by a joint-venture partner, often an international investor with a different philosophy. They state, 'We are tired of waiting for the business to transform, for baby-boomers to exit the business. We want answers now, we want to know our career and succession plans.'

Where the formal mentoring was initiated and did not work, the mentors felt helpless and dismayed by the size of the gaps in perceptions. The mines saw the graduates as a burden in terms of the time and effort required to integrate and develop them. Both parties in effect shut down on the relationship. The senior managers of the mine intellectually see the need to develop graduates, but experience it as one more burden in their mountain of obligations.

The lack of mentoring has contributed significantly to the high attrition rates of the graduates – though the graduates stay within the group, gravitating towards parts of the business with younger, more forward-looking managers, where they feel integrated and that they belong.

Lessons learned

This programme reflects a very common situation in South Africa, where companies embark on mentoring on a 'do-it-yourself' basis. Research I conducted in 2008[1] showed that less than 20 per cent of the schemes surveyed had used any external consultancy or training. Further, only 30 per cent of the people who designed the mentoring programme had any formal training in mentoring, and less than half the survey respondents networked with other mentoring programmes. Most of the designers of mentoring programmes used their own reading as the basis for the design and implementation.

In South Africa, HR practitioners often 'diagnose and prescribe' mentoring as an intervention without building a business case and obtaining top management buy-in. The study found that mentoring pairs were the most satisfied stakeholders in mentoring and top management were the least satisfied.

HR in this mining company have tried to raise awareness of the contribution that mentoring can make and to raise the profile of mentoring, for example, they sought to include mentorship as a key performance area for HR leaders in the mines. This has not yet been implemented.

The main issue raised in this programme is the chasm between espoused intent and actions. Mentoring has never moved from a 'group ownership' issue – this is something *we* must do – to an individual accountability issue – this is something that *I* am going to do. Mentors were simply not equipped to handle very difficult diversity issues and the mentoring relationships failed as a result. The lack of mentee training has resulted in graduates who do not have a clear understanding of their role in taking responsibility for their own career development, and who do not take on individual responsibility for constructive engagement on sensitive issues.

Reflection questions

1. Do you think mentoring is an appropriate learning support strategy for this company at this point in time?
2. What would help you to determine the readiness/maturity of this company to implement mentoring?
3. What could be some effective ways to overcome the huge 'values' gaps between mentors and mentees?
4. What needs to be in place for the mentoring to work effectively?

Note

1 P.M. Abbott (2009) The role of the coordinator in structured mentoring schemes, Master's dissertation 2009, University of Johannesburg.

Case study 24: Australia

Merryvale High: mentoring high school refugee students

Loshini Naidoo and Maggie Clarke

Introduction

Worldwide there has been and continues to be an influx of refugees into developed countries. Many young refugees arrive from war-torn countries with little or disrupted education and limited knowledge of English. Although in Australia, they are able to enrol in Intensive English Centres (IECs) for English language instruction prior to entering the mainstream education system, proficiency in academic English takes several years, especially for those from interrupted educational backgrounds (Brown et al. 2006).

This case study reports on a support program for refugee students in a secondary high school in the south-western suburbs of Sydney, Australia. The aim was to establish a safe learning environment, where students felt supported and could learn skills to assist in integration and acculturation in a new society.

Background

The Refugee Action Support Program (RAS) at Merryvale High School (a pseudo-nym) is an approach to literacy and the social development of refugee high school students. It is a partnership between the University of Western Sydney, the New South Wales Department of Education and Training, and The Australian Literacy and Numeracy Foundation, that uses pre-service teachers in the Master of Teaching (secondary) degree at the University of Western Sydney as mentors. These mentors provide academic support to refugee students in 12-week cycles. The program, first implemented in 2007 in four high schools, has since grown to serve nine high schools. It has evolved in each of the schools in different ways, to complement site-based structures and requirements and meet the needs of the refugee students. Initially, mentors receive 18 hours of intensive training on cultural orientation and literacy development. After this training they mentor small groups of refugee students, who have previously been enrolled in Intensive English Centres, but are now in mainstream high schools.

The partnership organisations have provided strong experience in how to work collaboratively to pursue an integrated literacy solution. This program addresses two of the challenges identified by Kanu (2008) in her research: (1) acculturation stress, which includes difficulties associated with literacy and numeracy; and (2) development of English language skills.

Merryvale's mentoring program was designed to support refugee high school students and their families and ensure that refugee students at the school have a positive experience. The school is situated in Sydney's most multicultural Local Government Area, with 133 nationalities represented and over 70 languages in use. The 2001 Census counted 92,420 people (51.5 per cent) living in the 27 suburbs, who were born overseas, principally from Vietnam, Italy, Cambodia, and Iraq (ABS 2006). Other represented groups originate from Laos, Iran, Turkey, Bosnia, Macedonia, Serbia, East Timor, Fiji, Samoa, Tonga and, more recently, Sudan (Southern), Congo, Burundi, and Nigeria (ABS 2006). Other groups are not recognised by country of birth categories (such as Assyrians, Macedonians, Kurds, and Tamils).

The program philosophy

The program philosophy is: (1) to provide specific assistance through a learning support teacher and mentor; (2) to require students to commit to attend at least twice a week over the school year to build a strong academic foundation; and (3) to address student social acculturation and learning needs with the support of the local community. Sometimes the school was fortunate to have mentors and teachers who were bilingual, which proved an additional asset. The philosophy of a specific support teacher and a mentor aligns with the structure of formal mentoring in that the mentor is allocated to the mentee/protégé and that the program is purposefully developed, monitored and evaluated by the teachers.

Program structure

Teachers and mentors work closely together to define expectations for mentors and students. They demonstrate empathy, flexibility, enthusiasm and energy. Mentoring is fundamentally a nurturing process and both teachers and student teachers from UWS play a significant nurturing role.

To encourage all students to attend the after-school sessions, individualised instruction is offered by learning support staff. Staff are encouraged to experiment with styles that best meet the students' needs. The program works because it attracts those most in need. According to the RAS co-ordinating teacher, the learning support faculty are 'trying to target those students, who are in the most need of literacy and numeracy support . . . not just students, who have just arrived but students who have been here a while, have slipped under the radar and have not been able to receive help' (Naidoo, cited in Ferfolja and Naidoo 2010: 28).

For any mentoring program to be successful, there needs to be an environment of trust and support where students feel safe (Clarke et al. 2002). As these qualities were developed, students began to feel encouraged in their own self-worth and

their achievements. Many refugee students have high expectations of their education and the school provided an environment to support them.

Successful mentoring programs are based on commitment from the whole
organisation, in this case, the school, the students, the parents and the wider
community. The norms and values of the program philosophy are shared by the
school community and this contributes to the professional community of the school
(Naidoo 2009b). The school altered its structure so that the learning support centre
became the hub of the school. The timetable is structured to give students longer
and less interrupted learning times, especially in the senior years. They can seek
assistance during junior and senior breaks as well as after school. This structure
during the school day demonstrates that learning support is highly valued and
encourages refugee students to attend the after-school mentoring program.

Within the school there is evidence of inter-faculty collaboration, a high focus
on student learning; reflective dialogue between teachers, management staff,
mentors and students and collective responsibility for refugee student learning in
the school (Hamilton and Moore 2003: 83). The faculty maintains profiles for all
students, develops individual transition plans if needed and engages in a range of
internal and external assessment. This collective responsibility is one of the key
factors in the outstanding success of this program.

Impact

The after-school intervention components integral to the success of the program
were: (1) teaching teams; (2) a structured setting for assistance with academic work;
and (3) a well-planned whole school teaching and learning support program for
students. This was pivotal in raising the confidence and status of the refugee
students within the school environment (Naidoo, cited in Ferfolja and Naidoo
2010). A previous study by Clarke (2000) had found that student teachers acquired
confidence-building skills through mentoring. Mentoring provided the time, place,
and structure missing from home for the refugee students. The consistency and
regularity of support strengthen its effectiveness (Naidoo 2008). Participants also
indicated that the welcoming climate of the after-school mentoring centre was
attractive, as it was also a place where emotions could be expressed through peer
and adult interaction, which was influential in the school adjustment (Naidoo
2009a: 268).

A key feature of this program is the way small group mentoring activities are
incorporated into the everyday activities of the school. The refugee students begin
to assimilate with other students and to feel less isolated. These everyday activities
also assist other students to begin interactions with refugee students and barriers
break down, enabling the refugee students to feel part of the school. For example,
each lunchtime (there is a junior and a senior lunch), there is a small program of
activities that include elements of the after-school mentoring. The learning support
staff assist students during the lunch hour in the production of assignments and

homework along with 'hidden' support by counselling students. As one refugee student commented: 'I really enjoy it because . . . I do the work and sometimes if I got a problem, I sit with the teacher and talk about it' (Naidoo, cited in Ferfolja and Naidoo 2010: 25).

The support and commitment of the teachers outside the classroom in the teachers' own time indicate to students the worth and value the teachers place on their learning and on achieving positive learning outcomes. So small group mentoring supplements individual mentoring. Mentors are able to model/scaffold work for the students; able to help students learn to better structure essays by breaking down assessment questions and assigned tasks and by using examples which relate to the students' lives, interests and experiences.

The mixing of mainstream students with English Second Language speakers and refugee students facilitated the acculturation process and enhanced the social integration of those students considered to 'be at risk' of failing. Subsequent to the growth in attendance, there was an improvement in the assessment results. Students remarked that they attended the after-school mentoring sometimes purely because they enjoyed being there. 'I go there if I don't have any assignments to do, I just sit and have fun, we have fun together laugh, stories . . . chat and yeah' (Naidoo, cited in Ferfolja and Naidoo 2010: 26). After a while, most refugee students build up their self-esteem and attend for other reasons. Achieving respectable school results orients them towards entering higher education.

There has been improvement in behaviour and motivation of refugee students in particular. As the program developed, the learning support staff have continually sought to involve students and now find that students come to them on their own initiative. Mainstream students from mainly Anglo backgrounds have accessed the program as a 'drop-in' basis. Refugee students and students who have low-income or non-English-speaking parents are not the only ones who may need and benefit from after-school mentoring assistance.

Lessons learned

Keys to the program's success are:

- Collaborative management, involving everyone in the process – managers, staff and students. They all share in the common sense of purpose, the values and the direction.
- All staff have ownership and share responsibility for the program.
- Support for staff is readily available from heads of department, and the Learning Support and Practicum co-ordinators, the leadership team and colleagues all help to maintain this collective responsibility.

> ### Reflection questions
>
> 1. Co-mentoring recognises the contribution that each person brings to the mentoring relationship and is based on reciprocal benefit (Jipson and Paley 2000; Kochan and Trimble 2000; Mullen 2000). What benefits would pre-service teachers gain from mentoring refugee students?
> 2. To optimise the acculturation and integration support provided to refugee students in this particular case study, how could this program of support be embedded into the practices of all schools?
> 3. The case study discusses strategies that work for refugee students. How does the structure of RAS (Refugee Action Support) at the school support not only refugee students but the school community more broadly?
> 4. Key stakeholders in the school have commented on the value of the RAS program. How could further studies analyse the impact of the program structure on refugee students' learning, acculturation and socialisation over the long term?

References

ABS (Australian Bureau of Statistics) (2006) *Statistics*. Canberra: Australian Government Publishing Services.

Brown, J., Miller, J. and Mitchell, J. (2006) Interrupted schooling and the acquisition of literacy: experiences of Sudanese refugees in Victorian secondary schools, *Australian Journal of Language and Literacy*, 29(2): 150–62.

Clarke, M. (2000) Mentoring skills: implications for portfolio development and professional learning. Available at: http://www.aare.edu.au/00pap/cla00017.htm.

Clarke, M., Power, A. and Hine, A. (2002) Mentoring conversations and narratives from the tertiary experience, paper presented at the Higher Education Research and Development Society of Australasia, Perth, Western Australia.

Ferfolja, T. and Naidoo, L. (2010) *Supporting Refugee Students Through the Refugee Action Support (RAS) Program: What Works in Schools*. Sydney, New South Wales: University of Western Sydney.

Hamilton, R. and Moore, D. (eds) (2003) *Educational Interventions for Refugee Children: Theoretical Perspectives and Implementing Best Practice*. New York: RoutledgeFalmer.

Jipson, J. and Paley, N. (2000) Because no-one gets there alone: collaboration as co-mentoring, *Theory into Practice*, 39(1): 36–42.

Kanu, Y. (2008) Educational needs and barriers for African refugee students in Manitoba, *Canadian Journal of Education*, 31(4): 915–40.

Kochan, F. and Trimble, S. (2000) From mentoring to co-mentoring: establishing collaborative relationships, *Theory into Practice*, 39(1): 20–8.

Mullen, C. (2000) Constructing co-mentoring partnerships: walkways we must travel, *Theory into Practice*, 39(1): 4–11.

Naidoo, L. (2008) Supporting African refugees in Greater Western Sydney: a critical ethnography of after-school homework tutoring centres. *Educational Research for Policy and Practice*, 7(3): 139–50.

Naidoo, L. (2009a) Developing social inclusion through after-school homework tutoring: a study of African refugee students in Greater Western Sydney, *British Journal of Sociology of Education*, 30(3): 261–73.

Naidoo, L. (2009b) Innovative dialogues: refugee students, pre-service teachers and 'Top of the Class', *Tamara Journal*, 8(8.2): 235–44.

Case study 25: Great Britain

Mentoring in the healthcare sector: the South West Strategic Health Authority Mentoring Programme

Louise Overy and Michail Sanidas

Introduction

The South West Strategic Health Authority was established in 2006 and is accountable to the Department of Health for the performance of the UK National Health Service in the South West. The South West SHA clustered with NHS South Central and NHS South East Coast to become NHS South of England.

The mentoring project was part of the Pacesetters programme in partnership with the NHS Breaking Through (BT) initiative. The Pacesetters programme was a transformational change programme in which the NHS worked in partnership with local communities to reduce health inequalities arising out of discrimination and disadvantage for patients and staff on account of their age, disability, ethnicity, gender, gender identity, sexual orientation, and religion or belief.

The Breaking Through (BT) initiative is a positive action programme, in place to improve the current severe under-representation of Black and Minority Ethnic (BME) staff at senior leadership levels in the NHS. Created in 2003, it involves a suite of innovative national development programmes for talented BME staff to support their career journeys in the NHS. Within the regional Strategic Health Authority (SHA) areas, BT Regional Coordinators work closely with Leadership Development and Equality and Diversity teams, to support and advise local networks and organisations. The programme included a cohort of 25 mentees and 22 mentors (Table 5.1).

TABLE 5.1 Composition of the mentoring group

	Mentees number (%)	Mentors number (%)
Ethnic origin		
White	0 (0)	16 (73)
Other white	1 (4)	1 (5)
Black African/Caribbean	19 (76)	1 (5)
Asian	4 (16)	4 (18)
Mixed heritage	1 (4)	
Gender		
Men	4 (16)	13 (60)
Women	21 (84)	9 (40)

Objectives

The programme objectives were the following:

- support progression of BME staff in the region and create a more diverse talent pool for senior clinical and leadership positions;
- reinforce the value that the SHA placed on a diverse workforce at all levels in the region;
- develop mentees' confidence, skills and knowledge so they were better equipped to progress their career by proactively creating and taking opportunities;
- raise the awareness of the importance of racial and cultural diversity among senior NHS managers;
- following evaluation of the programme, to provide recommendations on addressing barriers for the career progression of BME employees, and, where applicable for other under-represented groups, for example, employees with a disability.

Mentoring was defined as being about an individual providing off-line help to another person, developing skills such as:

- how to communicate effectively;
- how to increase confidence, self-awareness and autonomy to take on new challenges;
- how to develop networks;
- how to engage support and commitment of senior colleagues.

Mentees' expected behaviour

Mentees were expected to do the following:

- consider and clarify what they want to achieve from mentoring, setting objectives which crystallise these aims;
- consider what they need from a mentor to enable them to achieve their objectives, e.g. advice, exploring an issue, feedback;
- be prepared to discuss issues with their mentor, seek their advice and act on feedback;
- share responsibility with their mentor for an effective mentoring relationship by preparing for each mentoring meeting.

Mentors' expected behaviour

Mentors were expected to do the following:

- provide guidance and advice on career and development opportunities, on the clear understanding that this did not guarantee promotion;

- act as a sounding board to help mentees solve problems;
- stimulate and motivate mentees;
- listen and ask challenging questions;
- enable mentees to see themselves more clearly, particularly regarding how they come across to others;
- facilitate networking and access to others and provide insights about how things work in the department;
- act as a role model.

BME staff are significantly under-represented at all middle and senior managerial levels in NHS South West. Sir David Nicholson, Chief Executive of the NHS, has repeatedly urged all NHS organisations to find ways to change this, in order to benefit from a more diverse leadership and to make the most of all the talent in the NHS.

As a response to this identified need, the SHA decided to develop a mentoring scheme for BME staff across all organisations in the region, using resources from the Pacesetters and the Breaking Through initiatives. The project leads were the SHA Equality and Human Rights Manager and the Breaking Through Regional Coordinator. To ensure that the programme was based on best practice, expert providers were employed, who had significant experience of supporting diversity within organisational development. A regional stakeholder group was also developed and stakeholders were involved at all stages of development of the scheme. A reference group of interested senior managers across the South West provided initial support in scoping the project. Subsequently, regional networks of equality and diversity professionals and Leadership Development organisation leads provided comment and disseminated information. Getting messages through to the intended audience is often difficult within the NHS, and the project leads sought to overcome this by using as many communication channels as possible.

Marketing flyers were sent to all NHS organisations and the project leads hosted 'discovery days', to provide face-to-face information and to answer questions. FAQs were developed for potential mentees, their line managers, and mentors. Engaging and informing line managers was particularly important, as their encouragement, or lack of it, could affect an individual's ability to take up this opportunity. Explaining the background was important in overcoming any resistance.

Mentees were selected by application form and by attendance at a selection and orientation day. The purpose of both stages was to ensure that, given the limit on numbers who could be mentored (25), mentees had the self-awareness and motivation necessary to make the most of the opportunity offered.

The selection and orientation day also helped mentees to bond as a group, to understand and appreciate the aim for them as individuals and for their employer organisations and the wider NHS, and explore the principles of a good mentee/mentor relationship.

Because of limited availability of mentors, mentees were not able to select their own mentors. Instead, the project leads matched them using geography (travel time and cost are a big issue for many NHS staff in the South West) and the mentee's known aspirations. In practice, matching worked well, and no pairs have terminated early.

Handbooks for mentors and mentees were provided to remind and guide participants through the mentoring relationship; the information provided was reinforced by occasional e-mails from the project leads and by networking meetings.

Challenges

The greatest challenge was in recruiting sufficient mentors. Despite extensive publicity and the support of the SHA Chief Executive, volunteers were slow to come forward. Slowly and by different routes (personal contact, targeting beneficiaries of leadership development programmes, word of mouth), enough mentors were taken on to cover all the target number of mentees.

It was also difficult to get mentors to attend networking days. Generally 10–20 per cent of mentors attended. For some mentors, urgent meetings meant they could not attend. In other cases, mentors may have felt that the networking days were a 'nice to have' day and as such did not warrant priority in their diaries. Those who did attend gave positive feedback about the value of sessions, but fuller attendance would have benefited both mentees and mentors, through sharing and reinforcement of key learning.

Assessment

During the project design, we identified the following criteria to measure the project progress:

- number of mentors coming forward;
- number of mentees coming forward;
- feedback from mentors and mentees;
- career progression of mentees;
- number of applications, shortlisted and appointed candidates at the SHA from different BME backgrounds.

In terms of outputs, the pilot project managed to select 25 mentees and match 24 of them with a mentor. We organised two networking events over a period of nine months. The feedback for these events has been overwhelmingly positive. The participants appreciated the opportunity to reflect on the individual and organisation learning; it also provided them with an opportunity to network with the other project participants. In terms of career progression, three participants have been able to secure a promotion during the duration of the project. One secured a secondment opportunity within the SHA.

It is difficult to quantify the impact of this project in terms of recruitment data. While work is under way to increase BME staff in senior managerial and clinical positions, and the project team advocates the use of mentoring as an intervention to support a more diverse leadership base, the NHS is going through economic and structural changes that have severely reduced job opportunities. BME staff could be disproportionately affected by the reforms introduced by the Health and Social Care Bill, as in previous reconfigurations. Developing new relationships and exploring new avenues through mentoring can offer some protection against this.

Feedback from both mentees and mentors has been extremely positive. Mentees' comments include:

- confidence building, happier;
- gives direction, helps build priorities through others' perspectives;
- networking and contact building: meeting people higher up which puts career in perspective/gave a good relationship with senior colleagues;
- time to reflect and analyse yourself;
- learnt from each other; helped to be in a 'learning' zone and improve skills in current area;
- given motivation and a challenge in a positive way – to make you succeed and not highlight your weaknesses;
- helped lead to other things.

Other comments included:

> With the help of my mentor,I was commissioned to pick up a Review project with another NHS Trust. That has given me the skills of doing projects and since then I have got more projects in team.
>
> (Mentee)

> The programme can contribute to hopefully retain and develop someone with leadership abilities. It also gave me increased awareness of the challenges facing very different teams in times of organisational change.
>
> (Mentor)

> I have developed more experience due to the activities I undertook during the process. I am able to map my plan over the next three years both on a personal and professional level.
>
> (Mentee)

Mentors stated that the benefits of mentoring included:

- learning more about oneself;
- understanding front line perspectives;

- developing the skills of 'quiet leadership';
- that they would mentor again, encourage its practice, and look for a mentor themselves.

One mentor has since become Interim Chief Executive of his Trust, and enthusiastically headed up an equalities event for all staff recently.

All mentees agreed that they would now consider applying for roles, which they would not have done before mentoring. The implications of this are considerable – both in indicating this group's previous mindset and in making a positive step towards achieving the ultimate aim of improving representation of BME staff at more senior levels.

The increase in self-confidence and therefore the ability to be proactive are extremely significant. One participant described how she had e-mailed her Chief Executive to request a work shadowing opportunity – something she would never have contemplated before the programme.

An aim of the programme for project leads was to model to the wider NHS system how mentoring can benefit staff. This was also achieved (and continues to be built on), and exemplified by a participant, who described how others in his work area became interested in mentoring and subsequently found their own mentors.

> The health community in the region has learned a lot from this project. It has helped raise the profile of mentoring and the importance of a more diverse pool of future leaders for the local NHS. Networking events allowed participants to share learning with each other. We have also developed a series of resources for mentors and mentees that can be used to ensure the continuation of this programme, and are being circulated widely as word spreads. We have developed a community of interest, and some very strong advocates for mentoring, who hopefully will take over ownership and ensure that the scheme survives following the demise of the SHA.

Lessons learned

- Setting up a mentoring scheme may take longer than originally anticipated but it is a worthwhile endeavour.
- Key to the success is having a sufficient number of mentors. Mentors can be busy, but linking mentoring to personal development or corporate objectives can provide a critical mass of mentors.
- Although the mentoring scheme focused on BME staff, there is also an impact on non-BME staff.

- The project team did receive some queries at the start of the project on why it was focusing on BME staff. Some mentees mentioned that the mentoring scheme had a spill-over effect and non-BME staff sought to find a mentor as a result of hearing about this initiative.
- Good, regular, thorough communication to all stakeholders and beyond, including key learning after the end of the project, is essential to ensure the system makes the best of the investment, and to help spread and embed the mentoring habit.

Reflection questions

1. How would you deal with resistance by groups that feel that they are unfairly excluded from such a scheme?
2. How can you identify potential mentors and other influential stakeholders for the benefit of the programme?
3. How can you help busy mentors to keep engaged with the project beyond the mentee?

Case study 26: Denmark

AU Mentor: double mentoring

Susanne Søes Hejlsvig

Introduction

The AU Mentor programme involves the business community and Aarhus University, Business and Social Sciences (formerly the Aarhus School of Business, Aarhus University) jointly seeking to aid students as well as refugees and immigrants to integrate into the world of business and Danish society.

The programme was initiated by Pernille Kallehave, Director of Communication and External Relations, and Professor Steen Hildebrandt. It is conducted under the auspices of the Career Centre and is managed by career consultant Susanne Søes Hejlsvig. Professor David Clutterbuck has been one of the Mentor consultants and teacher. The Intercultural Network of the Women's Museum and the Danish Refugee Council's mentornetDK are partners.

Aims of the programme

The programme has two primary aims:

1 to train a group of Master's students to become socially responsible employees and managers for the purpose of integration and multicultural understanding;

2 to prepare the students for business careers through having a personal relationship with an experienced businessperson.

The programme offers Master's students the opportunity to have their own mentor from the business community. It also gives the students the opportunity to become mentors themselves by mentoring a refugee or immigrant. This could be called double mentoring and is a give-and-take scenario, where the student receives guidance and help from his or her mentor and in return gives something back to society. The string of meetings between the alumnus and the student and the student and the refugee/immigrant increases everybody's understanding of each other and contributes to tearing down prejudicial barriers.

Mentors and mentees meet each other at eye level as equals, creating the best possible starting point for getting to know each other. When, as a mentor, you know the other person and the other person's way of thinking, you can offer support or present challenges, depending on what feels right. Many participants in this three-party relationship meet each other at some point, in a meeting facilitated by the student.

Programme structure

Alumnus-to-student relationship

The programme runs for approximately nine months. We believe that a mentor relationship should be based on the mentee's need, so the mentee picks his or her own mentor. Each mentee is asked to make a top five list of the mentors they would be interested in having, based on the mentor profiles, which the mentees have access to on the AU Mentor website.

Once all applications have been collected, the career centre does the matching between the alumni (mentors) and the students (mentees). Everybody meets for an introduction day, alumni and students are divided during the training. Immediately after, they have their first mentoring meeting. The tension and excitement in the air are amazing, when the parties meet and make their first connection. The mentees are often very nervous to meet this person, who voluntarily has decided to spend time with him or her. Does the mentor live up to my expectations so far? Why will he or she spend time with me? What does he or she expect from me? Can I live up to that? Everything happens at the university, since this is a place everybody can relate to, and it is more informal for the students, since they are meeting on their home ground.

During the first two months, the mentor and the mentee get to know each other, and they both get a fairly good idea about what mentoring is about. The alumnus and the student meet approximately once a month for conversations lasting approximately 90 minutes. Halfway through the mentoring programme, participants are invited for an evaluation day, where everybody shares their experiences.

When the alumnus and the student have been working together for just over six months, their relationship is nearing its end, and there are two meetings left to round things off. The last two conversations must constitute the 'approach' to a good landing.

The AU Mentor programme has now been running for approximately nine months, and a final evaluation will soon be done to address such questions as 'Does what the student has gained from the mentor programme tally with what he or she put down in the contract?' and 'What were the alumnus' experiences along the way?' Although we do not have such summative data, we wish to present an example of the experience from one mentee's point of view.

Student-to-refugee/immigrant relationship

The relationships between the students (now the mentors) and the refugee/immigrants (now the mentees) are initiated one or two months after the relationships between alumni and students. It is important that the students gain a little experience of being a mentee before they become mentors themselves. Our partners from the integration environments train the students in their mentor role, focusing especially on the cultural differences they will experience in the relationship. Matching is made on the basis of interviews with both students (mentors) and refugees/immigrants (mentees). At the first meeting, the mentor and mentee sign a mentor agreement stating, e.g. their expectations, meeting frequency, topics to discuss and confidentiality. The agreement can be revised during the relationship. The mentor relationships between students and refugee/immigrants last for about six months and are also evaluated at the end.

Ehsan's story

In 1990, Ehsan emigrated to Denmark with his family. He was only 2 years old. His father became self-employed and has a kiosk, a restaurant and hair salon. Ehsan had for some time been helping his father out in the restaurant and was not sure what to do after finishing high school. He could stay and work in the restaurant if he wanted to.

Ehsan was in high school and unsure of his next step. He did not have anyone in his immediate environment who could explain the Danish educational system to him or the choice of education that he had. He heard about the possibility of getting a mentor and was lucky enough to be matched with Michael, a student at the business school. Ehsan says that at that period of his life, he was not being very responsible. Looking back, he says it was important that someone was looking after him, e.g. ensuring that he sent his applications for acceptance to educational institutions on time. Michael became both his mentor and his friend. Today Ehsan is studying to become a teacher.

Lessons learned

For Ehsan, it was easy to understand how his mentor could help. That is not always the case, so a lesson learned is to ensure both mentor and mentee are clear about the purpose and potential outcome of a mentoring relationship. It has to be tangible, with concrete suggestions for topics. Without a clear topic to discuss, the relationship tends to fade.

In most cases, mentors felt they could have been used even more – both more meetings and broader topics. Many of the mentees were surprised to learn how many topics they could actually cover with their mentor. And the more open the mentees were, the more fruitful the relationships.

Another learning point has been to clarify why someone should offer to be a mentor. What do they hope to obtain and learn from the relationship? Why do they even want to spend their spare time with a mentee? Some mentees have a difficult time figuring out what they can offer their mentors, as they feel they should pay back the favour. They see the relationship as very unbalanced and consider their mentors to be very superior. And some have a hard time asking for help, because they see it as a one-way relationship. Hence statements from former mentors explaining why they enjoyed the mentor relationship and what they learned and gained from it have been very useful in helping mentees understand that the mentors also undergo a learning experience and therefore gain from the relationship.

Every mentee who is meeting his or her mentor for the first time is nervous, so the preparation for that meeting is important. We learned to explain even more explicitly to both parties how to deal with their nervousness.

When asked the following evaluation question, 'What has made the deepest impression on you in this mentor relationship?', the mentees responded:

- My mentor's willingness to take this time for me.
- My mentor's willingness to help me on different levels.
- My mentor's openness and sincere desire to help me.
- My mentor's commitment and her eagerness to help me.
- My mentor's sincere commitment.

Looking at the mentors' reflections, it becomes evident that 'just' being able to help and contribute to a young person's development is in itself satisfying. Mentors commented:

- It is a great joy to be able to contribute with sharing and advice to a young person's challenges. I feel good about helping others becoming stronger, more motivated and finding the best solutions for them personally.

- I experience a personal joy in helping my mentee through tough phases of her studies.

Reflection questions

1. How can we manage the nervousness and expectations of both mentor and mentee?
2. How can we ensure that the mentor is used appropriately? To what extent is this important, relevant and necessary?

Case study 27: South Africa

Qualitative reflections on a pilot coaching programme in Pollsmoor Prison

Jonelle Naude

Introduction

Internationally, many calls have been made for more personal, narrative, relationship-based and social constructionist approaches (Thompson 2000; Gorman et al. 2006; Gregory 2006; Hayles 2006) towards working with the offender population. In September 2006, a coaching programme pilot was implemented in Pollsmoor Prison (Med A), in Cape Town, South Africa, to achieve this goal. The aim of this pilot programme was to coach three adolescent boys in gaining confidence and a positive approach towards themselves and their future. It was hoped that this would heighten their ability for successful and positive reintegration into society and possibly, over time, reduce recidivism (Gaum et al. 2006). I personally hoped the results of this pilot programme would highlight the effectiveness of coaching in this context.

It should be noted that definitions of coaching and mentoring – particularly in the developmental context – can often be contradictory and confusing. This project was labelled a coaching programme, but within the context of this book, it could equally be described as developmental mentoring, as it incorporates elements of both approaches.

Programme design

Some criteria were employed to identify the three adolescent boys for this pilot programme. They had to do the following:

- demonstrate a willingness to work on their future;
- commit to the process of behavioural change;
- commit to a six-month process (one-hour session every two weeks);
- have a release date within the next three months;
- consent to the research process and possible follow-up conversations in the future.

Having explained to them the process and all activities involved, we gained their verbal consent. We treated all the assessments in an empathic and respectful manner and kept participants' identities confidential.

For the pilot programme, three participants (P, Z and M) engaged in one-to-one coaching sessions for a total of six months: three months prior to their release date and three months after. While in prison, they were coached in a room that provided some degree of privacy to enable confidential conversations. Once released, coach and coachee chose suitable locations where they could meet to continue the sessions. Each participant had a two-hour introductory session, followed by one-hour coaching sessions, bi-weekly, for six months, ending with a final two-hour session for completion. Their experience and progress were measured through pre-coaching and post-coaching assessments. The assessments consisted of three sections: a multiple choice unit, a life satisfaction exercise, and an open-ended questionnaire. The open-ended questionnaire served as the primary source of data for this qualitative study, while the multiple choice section and life satisfaction exercise provided quantitative support to this qualitative study.

Approach to research

My approach as researcher was typically phenomenologically interpretative (Stanley and Wise 1993; Burr 1995). Phenomenology is concerned with the study of the experience from the perspective of the individual (Stanley and Wise 1993; Burr 1995). At the same time, the researcher becomes a visible part of the research, rather than invisible observer (Stanley and Wise 1993). So my reflections also form part of the data.

Qualitative thematic analysis (Benner 1985) was derived from pre- and post-coaching assessments, examining open-ended questionnaires, multiple choice questionnaires, and my observations and reflections. I approached the data by familiarising myself with the content and allowing themes to emerge. Once the data felt exhausted of themes, corresponding literature and theory were used to form a new framework in which to view the data. The data (and themes) were re-analysed – this time parallel to existing theory on the strengthening of the self.

Outcomes

The data analysis indicated that the central outcome of the coaching intervention was a 'strengthening of the self' (McAdams 1993). The self develops from incorporation of attitudes, ideas and beliefs as the person experiences life and the world and interacts with the human environment (Neihart 1998). In a sense, the self is a product of what the individual pays attention to and internalises from his immediate environment (Csikszentmihalyi 1993).

Adolescence is the most critical time for developing the self, when it is most clearly defined and established (Neihart 1998). Before a person can develop an identity, they must have a basic sense of self (McAdams 1993). Before adolescence, we have no life story and no real identity (McAdams 1993). According to self-psychology (Kohut 1977; Neihart 1998; Winnicot et al. 1989) the process of self-development and strengthening of the self include self-esteem, differentiation, authenticity, self-efficacy, integration of the self and self-regulation (learning to express your emotions, and managing intense emotions) (Miller 1981). These six factors were a framework to explore participants' experiences of the strengthening of the self.

Self-esteem

The boys were particularly vulnerable to distortions in developing their sense of self as they were faced with dire situational factors typical to life in the Cape Flats: poverty, violence, physical abuse and emotional abuse. When positive role models are absent, negative role models provide substituting narratives. From the data it emerged that the creation of a 'future self' took on a central process in increasing self-esteem. A visualisation called the Future Self (Whitworth et al. 1998) was used to create an internal personal role model for each participant. As discussed below, the future self seemed to facilitate greater self-esteem by providing an internal role model, by instigating dreaming and creating alternative narratives, and by inspiring and creating hope. The personal dreams and visions that adolescents conjure up entail limitless possibility for their future. Creating these personal fables (McAdam 1993) is a normal developmental process. Due to their harsh life circumstances, the participants all reported never having experienced this sense of future dreaming. The data indicated that once the participants discovered and connected with their

Future Self, they started dreaming and building their own personal fables. They also used this internal structure to get in touch with their own sense of 'better knowing'. Their internal role models seemed to inspire as well as create hope for the future. Moreover, they developed a greater sense of ownership and responsibility for their current lives:

> I want my future to be a bright future and I want to reach my goals, and I feel like I will – no matter what will happen . . . [I] feel my future is in my own hand.
>
> (P)

The role model of the 'future self' further assisted in the formation of a new narrative the participants could relate to as an alternative to the familiar offender/gang-member from the Cape Flats narrative. At the start of the coaching process, it was clear that all three participants identified with scripts of the incarcerated juvenile, gang member, school drop-out, or the boy who was a failure and disappointment to his family and community:

> I see my past as a child who was raised by his parents and teach him to go the right way. I had disappointed my parents. I was going deep inside the wrong way and I had done lots of mistakes.
>
> (Z)

> I feel embarrassed for what I have done. My family still sees me that way.
>
> (M)

Pre-assessment, Z said, 'I feel ashamed because I had disgraced my family and myself to the people who knew me and to God.' During the coaching process, however, a shift occurred from perpetrator discourse to survivor discourse. With the new narrative of becoming their future selves and rising above their circumstances, they could access greater self-belief and self-esteem. Z now said, 'I feel free [and] I feel very proud myself because I had gone through many difficulties . . . so that they can look at me as a good person and not a criminal.'

Differentiation

Participants' initial process of differentiation, attempting to develop the self (Neihart 1998), had led them to criminality and gang activity. Acting-out behaviour in adolescents often represents attempts to protect and differentiate the self (McConville 1995; Neihart 1998), and destructive behaviours could be seen as an attempt to preserve the self. The participants were now faced with the challenge to differentiate themselves once again from their current peer-accepted status as offender or gang member. Further differentiation took place as the participants increased in self-esteem and self-efficacy. The ultimate act of differentiation took place during the last two months of the intervention. Two of the three participants were loyal gang members. Not only did being gang members provide them with respect and a sense of belonging, it also kept them safe from other gangs. Breaking free from a gang is a perilous effort and members often pay with their lives in an attempt to escape. Both these participants had differentiated to the extent that they had successfully quit their gangs by the end of the six months. Their increased self-esteem and self-efficacy allowed them to differentiate from their gangster identity and develop an identity more aligned to their values and true self.

Authenticity

The inner critic is a schema personification of all limiting beliefs, self-doubt and self-sabotage. It really is the schema, the source, of all negative thoughts (Stone and Stone 1993; Carson 2003). Working with the Inner Critic made it possible to challenge and assist in separating it from the other selves (Stone and Stone 1993). Externalising an idea (or problem, feeling, etc.) linguistically shifts that construct from a subjective status to the status of an object (Bird 2000). Consequently, this construct (attribute or feeling) then shifts from being a significant part of the person, to being in relationship with that person. In this case, we were creating an externalised discourse to work with destructive and self-sabotaging behaviour without threatening the self. The participants could start separating their authentic self from the 'bad' voice that had reportedly caused them such conflict.

From the participants' assertions it seemed as if the future self was a useful tool in further uncovering and developing the authentic self. The participants demonstrated that they were indeed involved in this process of establishing and uncovering their authentic self:

> [I am learning] what kind of person I am deeply inside.
>
> (P)

> I am starting to realise who I really am.
>
> (M)

Once they had established a sense of their true self, they could augment this process by becoming more authentic. They achieved this by aligning their action with their authentic self and showing that to the world:

> [I] . . . had also realise[d] who I am and how to show my real person to people.
>
> (Z)

> I learn[ed] about how you can improve your life, and being myself, and listen to others' ideas, and live a normal life without crime.
>
> (M)

Self-efficacy

The participants' self-attribution of competence and efficacy (Powers et al. 2001) was reinforced and magnified through the coach's continued validation and acknowledgement of their efforts and personal work. An especially powerful coaching tool used in this regard is 'championing' where the coach stands up for the client who is hesitant about his/her own abilities. For example, when the participants doubted their ability to achieve their goals, the coach would emphatically cheer them on, reminding them that she had no doubt and knew they could do it. This particular skill is considered an effective application towards increasing a client's perception of self-efficacy (Irwin and Morrow 2005). In the post-assessments participants gave personal accounts of their new sense of self-efficacy and motivation (Schunk 1989):

> . . . because I am gonna prove my goals and hopes . . . I expect to achieve my goals and look to the future.
>
> (M)

> I make positive choices . . .
>
> (Z)

> I see that I have change[d] . . . [I have] change[d] friends, change[d] my life, change[d] my attitude, change[d] the way I approach others.
>
> (P)

Self-regulation

Self-regulation could be described as 'managing one's internal states, impulses, and resources' (Goleman 1998: 26). From the statements below it seems as if all three participants' ability to self-regulate had increased by the end of the coaching programme:

> I had learn[ed] how to control myself and how to think positively, how to be strong and avoid temptation.
>
> (Z)

> I have gain[ed] how to respond to other people; I also gain[ed] how to have power and be myself; I have also learn[ed] how to say no to bad things.
>
> (P)

> I [have] gain[ed] knowledge . . . I had learn[ed] how to express my feelings to . . . others.
>
> (M)

Integration

Although the participants were still in the process of forming their identities and true selves during the coaching programme, there was evidence in the data to suggest that some integration of the self had taken place towards the end of the coaching intervention. This was demonstrated by absence of internal conflict present at the start, as well as a general feeling of contentment and happiness. M said, 'I am happy about myself.'

One participant (P) integrated his past and 'old' self by reframing his criminality as 'bad' choices and 'lying to himself'. His capacity to integrate his 'old' self confirms that his current self-view has unfolded through the coaching process: 'I see my past as a bad choice; . . . I also see that I have wasted time; I have also lied to myself; I have done wrong instead of right.'

The newly developed sense of ownership and responsibility that emerged towards the end of the coaching could also be indicative of a greater sense of integration of the self. P stated, 'I feel my future is a right way; . . . That my future is in my own hands; I feel that I have to make the right choices for it; I have to be myself for the future.'

Finally, one participant demonstrated integration of the self in terms of a feeling of maturity that he had achieved by the end of the programme: 'P the boy has become P the young man.'

Quantitative support

The multiple choice section and life satisfaction exercises were also analysed to provide some quantitative content and support to this qualitative study. Participants' overall confidence and positivity in the self and the future increased by an average of 21.8 per cent. Their general life satisfaction showed an increase from 30 per cent to 90 per cent.

Coach reflection

The coach in this pilot study, as well as the coaches from the coaching programme that followed, agreed that the coach believing that the boys already had everything inside them to succeed had most impact. The coach(es) acknowledged how difficult it was at times not to collude with what 'circumstance' (or the societal/inner critic) predicts: that it is too difficult or impossible to change within their context. Reinforcing the belief that the coachees could move beyond their circumstances helped these boys to also start believing that they could. When these adolescents succeeded against all odds, it reinforced the powerful assumption that change is always possible.

Conclusion

The study found that 'strengthening the self' was the predominant outcome for the participants of the coaching programme. A major concern regarding normative rehabilitative measures is the tendency to objectify the offender, which reinforces the offender discourse and, as such, their sense of alienation from society (Hoffman 2005). This is maintained by the overriding authoritative approach embedded in most rehabilitation interventions or programmes. Coaching helped bridge the gap between an authoritarian institute, such as prison, and providing a meaningful vehicle for behavioural change.

After the pilot's success, this programme was adopted by the Dutch-based NGO Young In Prison 2007. Some 18 boys and 3 girls were involved in the programme with 6 coaches. All coaches remained under my supervision and received compulsory monthly supervision. Additionally, coaches received six hours induction training of pre-coaching supervision and training that included additional coaching tools, and working with an offender population. We were on target for 30 participants over year one when our momentum was halted in January 2008 by sudden and extensive changes within PollsmoorMedA (the male adolescent section). We had to halt the programme for several months. Since then, YIP has re-engaged with an adapted programme.

Lessons learned

It seemed as if the internal role model (in this case, the future self) played a central role in participants' development of greater self-esteem, The coach's constant validation and affirmation helped create self-efficacy, authenticity and facilitated greater differentiation. Continuously acknowledging the participants for who they were being (courageous, wise, big-hearted, scared) instead of only acknowledging their actions (saying no to drugs, doing homework, writing to their parents) made them feel validated and affirmed. Role modelling was therefore a valuable element of the programme. One-to-one relationships proved resource-intensive. A group mentoring programme would be more cost- and labour-effective. Future research could explore how we could retain the transformational quality of one-to-one coaching within a group mentoring scheme. Future studies could also explore long-term effects of coaching on recidivism. Finally, some words from a participant:

> By the time we started the programme last year in prison I was rebellious and I was always confusing myself with bad things, but as time goes by I learn how to be strong and to overcome the temptations and I had also realise[d] who I am and how to show my real person to people so that they can look at me as a good person and not a criminal. I had learn[ed] to express my feelings and how to control myself.
>
> (Z)

Reflection questions

1. How could this programme inform 'correctional services' as we currently know it?
2. How could the transformational quality of one-to-one coaching be retained within a group mentoring programme?

References

Benner, P. (1985) Quality of life: a phenomenological perspective on explanation, prediction, and understanding in nursing science, *Advances in Nursing Science*, 8(1): 1–14.

Bird, J. (2000) *The Heart's Narrative: Therapy and Navigating Life's Contradictions*. Auckland: Edge Press.

Burr, V. (1995) *An Introduction to Social Constructionism*. London: Routledge.

Carson, R.D. (2003) *Taming Your Gremlin*. New York: HarperCollins.

Csikszentimihalyi, M. (1993) *The Evolving Self*. New York: HarperCollins.

Gaum, G., Hoffman, S. and Venter, J.H. (2006) Factors that influence adult recidivism: an exploratory study in Pollsmoor prison, *South African Journal of Psychology*, 36(2): 407–24.

Goleman, D. (1998) *Working with Emotional Intelligence*. London: Bloomsbury Publishing.

Gorman, K., O'Bryne, P. and Parton, N. (eds) (2006) Constructive work with offenders: setting the scene, in K. Gorman, P. O'Bryne and N. Parton (eds) *Constructive Work with Offenders*. London: Jessica Kingsley Publishers, pp. 13–32.

Gregory, M. (2006) The offender as citizen: socially inclusive strategies for working with offenders within the community, in K. Gorman, P. O'Bryne and N. Parton (eds) *Constructive Work with Offenders*. London: Jessica Kingsley Publishers, pp. 49–66.

Hayles, M. (2006) Constructing safety: a collaborative approach to managing risk and building responsibility, in K. Gorman, P. O'Bryne and N. Parton (eds) *Constructive Work with Offenders*. London: Jessica Kingsley Publishers, pp. 67–86.

Hoffman, S. (2005) Rehabilitation of prisoners in a transforming South Africa, paper presented at the Criminal Justice Conference, Gordon's Bay, Western Cape, 7–8 February. Available at: http://www.csvr.org.za/confpaps/hoffman.htm.

Irwin, J.D. and Morrow, D. (2005) Health promotion theory in practice: an analysis of co-active coaching, *International Journal of Evidence Based Coaching and Mentoring*, 3(1): 29–38.

Kohut, H. (1977) *The Restoration of the Self*. New York: International University Press.

McAdams, D.P. (1993) *The Stories We Live By: Personal Myths and the Making of the Self*. New York: Guilford Press.

McConville, M. (1995) *Adolescence: Psychotherapy and the Emergent Self*. San Francisco: Jossey-Bass Publishers.

Miller, A. (1981) *The Drama of the Gifted Child*. New York: Basic Books.

Neihart, M. (1998) Creativity, the arts, and madness, *Roeper Review*, 21: 47–50.

Powers, L.E., Turner, A., Ellison, R., Matuszewski, J., Wilson, R., Phillips, A. and Rein, C. (2001) A multi-component intervention to promote adolescent self-determination, *The Journal of Rehabilitation*, 67(4): 13–19.

Schunk, D.H. (1989) Social-cognitive theory and self-regulated learning, in D.H. Schunk and B.J. Zimmerman (eds) *Self-Regulated Learning and Academic Achievement: Theory, Research and Practice*. New York: Springer Verlag, pp. 83–110.

Stanley, L. and Wise, S. (1993) *Breaking out Again: Feminist Ontology and Epistemology*. London: Routledge.

Stone, H. and Stone, S. (1993) *Embracing Your Inner Critic: Turning Self-Criticism into a Creative Asset.* New York: HarperCollins.

Thompson, N. (2000) *Understanding Social Work: Preparing for Practice.* Basingstoke: Macmillan.

Whitworth, L., Kimsey-House, H. and Sandahl, P. (1998) *Co-Active Coaching: New Skills for Coaching People Toward Success in Work and Life.* Palo Alto, CA: Davies-Black Publishing.

Winnicot, C., Shepherd, R. and Davies, M. (eds) (1989) *Psychoanalytic Exploration.* Cambridge, MA: Harvard University Press.

Case study 28: Great Britain

Middlesex University Mentoring Network

Julie Haddock-Millar, Nwamaka Onyiuke, Helen Villalobos, Tulsi Derodra, Gifty Gabor and Raymond Asumadu

Introduction

This case study reports on the development of the first Middlesex University Mentoring Network (MUMN) – created and developed by a group of diverse undergraduate and postgraduate students at Middlesex University Business School.

Middlesex University became a new university in 1992 and has since opened international campuses in Dubai and Mauritius. The university supports over 35,000 students worldwide, of which over 30 per cent are international students, and over 4,000 of those students study on the London Campus. Middlesex University comprises a culturally and internationally diverse range of students, studying in a variety of ways from work-based learning programmes to full-time on campus. Over 66 per cent of full-time students are from London or the South East.

The authors, three second-year undergraduate BA Human Resource Management (HRM) students, Asumadu, Gabor and Derodra, two MA Human Resource Development (HRD) students, Onyiuke and Villalobos, and one professional Doctoral student, Haddock-Millar, are a group of diverse students, originating from Ghana, Kenya, Nigeria and the UK, ranging in age from 19 to 41.

This case study describes their journey. In light of the growing concern around rising unemployment among graduate students, Haddock-Millar identified an opportunity to support career development, creating opportunities to enhance skills, behaviours and knowledge to help them succeed in the world of work. She discussed the concept with a number of postgraduate students, who were also practitioners. Two students, Onyiuke and Villalobos, offered to support the initiative and help to get the network off the ground, bringing together students, alumni, academic staff and practitioners through a formal Mentoring Network. Thus, MUMN was founded in November 2009.

Programme initiation

The founding team met with 37 first-year BA HRM students, asking if they would like to be involved in a Mentoring Network, and if so, what they would want from it. The discussion revealed that many students would value the opportunity to build their professional networks, which they recognised would be critical to enhancing their career opportunities in a challenging climate. There was significant interest and demand for a mentoring programme. Students were invited to meet potential mentors and the founding team and discuss the approach they would like to take in building the programme. Asumadu, Gabor and Derodra attended the first discussion and have been active members and mentees since.

Design of the programme

Coming from culturally diverse backgrounds, the team were conscious that they did not want to impose a particular framework based on preconceived ideas but rather, wanted to develop a programme that would 'best fit' the needs of the group. The design emerged organically from initial discussions on individuals' values and beliefs. Members identified four common values: commitment, care, community and creativity, which provided the basis of all future activities.

Support

The team secured funding of £3,000 from the Centre of Excellence for Work-Based Learning at Middlesex University. The team also gained the support from the Dean of the Business School, the BA HRM Programme Leader and other internal and external stakeholders.

Outcomes

Over a period of 12 months, the programme members have participated in the following activities:

- Twelve mentoring group sessions.
- Presented the project at the European Mentoring and Coaching Council Conference 2010, Annual Conference.
- Held the first MUMN 2010 Annual Conference, titled 'Unleashing your potential through mentoring' for 33 delegates, including students, alumni, academic staff and practitioners.
- Organised a mentee site visit to a large charitable organisation to understand HR management in practice.
- Developed the MUMN brand and logo with an external media company.

- Launched the MUMN website: www.thecoachvine.com.
- Collaborated with the International Centre for the Study of Coaching, MU, to launch and co-facilitate the first research-practitioner Conference in 2010.
- Been invited to author two case study chapters reporting on the development of the Network.

Reflections

MUMN aimed to raise the aspirations of group members, providing opportunities that might not usually arise within the context of their studies and stakeholder groups, enriching their personal and professional lives. Two learning outcomes have emerged from the activities of the group: (1) practical and emotional support has been provided for group members; and (2) a positive attitude towards difference has been developed.

Practical and emotional support: developing emotional intelligence

The Network has provided practical and emotional support for group members. During the monthly group meetings members have shared stories about their backgrounds, cultures and family origins, retracing the paths that led them to meet at the university. Such opportunities have enhanced cross-cultural awareness and understanding between participants. In one such meeting, Villalobos described how her mentor provided her with feedback which increased her self-awareness, helping her to reframe personal dilemmas and identify constructive ways of dealing with difficult situations. Asamadu described how his involvement in the Network helped him to develop greater self-awareness. In one of the sessions Asamadu participated in a discussion around the ability of learners to understand their own emotions, the emotions of others and how to manage emotional reactions to situations.

Asamadu states, 'Understanding my emotional intelligence, recognising my own feelings and the feelings of others has helped me to build stronger relationships with my colleagues at university and in the workplace.' He also describes how understanding non-verbal communication has made him more aware of his behaviours and how he interacts with others in everyday life, commenting that 'This could make the difference between me being employed or declined a position in an organisation following the interview process.'

Developing a positive attitude towards difference: enhancing mutual respect

Onyiuke provided Asumadu, Derodra and Gabor with an opportunity to spend a development day at her workplace, Jesus House for All Nations, a non-profit organisation. The mentees were able to experience and appreciate theory in practice, at the same time meeting people from a variety of cultural, educational and social backgrounds. The experience enabled the mentees to broaden their understanding of how people come together from different backgrounds to work together towards a common goal of discovering purpose and maximising potential within the community, free of prejudice and discrimination. Mentors tend to gain immense personal value and satisfaction from knowing that they have contributed greatly to another individual's growth and development (Klasen and Clutterbuck 2007). Villalobos explains that the mentoring journey has not been a job, but an exciting opportunity to nurture some very committed undergraduate students who made a decision to take their lives in their hands and shape it rather than let life lead them where it wanted.

Lessons learned

Five critical factors have contributed to the Network's success.

1 *Having a programme champion*: MUMN has benefited enormously from having a programme champion (Haddock-Millar) actively promoting members' achievements to senior members at the Business School and knowing how to access funding and develop project opportunities. Having a credible programme champion maintained visibility and ensured successes are acknowledged and celebrated.

2 *Allowing participants to shape their learning agenda*: MUMN is owned and driven by participants (students). The Network has grown organically and with flexibility rather than taking on a bureaucratic structure, and is shaped by the needs and aspirations of the participants in the context of the university's wider aims.

3 *Exploring flexible development opportunities*: The university has supported the Network to form new learning partnerships outside the classroom, giving access a wider range of participants (both mentors and mentees). The members experiment with both one-to-one and group mentoring approaches and seek out links with local organisations, such as Jesus House.

4 Identifying opportunities to link with like-minded professionals: Oniyuke and Haddock-Millar have both sought out opportunities to link with other organisations and professionals, who share the Network's values and recognise the importance of cultural diversity in talent management. In particular, they have given the members access to new role models who have a global mindset and strong cross-cultural empathy.

5 *Providing a clear sense of purpose*: MUMN does not see itself as a remedial programme, and the members choose not to label it as a 'diversity programme', as such. Rather the focus is on enhancing capability, making a contribution to the community and raising the aspirations of those involved, while exploring flexible ways to involve a wider range of participants.

Reflection questions

1. What role does emotional intelligence have in working with diverse cultures?
2. How can you recognise and develop the authentic nature of individuals within a culturally diverse mentoring group?
3. What role does organic growth play in future mentoring programmes and our society?

Reference

Klasen, N. and Clutterbuck, D. (2007) *Implementing Mentoring Schemes*. Oxford: Elsevier.

Case study 29: Australia

Aboriginal mentoring in Community Services[1]

Ann Rolfe

Introduction

New South Wales (NSW) is home to a third of Australia's population. With an area of 800,000 square kilometres, it is eight times the size of the UK, yet has a much smaller population density. The population is even more diverse than the landscape, with around a third of people born overseas and just over 2 per cent being Aboriginal.

Aboriginal people are disadvantaged, compared to the non-indigenous population, on every social measure. However, education rates and employment participation are improving (Fryer-Smith 2002). In recent years, a number of mentoring programs aimed at producing better outcomes for Aboriginal people have been implemented in education, health, government departments, Aboriginal community groups and the private sector.

Community Services[2] is a government agency promoting the safety and well-being of children and young people. It works to build stronger families and communities, providing services in child protection, parenting support and early intervention, foster care, adoption and help for communities affected by disaster. There is an over-representation of Aboriginal people as clients (overall, 30 per cent of the client base), and an under-representation of Aboriginal staff in management positions. So, developing Aboriginal staff in Community Services is vital to fulfil its commitment to 'build the capacity to deliver better service to the children, young people and families of the State' (Community Services website). The program was promoted to employees across NSW. Mentorees were mainly Aboriginal Case Workers from regional and metropolitan areas. Mentors in 2007 were non-indigenous managers but in 2010 both Aboriginal and non-Aboriginal leaders mentored.

Program objectives

The program aims to increase representation of Aboriginal staff in mainstream management positions. Specifically, the 2007 program aimed to do the following:

- support the professional and career development opportunities for Aboriginal staff through one-to-one mentoring relationships;
- recognise and maximise the diversity and skills of the Department's workforce;
- provide a blueprint for future mentoring programs.

Community Services described participants' roles as follows:

> A *mentoree* can be anyone who wishes to set and achieve profes-sional goals and learning goals, and has an interest in management. A mentoree may seek help in building specific capabilities, in discussing career options, or in understanding the organisation better. They may have a workplace goal they are passionate about, for which they need the assistance of a mentor to realise.
>
> A *mentor* is someone, who is genuinely interested in people and has a desire to help others. The most important qualities of a mentor include communication skills (including active listening and ques-tioning skills), respect for alternate opinions, honoring agreements and maintaining confidentiality. They should be willing to share their experience to assist the mentoree as they work towards their goals. In addition to these general attributes, the Mentor must be culturally sensitive to Aboriginal staff and their aspirations.

Program design

In 2006, an external specialist in mentoring facilitated a planning workshop for members of the Australian Bureau of Statistics and the Learning and Development unit. The group developed a definition of mentoring, realistic objectives for an Aboriginal mentoring program and a plan for the training and support needed.

The program was promoted at management forums, through e-mails to Aboriginal people and by word of mouth. Expressions of interest were sought from Aboriginal employees and potential mentors. In 2007, mentoring matches were made during the initial workshop with input from mentorees. In 2010, participants were paired by Learning & Development before they attended.

Mentors and mentorees in 2007 attended two workshops together during the program: an initial two-day session and a final event. In 2010, a mid-point review was added. In 2007, mentorees were invited to participate in a leadership workshop. In the 2010 program they completed an accredited Transition To Management program concurrently. Transition To Management is a four-day course offered by the Department to first level managers and supervisors or those aspiring to management roles.

The initial two-day mentoring workshop was highly interactive so that, as well as acquiring knowledge and skills for mentoring, participants and mentors got to know each other in preparation for the mentoring relationships. The workshops provided an orientation to the program, and covered communication skills, career planning (for mentorees in 2007, for all participants in 2010) and cultural awareness (for mentors in the 2007 program). The final event of the pilot program in 2008 included a review that gathered feedback – used in developing the 2010 program – and a workshop that enabled participants to select goals for the next stage of their professional development.

A midpoint review was added to the 2010 program. It proved to be important in re-energising some relationships by sharing participant successes and challenges. It allowed program managers to assist pairs who were experiencing difficulties. This review was also an opportunity for further skills development, with a workshop on giving and receiving feedback included on the day. The consultant facilitated the review session and the feedback workshop.

In both programs, participants were provided with three books by Ann Rolfe: *The Mentoring Conversation, The Mentoring Guide*, and *The Mentoring Journal* (see www. mentoring-works.com). One-page Mentoring Tips were e-mailed regularly.

Evaluation

The evaluation process sought information about:

- participant satisfaction with the process;
- the achievement of learning objectives;
- the application in the workplace;
- the impact on organisational goals.

In 2008, following the final event, a questionnaire obtained individual input on issues raised in the group review process. Participants rated the extent to which outcomes were achieved and commented on what they had learned, whether it was relevant to their situation, how they would apply it, and whether further information or support was required. In most cases, mentoring had achieved the stated organisational objectives and had contributed to positive personal outcomes.

However, some participants experienced difficulty with their mentoring relationship and others felt constrained by lack of support in the workplace.

The program called on participants to set their own goals for career, personal and professional development and life balance. In 2010, some focused specifically on job application and interview skills. As a result, one participant achieved a management position and another obtained an acting role. Others reported improved work practices, gaining insight and skills that enabled them to solve problems and increased self-confidence.

Lessons learned

Evaluation of the 2007 program identified areas for improvement including communication about the program, coordination and monitoring of the program, selection of mentors, matching and support over the life of the program.

The pilot program in 2007 was small and targeted. Beyond the actual participants and their managers, few people knew about the program. The strategic value of developing Aboriginal staff as managers was not well understood by co-workers and consequently, their support was not strong. The first program also lacked a go-to person as the central contact and source of advice for participants. There was limited individual follow-up, so problems were left unchecked. Some mentors found the time commitment difficult. Matches were made quite quickly, in the original program, during the introductory workshop. Some mentorees felt they'd 'missed out' by not getting their preferred mentor. Although a one-day workshop was offered mid-way through the first program, few participants attended. Essentially the group got together only at the beginning and the end of the program and suggested in their feedback that more frequent gatherings would have been beneficial.

Changes were made in each of these areas for the 2010 program. Unfortunately, coordination and monitoring of the program remain a challenge due to limited resources. This is one of many projects managed by Learning & Development and Aboriginal Services Branch in an organisation constantly under scrutiny. A clear understanding of its priority and value, matched with the allocation of dedicated internal resources, could increase program effectiveness. A program manager dedicated for the full 12 months and able to maintain regular contact with participants makes a significant difference to the effectiveness of a mentoring program. They can spot and react to problems early to maximise return on investment.

Typically, mentors and participants are highly motivated during initial training. They see the potential benefits, begin to set goals and commit to actions. This initial enthusiasm must be nurtured if it is to be maintained. Competing priorities, unexpected events and normal work and life stresses get in the way of mentoring. So people need to be supported and engaged over the life of the program. In 2010, participants received 'Mentoring Tips' e-mailed every second week. These acted as reminders and provided techniques, information and ideas to help them stay on track. The addition of a mid-point review workshop was welcomed, well attended and highly valued by participants. Most importantly, the Learning & Development unit provided follow-up and support to participants throughout most of the program.

Ongoing commitment by line managers to staff development is sometimes difficult to obtain in a workplace that can be stressful and demanding. The link between personal outcomes that improve their subordinate's performance and career, and delivery of services may not be clear to line managers. Releasing participants from normal duties so that they can attend courses or talk to their mentor can put an added strain on workloads. Managers are understandably likely to place immediate job needs above longer-term objectives.

Reflection questions

1. The organisation needs to develop people; the line manager needs to ensure work gets done. How can line managers who also face demands for operational performance prioritise strategic outcomes?
2. Employees can be prone to cynicism and jealousy when they see any particular group targeted for 'special' treatment. Can the diversity agenda be addressed without causing friction between employees and if so, how?
3. With so many demands upon finite resources, how can important strategic initiatives be made to remain a priority?

Notes

1 The Aboriginal Mentoring Program described in this case study won the LearnX Asia Pacific 2011 Platinum award for Best Mentoring/Coaching Program.
2 NSW Family & Community Services: http://www.community.nsw.gov.au

References

Australian Bureau of Statistics, National regional profile www.abs.gov.au

Fryer-Smith, S. (2002) Aboriginal Benchbook for Western Australian Courts: AIJA Model Indigenous Benchbook Project. Australian Institute of Judicial Administration: http://www.aija.org.au/online/ICABenchbook.htm

Case study 30: The USA

Pathways for Success: making a difference for minority students

Nora Dominguez and Tim Gutierrez

Introduction

The University of New Mexico (UNM) is a public research university located in Albuquerque, New Mexico, with a total enrolment of 34,674 students. As the largest centrally located institution of higher education in the state, UNM attracts a very diverse student body that includes 33.1 percent Hispanic students and 51.2 percent total minorities.

Background

Underrepresented populations in the United States are growing rapidly. In July 2009, it was estimated that underrepresented groups reached 107.15 million, making up 34.9 percent of the U.S. population (U.S. Census Bureau Report 2010). However, underrepresented students are not attaining post-secondary degrees at the same rate as their Non-Hispanic White peers, with particularly low rates among the African American, American Indian, and Hispanic populations. According to Ryu (2010), despite the increase in minority enrollment to 30 percent in 2007, only 12.72 percent of undergraduate degrees were awarded to minority students. In the same year, whites continued to receive the majority of master's and doctoral degrees (58 percent), while those earned by minorities represented only 20 percent. At the doctoral level, the number of degrees earned by whites was 60 percent, while the number earned by minorities represented barely 20 percent.

Disparity in the number of persons from Hispanic, American Indian, and African American populations in the number of degrees earned fuels the disparity in income when considering that average earnings in 2008 for people with a High School diploma were $31,283; with a Bachelor's degree, $58,613; and with graduate education, $83,144.

Educational attainment in New Mexico also lags behind the national average. Only 28 percent of New Mexicans (national average: 31 percent) earned a High School diploma, 14.3 percent (17.7 percent) obtained a Bachelor's degree, and 10.5 per cent (9.3 percent) earned a graduate degree (Digest of Education Statistics 2009).

Context

UNM has a total enrollment of 34,674 students. It is the State's flagship institution of higher education and is one of only three Hispanic-serving Institutions with a Carnegie Doctoral/Research Extensive classification in the USA. Of the total student enrollment, 51.2 percent are minorities. In addition, about 46 percent of incoming freshmen are first-generation students, meaning that they are the first members of their family to attend college. In a state that ranks high in poverty and 39th in college attainment, UNM is committed to providing broad access to world-class education and research for New Mexico's residents.

In 1994, UNM's retention rate to the third semester of incoming freshman students was 69.3 percent, while its six-year graduation rate was 39.7 percent. Both figures were unacceptable for New Mexico's flagship post-secondary institution.

The first step in creating a pathway for students to attain a college education was an outreach program to increase the recruitment and readiness of secondary students from low-income and first-generation college attendance backgrounds. In 1997, the College Prep Program was inaugurated. By 1999, with the addition of the Research Opportunity Program and Ronald E. McNair Post-Baccalaureate Program, the division established the department of Special Programs – now called College Enrichment and Outreach Programs (CEOP). By developing a set of programs with similar goals under one area, the division was able to create a seamless pathway for students all the way from mid-school to graduate school.

Program design

The program, Pathways for Success: Making a Difference for Minorities in New Mexico, provides educational opportunities that will have a positive impact on individuals of diverse backgrounds. Our mission is to create a support structure for students in the development of skills to achieve post-secondary education, professional skills for life, and strong values to become productive members of society.

Pathways for Success provides opportunities for educational, social, and cultural experiences through the application of a comprehensive and holistic model of support, which includes peer and professional academic Advising, Tutoring, and Mentoring (ATM). By capturing students as early as possible, Educational Mentor-Tutors (EMTs), advisors, and program staff seek to create a nurturing and welcoming environment for developing strong long-term relations where mentoring, tutoring, and advisement take place.

The Mentoring Institute was created in 2007 to enhance the quality of mentoring services provided. It seeks to create a state-wide mentoring culture to increase engagement, retention, and graduation rates in P-20 (Preschool-Graduate School). With an investment of approximately $3.5 million in state, federal, and UNM instructional and general funds, more than 8,000 students receive individualised mentoring, tutoring, and advising services per academic year.

The program is composed of 12 distinct initiatives that work in two venues: Outreach Programs to promote college readiness, and Higher Education Programs to increase retention and graduation rates at the college level. All the programs work under the principle that mentoring is a strategy that involves establishing, cultivating, and nurturing a relationship between a mentor and a mentee to promote the learning of the participants. Complex variables affect graduation and retention rates. To respond to this challenge, we have integrated a variety of services that embrace three critical factors in educational attainment: academic advisement (A), tutoring (T), and mentoring (M). We also work on the premise that our students require different services at distinct developmental stages, focusing on psycho-social functions and cultural assimilation during the students' freshman year; professional development and skill development functions during the sophomore year; career development during the junior year; and networking and sponsorship functions during the senior year. The expected outcome of this model (Figure 5.1) is the development of solid mentoring communities of practice where all partici-pants have a dual role as a mentor for one person and as a mentee of another. It is our aim to provide intentional and positive role models to all of our students throughout their college education.

We recognize that in our particular context, for mentoring to positively impact academic achievement and persistence, initiatives must 'promote socialization,

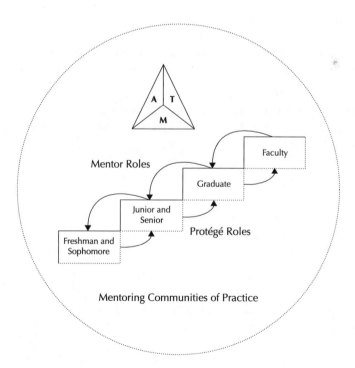

FIGURE 5.1 The mentoring model

learning, career advancement, psychological adjustment, and preparation for leadership' (Johnson 2007: 4). In addition, according to Johnson and Ridley (2004: 82), excellent mentoring 'demands an interplay of foundational character virtues, salient interpersonal and emotional abilities, and acquired mentoring skills'.

Therefore, the programs in Pathways for Success have been designed to include an array of tutoring, advisement, counselling, and mentoring services in a culturally sensitive environment, specially designed for low-income, underrepresented, first-generation college students. In addition, the Mentoring Institute has focused on developing an appropriate curriculum in mentoring, with a view to increasing the graduation rate of Hispanic students and enhancing their preparedness to assume leadership positions after graduation. So EMTs, orientation leaders, advisors, and program staff receive formal mentoring education, training, and certification services.

An initial eight-hour mentoring training and orientation session at the beginning of each academic semester focuses on developing a basic understanding of mentoring principles, theory, and practice. In an interactive and constructivist approach, mentors address topics such as concepts and definitions of mentoring, types and functions of mentoring, effective mentoring behaviors in the context of the program, and practical guidance in preparation to make the most of mentoring relationships. Accountability and responsibility are emphasized, with participants encouraged to keep records and document effectiveness of mentoring sessions using program templates and scorecards.

A comprehensive mentoring educational program has been developed, which includes three certification modules, each one lasting 40 hours, in the following areas:

1 *Mentoring for Career Development*, which focuses on developing mentees' competences and capabilities. It includes the development of career patterns and plans for mentees.

2 *Mentoring for Leadership Development*, which emphasizes the development of mentors' competences and capabilities, with emphasis in the development of leadership skills.

3 *Coaching, Advising and Mentoring*, which is a module that highlights the development of associated skills required for mentors' success to facilitate learning and high performance.

Furthermore, participants are required to participate in the Mentoring Annual Conference held each year at UNM main campus during the fall semester. The conference brings national and international experts together for the purpose of sharing and disseminating mentoring best practices. With annual attendance of more than 250 participants, the conference has become the place for students, staff, and faculty to exchange ideas for knowledge creation, know-how transfer, and innovation.

Assessment

The ability to show that programs are successful directly impacts our ability to keep current funding, and demonstrates our ability to be successful to new funders. Since Pathways for Success is made up of a number of different programs with similar goals but distinctly different objectives, each program has its own measurement tools. However, all of the programs under the AVP for Student Services' umbrella have the common goal of student retention and graduation.

Overall, these programs have succeeded in increasing the number of participants recruited and retained. In addition, all the programs also have satisfaction and retention rates above UNM's averages. UNM has increased retention rates in the third semester from 69.3 percent in 1994, to 79.2 percent in 2008; graduation rates have also increased from 39.7 percent in 1994 to 43.10 percent in 2003 (last cohorts evaluated).

Formative and summative evaluation processes measure the effectiveness of the courses/workshops using Donald Kirkpatrick's four-level model of training evaluation:

1 Reaction to education/training.

2 Accomplishment of learning objectives and outcomes per session.

3 Transfer of learning for behavioral change, capability improvement, and implementation/application of effective practices, skills and competencies for mentorship.

4 Results and impact of application of mentoring best practices and competencies model in students' engagement, satisfaction and retention rates.

On a 5-point scale, average evaluation in reaction to training is 4.5, while accomplishment of learning objectives average is 4.4. Transfer of learning is measured only in the certification programs with satisfactory results using observation rubrics. Impact in retention and graduation rates vary per program, but all programs surpass UNM's averages.

Lessons learned

During the past decade Pathways for Success has made a difference to UNM's underrepresented, low-income, first-generation college students in pursuing higher education, providing them with access and opportunities to achieve their academic goals. Having all the programs under one umbrella, there is daily communication on the strengths and weaknesses of each. To enhance communication with stakeholders, the AVP for Student Services holds bi-weekly staff meetings, uses a departmental newsletter/list-serve, and holds monthly directors' meetings to develop strategies for consistent and quality training. The Mentoring Institute works with all of the programs in developing training events.

The challenge continues as the state of New Mexico and the nation confront major crises; innovative and new approaches need to be developed to sustain the successes achieved. As underrepresented, low-income, first-generation college populations continue to grow, increasing access and opportunity for these populations are critical.

Reflection questions

1. What other strategies are needed to increase enrolment and retention of minorities?
2. As budgets are threatened, how can we ensure continuation and expansion of mentoring programs?
3. What processes can be applied to improve our mentoring services and to create a vigorous mentoring culture across campus?

References

Digest of Education Statistics (2009) *Educational Attainment of Persons 18 Years Old and Over, by State: 2000 and 2005–07*. Retrieved on December 14, 2010 from: http://nces.ed.gov/programs/digest/d09/.

Johnson, W.B. (2007) *On Being a Mentor: A Guide for Higher Education Faculty*. New York: Lawrence Erlbaum Associates.

Johnson, W.B. and Ridley, C.R. (2004) *The Elements of Mentoring*. New York: Palgrave Macmillan.

Ryu, M. (2010) *Minorities in Higher Education*. Washington, DC: American Council on Education.

U.S. Census Bureau Report (2010) *Population Estimates*. Retrieved on December 14, 2010 from: http://www.census.gov/popest/national/asrh/natasrh.html.

Case study 31: Great Britain

Mentoring immigrant schoolchildren

Coral Gardiner and Keith Whittlestone

Introduction

This is a case study of a secondary school in Walsall in the West Midlands that has developed a school-mentoring ethos due to the vision and leadership of its

Headteacher, Keith Whittlestone. Joseph Leckie Community Technology College takes the lead in a local cluster of nine schools. All schools within this cluster cater for ethnically diverse populations drawn from areas of significant deprivation. It has approximately 1,100 students, of whom 76 per cent are from ethnic minorities, principally from Pakistani, Bangladeshi, India, and increasingly eastern European backgrounds. The College accommodates 11–19-year-old students in mainstream education. Some 42 per cent of students are entitled to Free School Meals and a high proportion of students live within a ward where over 46 per cent of children live in poverty. The area itself is fifth from bottom of the 34 West Midlands' councils in relation to child poverty.

The 'Extended Schools Agenda', introduced nationally in 2004 by the then New Labour Government, involved providing services to the local community beyond the school's educational remit. At Joseph Leckie, this involved providing a new range of services to local communities and a model for other schools to learn from. The college was also designated as a Behaviour Improvement Programme priority school, with extra funding to improve behaviour and inclusion. In particular, there had been community cohesion issues within the local community which had impacted on the college and the interaction between students as well as stretching relationships within and between the local communities that the college serves.

Prior to its Extended Schools designation, Joseph Leckie was a typical traditional community school. There were some community partnerships and community use of facilities already at the college, but few of the developed multi-agency relationships and targeted support services existed, which are evident today. In 2005, the College employed an Extended Services Manager with expertise in mentoring. With the support of the Headteacher and the whole college, this paved the way to becoming a college with a strong mentoring ethos and an opportunity to transform teaching and learning.

For the purpose of this case study, it is important to define what is meant by mentoring in this context, so the college adopts the approach of 'Professional Friendship Mentoring' (Gardiner 2008) and defines the process as: 'A care-full mentoring relationship in a formal setting, successfully involving an experience for learning and change in which mentor and mentee utilise a range of core components including, honesty, trust and respectful listening.' The college uses this definition to describe the expected behaviours and roles of all its mentoring participants.

Joseph Leckie houses a school within its own walls and this is a West Midlands-wide 'Mentoring Academy'. Since 2010, it has trained over 400 students in mentoring. Its dual role is to both train mentors inside and outside college and to provide mentoring experiences for everyone involved. In addition, it provides training and qualifications to multi-agency professionals, the unemployed and new college staff, helping them to enhance their mentoring skills in their various roles. The following programmes are currently in operation through the college and/or the mentoring academy providing mentoring for a wide variety of groups and purposes:

- Year 8s to Year 6s (13 years mentoring to 10/11-year-olds in Primary and Secondary education in the area);
- Reading mentors (6th form to Year 7s, 11 years mentored in their tutor groups by 19-year-olds);
- Peer mentors (same age);
- Year 8 to Year 7 (13 years to mentor 11-year-olds, called transition mentors);
- Year 10 to Year 8 (14/15 years to mentor 12/13-year-olds);
- 8Aim Higher Mentoring in 6th Form (university students aged 18–21 to mentor 16–19-year-olds, mentoring 6th formers);
- 6th Form Mentors (16–19-year-olds) in vertical tutor forms (mentoring conversations);
- Intervention mentoring (ex-students as role model professionals);
- Ethnic Mentoring;
- Year 11s (15/16-year-olds) (mentored by senior and middle managers or other teachers for academic mentoring);
- Mentoring of middle managers by senior managers;
- Mentoring of Initial Teacher Trainees by Advanced Skills Teachers;
- Mentoring of those individuals who are Not in Education, Employment or Training (NEETs) by Connexions P.A.;
- Mentoring of Year 10 (14/15-year-olds) by Education Business Partnership professionals from businesses and enterprise.

From members of senior management mentoring students who are potentially underachieving to Sixth formers mentoring Year 7 and 8 students, the college has developed mentoring as one of its key strategies, leading students/staff to feel safer, better supported and more confident within their college life and work.

Each programme builds on the others and this leads to young people in the college feeling more self-assured, and maintains a greater sense of collective inclusion, mobility and cohesion between students and staff. Inspectors reviewing standards at Joseph Leckie commented that, through mentoring, 'The school encourages students to take responsibility to support and help each other. Mentoring also appears in the school's Improvement Plan and is highly valued by staff and students.'

Recent developments

Over the past two years, the college has reorganised its tutor groups and saw this as an ideal opportunity to further develop peer mentoring as an additional support and intervention strategy. Rather than having each year group as separate entities, tutor groups are now made up of three or four students from each year group, including the Sixth Form. These Sixth Formers are trained in mentoring and are encouraged to motivate and support younger students with their reading and literacy skills. All mentees receive mentoring training that is appropriate to their age. In addition, they may receive training as peer mentors. The initial Sixth Form training programme involved two days out of college undertaking a full, interactive mentoring programme covering a variety of topics.

For many of the students, becoming a peer mentor seemed like a natural thing for them to do. Peer mentors also receive training in practical issues and what to do if a child protection issue is disclosed to them in the college. There are no mentoring programmes operating outside of the college day.

Two brief examples illustrate the effects of the peer mentoring. Student N, a Year 11 student, felt that peer mentoring would be a good way to develop the skills she needed for her future career as a teacher. She felt her communication skills improved through being a peer mentor and that she became more aware of the help some Year 7s and Year 8s needed and how she could support them. She found that, through reading with younger students, she could create a relationship of trust, so when the mentees had particular questions (e.g. on course options), she could help them make better informed decisions. As the mentoring takes place within tutor time in the morning, no lesson time is lost and mentees are set up positively for the day ahead.

Student R, a Year 11 peer mentor, has commented that the mentoring 'helps the younger students to engage with learning, making them more prepared for the rest of the classes which they were due to attend each day'.

This programme is monitored by individual form tutors. Tutor X describes the impact of the programme:

> It has been great to see positive relationships evolve between students. Although there was some reluctance from some of the students to begin with, they are now all keen to work with their mentors and learn from them. Students also reported that they were pleased to know someone within the Sixth Form, which helped them to feel safer within the college. It is easy to see the impact the programme is having on the students. In the case of student V, a Year 8 mentee, she said her mentor 'really helped her improve her English' and that she has increased her grade in English from Grade 4/5 in Year 7 to Grade 7/8 in Year 8. She also feels that the programme has helped her to become more confident as it has given her someone to talk to about other things. Student M, also a Year 8 mentee, pointed out that the benefit of having a peer mentor has been the ability to make new friends throughout the college. Spending time with her mentor has given her the confidence to be more outgoing and to talk to other people. It has also made her feel safer because she knows that she can tell her peer mentor if she has any problems with 'bullying or learning or anything'.

A whole-college mentoring ethos

The key ingredient in making the mentoring endeavours at the college successful is that it is part of the college ethos. The mentoring objectives of our college are integrated with the purposes of the extended school, described in our Improvement Plan – and hence included in all we do.

Staff and students receive mentoring training and are encouraged to support others who may be struggling in the college and within the community. By featuring mentoring in the College Improvement Plan and by training Sixth Formers to be mentors, the college has unleashed a wealth of talent and experience in its students and enabled them to take part more fully in the life of the college.

The targeted mentoring programmes are of course intended for particular groups of students. Students are selected for these intervention programmes on the basis of need/concerns from staff/disclosures from students as well as the close interrogation and rigorous monitoring of the academic progress data provided on a regular basis to tutors and staff.

Objectives

The mentoring programme objectives are:

- to contribute to the key issues of raising student attainment and achievement;
- to contribute to improving behaviour and attitudes to learning;
- to contribute to raising levels of attendance and punctuality;
- to continue to develop community and adult programmes of mentoring working with partner agencies to identify need and target services.

The College Improvement Plan

The College Improvement Plan is the overall planning document for each aspect of the college's operation. It includes development plans for delivery of the college's priorities, including specialist status, extended and mentoring services. It demonstrates that the aims of extended services including mentoring are fully embedded within the ethos and overall aims of the college. The range of services at the college include:

- Free breakfasts to all students requesting them
- After-college revision and homework classes, holiday booster classes and additional revision opportunities after college and at weekends
- Home language tuition
- Urdu lessons on Sundays

- Family/friends/student use of independent learning from Rosetta Stone language software
- After-college clubs
- Holiday activities
- Community classes
- Sporting competitions
- Mentor/Peer Mentoring Training and Development
- Childcare provision
- Health Agency support
- Support for parents
- Community social events.

The Office of Standards in Education (Ofsted) Reports from inspections of the college state:

> Many changes have occurred resulting in the high outcomes ratings. An example of this is using mentoring as an agent for change through the Pastoral re-structuring and Peer Mentoring programme. This programme established to embed changes to a vertical tutorage (pastoral) system with the college divided into 4 houses, each having 12 vertical tutor groups with students of all ages. This system provides the structure for effective peer mentoring arrangements in which students are coached, advised and supported by their peers. It provides peer mentoring qualifications for large numbers of students within the college in all year groups.

In 2005, the Ofsted report graded the college as inadequate for overall effectiveness in achievement and then came the mentoring strategies. The Ofsted report of 2007 recognised the impact of extended services including mentoring on supporting students and the community, contributing to an overall inspection grade of Satisfactory. By 2009, the benefits of additional services were again recognised by Ofsted in the overall grading of Good.

The data sources behind these inspection findings show that the impact of the mentoring programmes includes significantly improved:

- individual student attainment
- self-confidence
- motivation
- attendance
- reduction of exclusion rates.

In particular, mentoring has better enabled teachers to focus on teaching and learning and enhanced children's and families' access to services. Learning outcomes for participants and programme managers also show the following key areas have been improved:

- Students developed more positive attitudes toward the college and their college work as identified in the college survey carried out in the summer of 2009.
- Students achieved higher grades in English and Maths.
- There are improved relationships with adults, and improved relationships with peers.

Lessons learned

Reflecting on what we would do differently, if we were setting up programmes based on what we have learned, we would do the following:

- Train and support teaching staff to have a common understanding how they can utilise a mentoring approach within their own role within the classroom.
- Offer training to develop mentoring skills in and outside of the classroom to teaching staff.
- Train all school support staff (non-teaching) in both mentoring skills and how to target their mentoring approach to specific learning outcomes for students.
- Train students entering the college in the skills required for mentoring.
- Further develop the mentoring skills base of students as they move up the college to acquire age-related differentiated learning.
- Recruit local people from the community as volunteer mentors to support children and young people in the area.
- Dedicate a day in the school calendar when everyone can meet their mentor for a mentoring session.
- Recognise there is great potential to utilise the skills and knowledge of the local communities that the college serves and which has so far been relatively untapped, particularly for cross-cultural and ethnic mentoring.
- Ensure that mentor contact during the summer and other school holiday periods is supported via the available technologies.

As Headteacher, I (Keith) think that it is of paramount importance that we provide ongoing positive reinforcement to all of our mentors. We need to do whatever is possible to show mentors what they are accomplishing, including conveying positive feedback from the student, teacher, or student's parent/guardian. We should also actively solicit feedback from mentors and mentees regarding their experiences; and use the information to refine the overall programme and retain mentors.

We should explore the potential of awarding our own college certificate for all mentors who have undergone training and seek to have it certified by an academic institution such as Wolverhampton University.

Reflection questions

1. Who in your organisation has day-to-day responsibility for the school-based mentoring programme? (In a school/college that person might be called a mentoring coordinator, or in our case, Head of House.)
2. Which staff member at the school acts as the programme liaison?
3. Who is responsible for what tasks?
4. Which responsibilities will be shared?

Reference

Gardiner, C.E. (2008) Mentoring: towards an improved professional friendship, PhD thesis, University of Birmingham.

Case study 32: Great Britain

Cross-cultural mentoring: the United Kingdom and Lebanon

Carol Whitaker

Introduction

This mentoring case study of a young female entrepreneur based in Lebanon demonstrates how mentors can share their experience and help unlock potential – even at a distance. The mentees' story describes the resilient culture that has been developed in Lebanon and how this hope inspires and gives comfort and encouragement for the future of the Middle East. This entrepreneur's aim is to build a local business that operates internationally, but strengthens the local community and provides job opportunities for young people. However, the lessons learned are not confined to the Middle East. There are many parallels both with mentoring programmes across different cultures and where different generations learn from each other.

The mentoring programme was organised by the UK-based charity Mowgli, which offers mentoring programmes in the Middle East. The aim of the organisation is to support the nurturing of young entrepreneurs and help them grow their businesses and employment opportunities in the volatile Middle East environment. The carefully selected mentors had a two-day intense programme of emergence in Lebanon. One of the team of mentors was Lebanese. This helped to raise the awareness of both the differences and similarities in the cultural backgrounds of both mentors and mentees. But what was soon evident was the need for all to be curious, to suspend judgement and for the mentors to hold a safe space for both the mentor and mentee to explore and raise self-awareness. We present an example of one team (mentee and mentor) and their journey to share the programme and its outcomes.

Forming the mentoring relationship

The mentoring relationship started with matching. Mentees had the opportunity to meet all the mentors and discuss aspects of their businesses with them. The programme facilitators observed this process and, with information on the mentees' applications, matched them. Both parties were able to declare in confidence any matches that they thought would not work. The next day was spent with the matched pairs developing their rapport and trust. Both parties shared their personal and business backgrounds and formally contracted how to work together. This intense time spent together helped when the relationship was continued by Skype. We used webcam, but because of technical issues and sometimes weak signals, only for the first 5 minutes to check in. This opportunity to see each other helped to remind both parties of their time together in Lebanon. We also met up in London when the mentee had a meeting with her UK client and this further cemented the relationship.

A tool used part-way through the process was the Cross-Cultural Kaleidoscope developed by Jenny Plaister-Ten. This provided a number of headings, under which to consider and discuss cultural stories. These 'stories' fell into the categories of history/arts, economic, political, education, legal, religious/spiritual, community/family, geography/climate as manifested by cultural behaviour, habits and norms and informed by cultural theory.

The mentee is in her mid-thirties. She had been educated in Beirut within the French system until university level. She acquired a Master's Degree at Reading University, UK, before joining a market research organisation based in Beirut for five years, then set up her own agency.

Lebanon has a varied history. In the past 100 years it has been a French protectorate and was also under British rule for a short time, but is now independent. Being a trading post for both the East and West has had a major impact on its culture and contributed to the economics of the region. Politics is an issue – there has been no government for two years and the last president was assassinated, but no one has yet been prosecuted. Business is done with people whom you know.

The future is still unstable due to the majority population of Muslims increasing in numbers at a faster rate than other sectors and the difficult issue of Palestinian refugees still being stateless. There are no effective employment laws and politics has become corrupt. Despite elections, the same families remain in power in civil law and politics.

The issue of diversity that emerged for the mentee was around the role of religion in Lebanon. The mentee felt that her Christianity defines her social sector to a much greater extent than it would in the UK. She felt that being a Christian in Lebanon meant she socialised and did business with Christians. She was very aware of being a minority in a mainly Muslim country. She felt that her religion defined her and that prospective employers could identify her faith by knowing which school she went to, where she lived, or even her name and that this meant some jobs would not be open to her. The background of turmoil has made her more resilient. It has also given her an awareness that she lives in a protective bubble within a Christian community and in the future this bubble might burst.

The mentor is in her sixties with a background in HR (which included 10 years for an international market research organisation). She has over 15 years of experience of coaching and mentoring, of which the past eight years has included running her own business. She has also held a number of non-executive director roles and is currently Vice-Chair of a Housing Association. She is of Irish/English descent and her parents were from different religious traditions. She was brought up in the Church of England although her father was Catholic. She had had personal experience of feeling in a minority when at the age of 10 she went to a Catholic convent day school, as there was only one other girl there whose parents were of a different religion.

Outcomes

This was an intergenerational relationship in which each party was able to learn from each other. The mentee was able to talk things through with someone who had experience of working in a number of industries and countries both in Europe and the Middle East. The mentor was able to gain insight into the influence on the younger generation of social media and technology and the blurring of cultural differences with the acquisition of more information and cultural knowledge.

The mentee feedback is that she has increased her self-awareness and been more self-confident in following up business opportunities. She displayed her resilience when, having worked for many months on securing a contract in Syria, the troubles broke out and the project was suspended. She quickly moved on and pursued opportunities in Dubai and other less volatile areas in the region. She also approached her UK-based client and expanded her global projects. She had a very pragmatic attitude to the issues that were presented.

Work with this mentee over the last 12 months has raised the mentor's sensitivity of how her own ancestry has affected her values.

Lessons learned

The greatest lesson for the mentor is that cultural identity is not fixed. It develops as a result of how people adapt to their environment. She discovered that individuals have the capacity to shape and reshape themselves. The mentor can support the mentee to develop their authentic self. The mentoring process is a journey of discovery but there is a need to suspend judgement and develop a sense of curiosity.

Reflection questions

1. What drives the current generation to have a different attitude to the use of technology and to the access of information than previous generations?
2. What is the impact of the increase of young global nomads? With the increase of global organisations, many young people will have been born in one culture, educated in another and now be working in a third. They may feel they do not belong anywhere – what impact does this have on social cohesion?
3. What impact does our cultural background have on the mentoring relationship?
4. What impact is the increase in fundamentalism going to have on the way countries work together?
5. What are the implications for organisations operating globally?

CHAPTER 6

A comprehensive view of mentoring programs for diversity

Frances Kochan

Introduction

The authors of our case studies have presented critical insights into issues related to diversity based upon gender, race, ethnicity and culture, and disability. There are many variations in program purposes, design, delivery, and outcomes. However, there are also similarities related to the mentoring process with populations not traditionally viewed as part of the mainstream or who face barriers in society based simply upon who they are. These similarities provide guidelines into how to create successful programs for these populations and also point to avenues for additional research and study. As noted in the Foreword to this book, this chapter is unique because of the manner in which it was developed. Initially we asked all authors to read the case studies in the chapter to which they had contributed and to share their responses to four questions:

1 What trends can you identify in how programs are structured, funded, evaluated and managed?

2 What recurrent challenges do you see in these case studies for diversity mentoring programs?

3 What lessons would you draw from the cases as a whole?

4 What significant questions do the cases suggest to you, as designers of future diversity mentoring programs?

The editors conducted a similar analysis of the chapters and combined the findings to create this chapter. We believe it is the first of its kind, drawing from a broad range of researchers' thoughts. As such, we view this chapter as a substantial contribution to the literature and to the field of practice.

This chapter seeks to capture responses to these questions by reporting on three issues that incorporate them. The first section examines trends by discussing the ways in which the programs are structured and delivered. This includes information about program purposes and the elements that appear to be essential in developing and implementing successful programs for populations traditionally left out of the mainstream. The challenges and lesson learned are presented in the next section, which deals with the cultural and contextual factors in the environment that appear to hinder success and the strategies used to overcome them. The final section provides areas for future study and reflection.

Program development and structures

Mentoring programs are organized and implemented in a variety of ways. This section deals with these two elements by addressing commonalities and differences among these programs. It is presented around two foci: program organization and program processes.

Program organization

Strong mentoring programs require extensive planning; effective leadership and management; adequate resources; and comprehensive evaluation if they are to operate successfully and be sustained over time (Kochan 2002). A common theme of case study authors was that it is essential to take time to consider all the program aspects before embarking upon implementation. This includes considering all aspects of the program including such things as scope, management, primary purposes, funding, mentor/mentee selection, training, operational processes, evaluation, communication strategies, and project sustainability. While this may be true of all mentoring programs, the complexity of the issues faced when working with individuals, who are often excluded from the environments or opportunities they are seeking, appears to make comprehensive planning especially critical.

The programs vary in size and scope. Some deal with a few individuals in a single setting (Cordell, Naude). Some operate in individual institutions or organizations (Okhai and Quinn), or deal with a few people, but operate across multiple organizations (Mertz and Pfleeger). Others are large in scope involving mentoring programs at multiple sites and with multiple groups (Møller-Jensen; Wagner and Wagner).

Most programs involve more than one goal, recognizing that the mentoring approach must be holistic in nature due to the variety of issues these mentees face. Within this framework of multiple purposes, there were numerous foci such as impacting the economic well-being of individuals and helping them balance life and work (Bujaki, Lennox Terrion, Mavriplis and Moreau; Johnson); supporting them in entering the job market (Møller-Jensen); assisting individuals to move up and succeed in the organization (Dixon, Birch, Sontag, and Vappie); helping individuals form their own business (Potts); integrating individuals into the organization, community, or society (Monserrat); and building the personal strength and/or self-esteem of the mentee (Naidoo and Clarke; Naude). No matter what the specific purposes, all of these programs are working toward enhancing individual capacity to succeed, breaking down barriers to success, and fostering the nobility and value of the mentees. As a group, they center upon building individual, organizational, and societal capacities.

Authors emphasized that no matter what the goals are, it is essential that they be made clear to all. Not doing so results in serious problems (Abbott; Haddock-Millar et al.). Likewise, they stressed the need to assure that the program is designed to be an integral part of the organizational or institutional base, rather than being perceived as an add-on, which could easily be dismantled when funding becomes an issue or leadership changes (Gardiner and Whittlestone).

In terms of management and leadership, one of the important traits for most of these programs is that they needed someone to serve as the cheerleader/the torch-bearer to motivate mentors and mentees and the organization and to keep things going. Concerns exist over what happens when this person leaves or is unable to continue to serve. This seems particularly crucial with the groups served in these programs, who so often need an advocate. An important lesson from this finding is the need to build in a team approach to leadership that will aid in sustaining the program over time, rather than depending on a charismatic or powerful leader to ensure longevity. Some programs spoke to this issue by creating a steering group or advisory board (Wagner and Wagner) to provide a stronger leadership base. Others, such as the Integrated Women's Mentorship Program (Cruz) and the South East Mentoring Network for Women (Hartshorn), built in multiple links with a variety of agencies to help ensure systems of support and sustainability (Naidoo and Clarke).

Program processes – matching

Program processes involve the activities and tasks that comprise the program. Among the most prominent issues addressed in these cases was the issue of mentor/mentee matching. The issue of matching is controversial in the literature. While some researchers claim that, when working with diverse populations, it is essential that the pairs are matched by the diversity feature (i.e. gender, race, disability) (Liang and Grossman 2007; Orland-Barak 2003), other researchers suggest that multiple diversity issues should be considered when creating mentoring matches (Clutterbuck 2001). There is also some indication that preconceived negative notions based on diversity issues can make it difficult for mentoring pairs with dissimilar backgrounds to succeed (Kochan and Pascarelli 2003). Other researchers found that such differences were not a problem in creating successful mentoring relationships. For example, Wales (2003) found no differences in male/female and female/female pairs in a business setting, and Davis (2008) suggests that matching should focus on organizational individual issues that might cause problems instead of issues relation to individual diversity. Finally, a number of researchers indicate that the level of success of mentoring depends more on attitudes and beliefs than on such as race and gender (Lee 1999).

Our authors reported multiple realties in regard to matching based on similarities and differences. In some instances (Alake and Sonaike; Cordell), having a mentor with the same diversity feature as the mentee enabled the mentors to share their own stories in ways that built mentee confidence. In some settings, having a different background caused difficulties (Monserrat). In other situations, it did not appear to matter (Potts, Wagner and Wagner). In fact, Hejlsvig views such difference as integral to the program, labeling it as 'double mentoring' in which both mentor and mentee gain from coming from differing cultures. Likewise, Whitaker reports that mentors from differing generations and cultural backgrounds felt they had gained something of importance from the experience.

Most programs included mentor training. In addition, many programs also included mentee training (Dominguez and Gutierrez). Numerous authors stressed the importance of training mentees because there is often a need to assist them in building confidence to foster their ability to overcome some of the obstacles they face.

In our view, and based on our experience, it is a matter of context and purpose as well as a good understanding of the individual participants which kind of matching should be preferred. Matching across the diversity dimension adds more learning for both mentor and mentee, and in some programs it is important that the mentor, who comes from the privileged group, gains new insights into the diversity issue. In other programs it may be better to match mentors and mentees with the same diversity issue so the mentee can learn about the mentor's coping learning journey and coping strategies.

Program processes – mentor and mentee training

Program developers used a variety of approaches for training both mentors and mentees. Some examples include workshops and internships (Cruz); electronic mentoring (Corinaldi; Hartshorn); reflection workshops (Knott and Poulsen); phone, small group (Dixon, Birch, Sontag, and Vappie); peer, individual and group mentoring (Bujaki, Lennos Terion, Mavriplis); university partnerships (Haddock-Millar et al.); junior/senior, near peer, and peer mentoring (Mavriplis, Heller, Sorensen); and multi-level and community building workshops (Cruz). There appears to be a strong recognition that there is not one way or a right way to provide mentoring. Rather, programs must assess the needs of the mentees and make adjustments as required.

All the programs emphasized the importance of building trusting relationships between and among those involved. This appears to be of particular importance when mentees come from groups that have been discriminated against or who have been or have felt excluded in some manner. They need a safe place where they can be free to express their needs and concerns. Although this is important in all mentoring programs, it appears to be of even greater significance in these settings since many individuals being mentored have experienced barriers to success and work opportunities.

These authors also recognize that evaluation is an integral part of successful mentoring endeavors. This is unusual since evaluation is often neglected in the implementation of mentoring programs (Kochan 2002). The definitions of success and the manner in which evaluations were conducted varied. They included techniques such as pre and post surveys and questionnaires (Mavriplis, Heller and Sorensen); examining growth in self-knowledge (Okhai and Quinn); determining levels of satisfaction with the program (Monserrat); measuring job progression (Overy and Sanidas); monitoring job placement (Ekeland); and determining the impact on organizational goals (Rolfe). Many authors emphasized that evaluation must be comprehensive and continuous; should gather data from multiple groups; and should be used to enhance and improve program attributes and operations. Two major issues facing these program developers are how to gather meaningful summative data and how to capture the intangibles inherent in program success.

Overcoming barriers

All mentoring programs face difficulties and some of the problems faced by these program developers are similar to those identified for most mentoring programs. Some of them, such as long-term funding and gathering summative evaluation data, were dealt with in the previous section on program operations. However, because many of these programs are working with excluded populations, the obstacles they face may be somewhat different than those of programs working with other groups. The obstacles we review here are organized around two topic areas: cultural and contextual issues and individual constraints.

Cultural and contextual issues

One of the most prominent challenges for program developers was gaining and maintaining the support of others in the organizational or cultural setting (Johnson; Knott and Poulsen; Abbott).

Some in the organization questioned the legitimacy of programs that, from their perspective, gave special privileges to others (Rolfe). At times, those within the organization did not understand why a person with a disability, or someone from another culture, should need additional assistance. Sometimes, there was a lack of understanding on behalf of the employer as to what the condition involved and what was required to overcome some of the barriers individuals faced (Overy and Sanidas; Abbott). These perceptions were sometimes based upon a prejudicial view and at other times, may have been based upon a lack of understanding or empathy. Whatever the cause, they served as obstacles to success. This lack of understanding, particularly from upper level administrators caused numerous problems (Johnson). Among the most prominent was struggling with finding time for mentees and mentors to meet. Some supervisors viewed this as detracting from productivity – not seeing the long-term positive impact the outcomes might bring. This caused pressure for both parties and served as a hindrance to success.

Program developers recognize that mentoring must be viewed as a core activity that positively impacts those involved and the organization and that there is a need to visibly link these programs with corporate or societal needs to assure success (Naidoo and Clark; Overy and Sanidas). They used a variety of strategies to make these connections and overcome cultural and contextual barriers to success. Among these were gaining support from high level administrators who would foster program acceptance; involving a broad range of people in the organization, incorporating the program goals into the goals of the business or organization; assuring that program goals and outcomes were widely disseminated; and consistently demonstrating the value of the program in a wide variety of venues and to a broad audience. Advisory councils and steering committees, previously mentioned as a part of shared leadership, were common vehicles in creating active involvement of these individuals. A common thread in these case studies was the necessity of continually communicating the value of these programs in terms of human development and organization success. Most authors appear to agree with Ekeland that 'we can never inform enough'.

Another contextual barrier to program success was finding appropriate mentors. While many programs had adequate volunteers, others struggled with finding mentors who were willing and able to give the time needed to support their mentees. Sometimes this was related to a lack of support on the part of the organization to provide the mentors and mentees the time they needed. At other times, it was because of a lack of understanding about the importance of the mentoring role. Conversely, in some settings, individuals wanted to be mentors, but were not suited to the role and/or did not see the need for training (Mertz and Pfleeger). Authors stressed the necessity of training, even for those who are already well suited to the role. They tried to overcome this difficulty by making training mandatory, but negative attitudes toward mentoring are not easily overcome and the issue of who should be a mentor requires some additional study. In our experience, one of the most important factors to motivate mentors for the role is that mentors are also able to see the benefits of taking on the role. In diversity mentoring the potential for the mentor's learning is even greater than in ordinary corporate mentoring programs.

One of the most important difficulties was the need to assure that mentors truly understood the world in which the mentee existed and were empathetic, while still not taking ownership of the issues the mentee needed to cope with. At times, this was easy as the mentor and mentee had the same diversity feature (Cordell), but it became a barrier when the mentors could not grasp the issues the mentees were facing (Abbott). Overcoming this barrier was addressed through training and discussion. Within these endeavors, it was vital to include 'cultural training'. This means providing opportunities to ensure mentors' understanding of the cultural aspects of difference – in all its realms. Among these realms is the disability itself, the accommodations that might be needed to address it, and the organizational, structural, and the societal barriers that must be addressed and overcome. Some programs dealt with the issue of assuring that mentees had mentors with a broad understanding of the issue by assigning multiple mentors to the mentee, including peers (Mavriplis, Heller and Sorensen), and expanding the dialogue and mentoring resources through the use of mentoring networks (Millar et al.).

Often the barriers to success went beyond a single organization or institution as there were issues within the culture of the society that were beyond the ability of the program developers to overcome. In fact, it is partially these obstacles that make such programs necessary. It seems to be more likely such obstacles will be overcome in situations where a government has established the program as part of a national policy (Ekeland; Saunders). However, even when there is a political move to create change, remove barriers within a society to accept individuals and to change mores that allow open access and opportunities for all, such change is difficult to achieve and may often take generations. While strategies for educating the public at large were often implemented, part of the solution also appears preparing the mentees to cope with the situation and to serve as advocates for themselves. This leads to the second barrier, the attitude and perception of the mentees.

In addition to gaining support from those within the organization or institution, the authors emphasized the need to prepare mentees with the skills they needed to overcome resistance from others and to build their own self-confidence. It was often the case that the mentee came to the experience with their own concerns about whether this was a good thing for them to do. Some viewed it as possible recognition that in some way they were deficient and were concerned about whether their involvement would stigmatize them. Others had low self-esteem, felt depressed, or had little hope for their future and did not believe that mentoring would help them. These attitudes had to be dealt with in order to enable the mentee to grow and develop.

Strategies to overcome these obstacles included assuring the mentors understood these issues and how to cope with them (Bujaki et al.); enabling the mentees to perceive a different future for themselves (Mossop et al.; Naude); and creating support networks to expand communication and provide long-term support (Corinaldi). An interesting perspective on this issue was noted by Parsonage and Wilson-Gotobed, who discussed the need to point out the 'positive aspects of dyslexia' and Johnson, who wrote about the 'highly original mode of thinking and cognition' of individuals with Asperger Syndrome. This focus upon the strengths of a disability is often overlooked by society which tends to look at something commonly known as a disability, without considering the possibility that there could also be a strength that accompanies it. Thus, a deaf person may have perceptions, understandings and wisdom lacking in those who can hear. Likewise, a person who has been in prison might have greater empathy with others than someone who has not had such an experience. These strengths can be used in powerful ways and recognizing and valuing them can make a difference in the self-perception of the mentee, the understandings and actions of the mentor, the level of acceptance of the organizational supervisors, and the society at large. This is an important element, which should be considered in the mentoring process when working with the mentee, the mentor, and the organizational or societal setting in which mentoring occurs.

Questions for reflection and further study

Our review of the case studies in this book has resulted in a broad range of approaches and strategies that can be used to assure that programs such as these can be successful. We present six questions for reflection that deal with issues we believe have not been fully addressed. We hope they will stimulate further thought and action as we seek to use mentoring as a means of fostering social justice for all as well as ensuring that the resources and talents of all the population can be put to good use for the benefit of the individual, corporations and society.

1 When adopting successful mentoring programs in differing sites, how can we determine needed adaptations based upon the environment in which one is working?

2 To what degree does matching like and unlike individuals add or detract from the mentoring process and which factors matter?

3 How can we build evaluation and assessment systems that capture the intangibles inherent in these programs and make them visible?

4 How can we assess the need for long-term support of mentees and mentors and what is 'enough'?

5 What is the proper balance between adaptation, integration, and individuality? To what extent should the society rather than the person adapt?

6 What additional strategies should be built into mentoring programs to foster deep cultural changes in organizational, societal, and cultural mores?

Concluding thoughts

We view the programs presented in this book as a light to the world. Their ultimate purpose is to create a society where all are valued and given the opportunity to share their gifts in meaningful ways. We close this chapter and our book with some quotes from the case studies which capture the true impact of the programs that have been shared. We hope they will inspire our authors to continue in their work and will encourage others to engage in similar endeavors.

> Mentoring changed my perception of myself in my job.
> (Parsonage and Wilson)

> I want my future to be a bright future and I want to reach my goals, and I feel like I will – no matter what will happen.
> (Naude)

> I am so ill often and so my business is very small, but it has given me an empowerment I couldn't have predicted would be so personally

valuable. I could at last give an answer to 'What do you do?' And for this, I will be eternally grateful.

(Potts)

You gave me hope. I can dream again.

(Mossop et al.)

I do not think of myself as a loser any more.

(Alake and Sonaike)

References

Clutterbuck, D. (2001) Building and sustaining the diversity-mentoring relationship, in D. Clutterbuck and B. Ragins (eds) *Mentoring and Diversity: An International Perspective*. London: Butterworth-Heinemann, pp. 87–113.

Davis, D.J. (2008) Mentorship and socialization of underrepresented minorities into the professoriate: examining varied influences, *Mentoring and Tutoring: Partnership in Learning*, 16(3): 278–93.

Kochan, F.K. (2002) *The Organizational and Human Dimensions of Successful Mentoring Programs and Relationships*. Greenwich, CT: Information Age Publishing.

Kochan, F.K. and Pascarelli, J.T. (2003) Culture, context, and issues of change related to mentoring programs and relationships, in F.K. Kochan and J.T. Pascarelli (eds) *Global Perspectives on Mentoring: Transforming Contexts, Communities, and Cultures*. Greenwich, CT: Information Age Publishing, pp. 417–28.

Lee, W. (1999) Striving toward effective retention: the effect of race on mentoring African American students, *Peabody Journal of Education*, 74(2): 27–43.

Liang, B. and Grossman, J.M. (2007) Diversity and youth mentoring relationships, in T.D. Allen and L.T. Eby (eds) *The Blackwell Handbook of Mentoring: A Multiple Perspectives Approach*. Oxford: Blackwell Publishing.

Orland-Barak, L. (2003) In between worlds: the tensions of in-service mentoring in Israel, in F. Kochan and J.T. Pascarelli, *Global Perspectives on Mentoring: Transforming Contexts, Communities, and Cultures*. Greenwich, CO: Information Age Publishing.

Wales, S. (2003) Breaking barriers in business: coaching women for career advancement in the United Kingdom, in F.K. Kochan and J.T. Pascarelli (eds) *Global Perspectives on Mentoring: Transforming Contexts, Communities, and Cultures*. Greenwich, CT, Information Age Publishing, pp. 165–90.

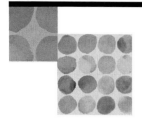

Index